Beachy Weekend Getaways from
New York City

BEACHY WEEKEND GETAWAYS FROM

New York City

Short Breaks in the Hamptons, Long Island, and the Jersey Shore

Teddy Minford

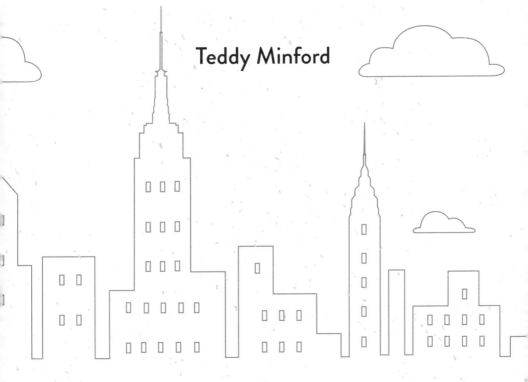

The Countryman Press
A division of W. W. Norton & Company
Independent Publishers Since 1923

We would appreciate any comments or corrections. Please write to:
Countryman Weekenders Editor
The Countryman Press
A division of W. W. Norton & Company
500 Fifth Avenue
New York, NY 10110

For information about permission to reproduce selections from this book, write to
Permissions, The Countryman Press, 500 Fifth Avenue, New York, NY 10110

For information about special discounts for bulk purchases, please contact
W. W. Norton Special Sales at specialsales@wwnorton.com or 800-233-4830

Manufacturing by Versa Press
Series book design by Faceout Studio, Amanda Kreutzer
Production manager: Devon Zahn

The Countryman Press
www.countrymanpress.com

A division of W. W. Norton & Company, Inc.
500 Fifth Avenue, New York, NY 10110
www.wwnorton.com

978-1-68268-372-9 (pbk.)

10 9 8 7 6 5 4 3 2 1

For Gaga

// An epic sunset at Montauket, one of the best places on Long Island to watch the sunset

Contents

Welcome

When temperatures rise and New York City turns into a sweltering garbage heap, the beach beckons.

The Hamptons serve as New York City's summer playground. An artsy and beautiful paradise for the rich and famous, this lush, green region at the eastern tip of Long Island has somehow remained a mystery for many—even though it's easily accessible from New York City.

From pristine beaches with an up-and-coming surf culture to trendy restaurants and bars to under-the-radar art museums and sculpture gardens, this region of Long Island offers a true escape from New York. While some may see the Hamptons as stuffy, it's actually quite the opposite—laid-back, artsy, bohemian, and ready to show visitors a good time.

The Hamptons are almost a caricature of themselves: quaint streets lined with sports cars,

// Georgica Beach in East Hampton

Indigenous History of Long Island

Before colonizers arrived from Europe, Long Island was known as *Paumanok*, which means "land that gives tribute." The first people to settle on this land were the Algonquian-speaking Shinnecock Nation, now headquartered on the Shinnecock Reservation in Suffolk County. Native American culture is alive and well on Long Island, and there are myriad ways to discover and engage with the indigenous past, present, and future of Long Island.

Annual Shinnecock Indian Powwow
shinnecockindianpowwow.com

Garvies Point Museum
garviespointmuseum.com

Montauk Historical Society
montaukhistoricalsociety.org

The Shinnecock Nation Cultural Center and Museum
shinnecockmuseum.com

Southold Indian Museum
southoldindianmuseum.org

Suffolk County Historical Society Museum
suffolkcountyhistoricalsociety.org

shops on Main Street selling $900 sunglasses. It's impossible to go out to a sit-down dinner here and not spend at least $60 per person (and that's only with one glass of wine). This is the land of private clubs, where billion-dollar deals are signed on the golf course by day and record-breaking real estate deals happen every week.

But despite all that, the Hamptons are truly wonderful. For every obnoxious stockbroker in the throes of a midlife crisis, there are multiple surfers, environmentalists, artists, bakers, farmers, landscapers, chefs, architects, and philanthropists who contribute to this great community. People love this place despite the ostentatious wealth, not because of it.

It's the natural beauty of the Hamptons that's most striking. Long, pristine white beaches and magnificent blue waves have been capturing the hearts of people as long as people have been here. The Shinnecock Indians were here first, followed by early settlers in the 1600s, followed by the fishermen of the 18th and 19th century, the artists and writers of the 20th century, the celebrities, surfers, and stockbrokers of today—and now you.

With beaches that rival any on the eastern seaboard, it's easy to see why so many people call this place home—if only on the weekends.

Beyond the Hamptons, Shelter Island and the North Fork offer authentic getaways without the glitz and glamour of the Hamptons—but you'll still find world-class restaurants, lush farms, and scenic vineyards. The hard-to-get-to oasis of Fire Island ranges from a multi-generational vacation destination frequented by families who visit every year, to wilderness campsites along the forested coast, to raunchy all-night parties in a Dionysian playground.

Oyster Bay and the surrounding area give visitors a taste of old-school WASP life, with cozy inns, rocky beaches, and seaside restaurants perfect for sipping a gin and tonic as the sailboats pass by.

The underrated Jersey Shore has bounced back from Hurricane Sandy, with secret National Park beaches on Sandy Hook and gritty hipster magnets like Asbury Park. Doable in just a weekend, these destinations all offer us a way to break out of the city, in most cases without a car.

The Hamptons Primer

Absolutely nothing is cheap in the Hamptons (don't say we didn't warn you). But while Shelter Island, Montauk, and the North Fork have a much more laid-back vibe, you'll find that the prices are just as chichi as they are in the Hamptons. However, it's possible (and even fun!) to visit if you're not a billionaire. With well-endowed communities come free museums and cultural events, meaning that you don't have to miss out on all the glitz and glamour just because you're not a celebrity. And while nobody blinks an eye at a $30 lobster roll here, there are deals to be had. We'll show you where to stay and eat without spending your whole paycheck in one weekend.

This insider's guide to the Hamptons, Long Island, and the Jersey Shore will show you how to have a good time on the East End, whether you're here for romance, parties, or simply a little bit of peace and quiet.

Before you get started, you'll need a primer—especially if it's your first time. Here's everything you need to know before you go to the Hamptons.

1 • The Ocean Is Not Your Friend.

Even on days when the ocean looks calm, it can be dangerous. Riptides are currents that run the opposite direction of the waves, pulling swimmers and surfers out to sea. If you find yourself in a riptide, the best plan of action is to swim parallel to the shore. Whatever you do, don't expend all your energy trying to outswim the current—it won't work. Pay attention to lifeguards, because in most cases, even though they might only be 17 years old, they know more about swimming than you do. Green and yellow flags mean it's ok to swim, red flags mean it's not. If you plan on surfing, learn the etiquette first. Don't drop in on somebody's wave, and understand the lineup before you get out there.

2 • This Is the Land of 1 Percenters.

Do you know how much the most expensive house in the Hamptons sold for? In August 2017, a Southampton estate sold for $175 million, which is more money than you and everyone you know will ever have in your lifetimes, combined. Even a modest, non-beach condo can cost upwards of 1 million in the Hamptons. But that's not to say every single person here is privileged—just like any community, there are people struggling below the poverty line.

But just because you don't have money doesn't mean you can't have a good time here. In general, restaurants are exorbitantly priced on Long Island, especially on the East End. To get the most for your money, go out to fancy restaurants for lunch instead of dinner, and don't eat all your meals in a restaurant. You can pick up a picnic at a deli or visit one of the bountiful farm stands to have a fresh and healthy meal.

3 • It Can Be Hard to Access.

Geographically speaking, the Hamptons are quite easy to access—by plane, train, and automobile. But once you're here, you can sometimes feel a little left out of the loop; some people might not quite get what's so great about the Hamptons on their first visit. For New Yorkers, it depends what you're looking for. For a sceney party and California surfer vibes, head to Montauk. Those looking for a quiet beach should visit East Hampton or Amagansett. If you want to party all night, try Fire Island. History buffs will love the Gold Coast mansions of the North Shore. For peace and quiet in a lush green setting, try Shelter Island, and for some of the best food and wine experiences in the state, visit Greenport and the North Fork, where farms and wineries abound.

If you come to any one place expecting all of those things, you might be disappointed. Each town on Long Island has its own personality, and while it's possible to experience them all in a weekend, it's best to take it slow and get to know a place gradually.

4 • It's All About Nature.

Some people forget why the Hamptons became popular in the first place, but once you put down the rosé and get away from the crowds, it's easy to see why this place is so popular—it's absolutely gorgeous. From marshy preserves in Peconic Bay to windswept sand dunes in Amagansett to the incredible rare sand forest of Fire Island, the natural beauty of Long Island is stunning. But the land isn't only beautiful—it's also fertile and productive, bringing forth organic local produce that's incomparable to anything you'd ever find in a grocery store. From tomatoes and corn to peaches and Chardonnay grapes, the bounty of Long Island is endless. (And we haven't even mentioned seafood yet!)

5 • Don't Discount the Off Season.

The summer communities of Long Island are busy from Memorial Day to Labor Day, without a doubt. That's when most season-long rentals begin and end, when most offices allow summer Fridays, and when the kids are home from college. Summer out here is idyllic—it's never too hot, with icy cold oceans under a perfect blue sky, with occasional thunderstorms. But all the people who leave after Labor Day are missing the best time of year out here. September is pure magic, with no crowds, sunny weather, and an ocean that's finally warmed up enough to swim. The late fall is nice too, with bright foliage, leaves crunching underfoot, and a spooky chill in the air—a great time to explore Long Island's historic mansions.

6 • It's OK to Be a Tourist.

You might think that visiting the Hamptons is all about shopping in the hippest boutiques and being seen at the coolest restaurants. But it's not. There's so much to see in the Hamptons and Long Island that even some locals don't know about. Visit a museum, check out a historic farm, or go for a walk in a nature preserve. There are events all summer long, from concerts and lectures to stargazing parties and fundraisers. Check the calendar and do some exploring.

7 • Just Don't Be Tacky.

There's a reason why the Hamptons is a celebrity enclave, and it's because the real Hamptonites truly *do not care*. Don't snap photos or ask for an autograph from a celebrity—even if it's your number one favorite actor/musician/artist/writer in the whole world. It's tacky, but it's also pretty disrespectful to interrupt a stranger's dinner and demand their attention.

8 • Avoid Traffic and Parking.

As the land mass of Long Island narrows on the East End, traffic can become extremely congested. Small towns with just one-lane highways become parking lots on holiday weekends, with mobs of people road raging their way to brunch. It's nice to have your own wheels, but make sure your hotel or rental has parking on site. Keep in mind that parking is an issue in Montauk, with bars and venues in residential parts of town allowing no street parking whatsoever. If you must head into town, try to do all of your errands at once. When in doubt, you can ditch your car at the train station parking lot and ride bikes around.

9 • Don't Bring Music to the Beach.

This one is pretty simple—this land is not your land, so don't be obnoxious. Sure, you might like listening to top 40 while you chug beers and play beach volleyball, but be considerate of other people. This also goes for: yelling into your cellphone in public, asking to speak to the restaurant manager when your server makes a mistake on your order during Fourth of July weekend, or any other attitude of general entitlement. The Hamptons is by no means an asshole-free zone, but we can all do our part to be kind, especially to the people who call this place home 365 days a year and not just on summer weekends. Your problems are no more important than anybody else's. If you're reading this book, that means you'll never be a local, so know your place.

10 • It's Not the Only Cool Place on Long Island.

Sure, the Hamptons might be the "it" destination for beach-bound city folks, but that doesn't mean it's the only place to go. Be open-minded and visit other places—you might be surprised at the beautiful beaches of the Long Island Sound or the chic restaurants hidden away in the suburbs. Beaches close to the city are surprisingly clean, with a totally different vibe than the preppy surfer enclaves out east. And if you've never been to Asbury Park, you're really not allowed to judge the Jersey Shore. Sure, parts of it are tacky, but that's what makes it loveable. And Asbury is cooler than you think, with venues, shops, restaurants, and hotels just as hip as anything you'll find in Brooklyn. Get out and explore.

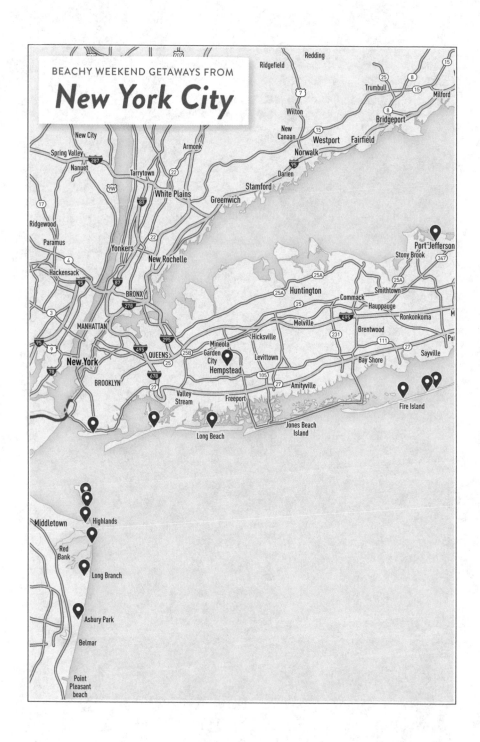

BEACHY WEEKEND GETAWAYS FROM

New York City

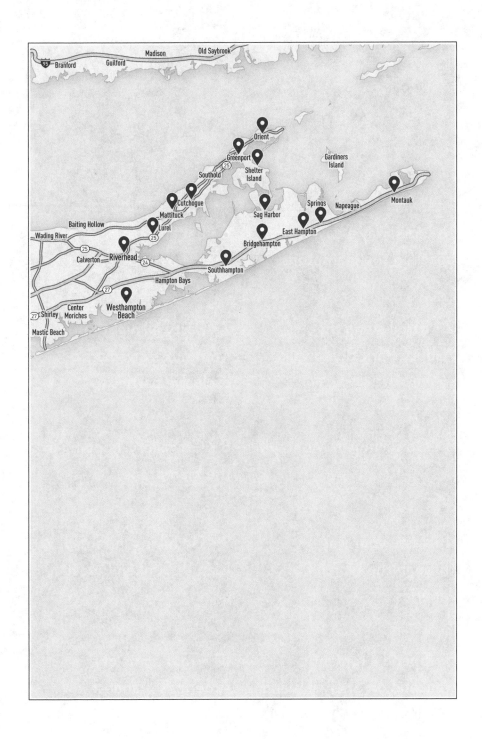

Top 10 Experiences

1 • Laze away a day on the beach in the Hamptons
(Chapter 2)

2 • Stroll along the Asbury Park Boardwalk
(Chapter 2)

3 • Go surfing in Montauk
(Chapter 6)

4 • Taste your way through the North Fork's wineries
(Chapter 4)

5 • Spend a romantic weekend on Shelter Island
(Chapter 8)

6 • Eat Peconic Bay oysters and clams in Greenport
(Chapter 4)

7 • Party all night in Montauk's dive bars or exclusive parties
(Chapter 5)

8 • Go gallery-hopping in the Hamptons
(Chapter 3)

9 • Go hiking in Fire Island's Sunken Forest
(Chapter 6)

10 • Tour some of America's grandest historic estates at Sands Point Preserve
(Chapter 3)

1 Experience 2: High Voltage Cafe, Asbury Park, New Jersey
2 Experience 6: Little Creek Oyster, Greenport, New York
3 Experience 1: Georgica Beach, Long Island, New York

Getting Here and Where to Stay

How to Plan Your Escape From New York

Friday afternoons in New York City during the summer are one of the world's great migrations. When the clock strikes 4:55 p.m., millions of workers rush to the nearest commuter hub to go home and rest—or make their great escape for a weekend at the beach.

To reach the outer ends of Long Island on a Friday night (while retaining your sanity) is a matter of skill, luck, ingenuity, and timing. There are myriad ways to arrive (and myriad prices for these choices), but the most important thing to consider is timing and traffic.

≡ Getting Here

THE SOUTH FORK | *The Hamptons, Sag Harbor, Amagansett, and Montauk*

Getting There

BY CAR | Montauk is located at the far eastern tip of Long Island, past the Hamptons. It's as far as you can get from the city. On a good day with no traffic, the drive all the way out to the end of the island can take as little as 2.5 hours, but it's a good idea to factor in at least 3 hours of driving time to get to Montauk. Even if there's no traffic on Long Island, keep in mind that there will always be traffic leaving the city. The fastest way to drive to the Hamptons and Montauk is by taking I-495 (Long Island Expressway) East from either the Brooklyn-Queens Expressway in Brooklyn or the Queens-Midtown tunnel from Manhattan. Those coming from the Bronx can access I-495 East from the Throgs Neck Bridge and I-295.

From I-495 East, it's a straight shot to the town of Manorville, where you'll take County Road 111 in order to access Highway 27. Highway 27 starts near JFK Airport and runs the whole length of Southern Long Island. It's possible to take the highway all the way from Brooklyn, but it will take much longer. However, if you're looking for a more scenic route that takes you through towns along the way, the scenery (and don't forget the stoplights) along 27 are far more interesting than I-495.

Highway 27 runs through Westhampton, Hampton Bays, Southampton, Bridgehampton, East Hampton, Amagansett, and Montauk. To get to Sag Harbor, turn onto the Bridgehampton-Sag Harbor Turnpike in Bridgehampton.

Traffic on the route out to the Hamptons can be life-ruining. A trip that can take as little as 2 hours with no traffic has been known to take upwards of 5 hours if it's not timed correctly. If you can't depart before 8 a.m. on a Friday, you will be stuck in miserable traffic—especially on a holiday weekend. Do not try to leave New York anytime between 9 a.m. and 7 p.m. on a Friday, any time of year. After 7 p.m., it should be smooth sailing. On other days of the week, it's fine

PEAK OR OFF-PEAK?

Eastbound Long Island Railroad trains that leave New York City between 4 p.m. and 8 p.m. are considered "peak" trains, which means they are charged at a higher rush-hour rate. Westbound trains scheduled to arrive in New York City between 6 a.m. and 10 a.m. will also be charged at the peak rush-hour rate. All other trains are considered "off-peak", which means the ticket costs less. Tickets for the Long Island Railroad can be purchased at platform kiosks or through the MTA app (highly recommended). Tickets can also be bought on board, but there's a $5.75 charge.

to leave midday, but try to avoid regular commuter times of 4 p.m. to 6 p.m. If you're hoping to get an early start on Saturday morning, you are out of luck—this is when local Long Island families get up and go to the beach, so you'll be battling traffic the whole way there.

When leaving the Hamptons or Montauk on a Sunday at the end of the weekend, later is always better. Stick around, enjoy an early dinner, and leave as the sun is going down. You'll still make it into bed before midnight, and you'll have missed all the traffic.

BY BUS | **The Hampton Jitney** takes New Yorkers to The Hamptons 365 days a year. It's probably the most reliable (but not the most enjoyable) way of getting here. There are stops throughout Manhattan near easy access points like Grand Central Station and 86th Street, as well as stops in Lower Manhattan and Brooklyn, depending on your destination. There's also an airport connection (for both JFK and LGA) stop on some departures, making this an easy option for those flying in for the weekend. From there, most Montauk-bound Jitneys make stops at Manorville, Southampton, Water Mill, Bridgehampton, Wainscott, East Hampton, Amagansett, and Montauk. Sag Harbor passengers can either take a taxi from Bridgehampton, transfer to a different bus, or choose a departure that stops in Sag Harbor.

Schedules vary by season and can change during holiday weekends, but you can usually count on a bus every hour from 7 a.m. to 11 p.m. during the busy summer months, with extra eastbound departures on Fridays and extra Westbound departures on Sundays. The ride usually takes at least 3 hours to Bridgehampton, but buses are subject to the same traffic that cars are, so it's not unheard of for a Jitney to take 5 hours or more. See the note about timing above.

Hampton Jitney runs two types of buses: their regular coaches, which cost $34 per one-way ticket, and the more luxurious Ambassador line, which costs $50 per one-way ticket. Advance reservations are recommended, as these buses usually sell out during the busy summer season. If you pay ahead of time, you can save $5 on your fare. Water and snacks are served on board, and there's supposedly free Wi-Fi, but it's often broken.

See the website for up-to-date schedules and to make a reservation: hamptonjitney.com.

For a slightly more upscale alternative (but still on a bus) the **Hamptons Luxury Liner** departs from multiple points in Manhattan and stops at the airport connection (for both JFK and LGA) before making stops at Southampton, Water Mill, East Hampton, Amagansett, and Montauk. Some buses also stop at Westhampton, Hampton Bays, Bridgehampton, Sag Harbor, and Wainscott—check the website for the most up-to-date schedule. There's about one departure per hour, both ways, from 9 a.m. to 10 p.m. during the summer, with extra eastbound departures on Fridays and extra westbound departures on Sundays.

The company offers three classes of buses: Coach Class, which costs $29 for a one-way trip; Luxury Class, which costs $39 for a one-way trip; and VIP Class, which costs $59 for a one-way trip. You can select your own seat for an extra $4 each way.

Check the website for schedules and to make reservations in advance: hamptonsluxury liner.com.

TAXI OR UBER | An Uber or private car to the Hamptons will usually cost around $200–$400. It's not recommended, although in the case of a middle-of-the-night airport arrival, it might be necessary.

BY TRAIN | The train is the most popular, the most economical, and possibly the most stressful way of getting to the Hamptons. Trains depart from Penn Station on Long Island Railroad daily. Trains are assigned a track about 8 minutes before departure, and this assignment is broadcast over the loudspeaker and on schedule screens throughout the LIRR waiting areas. All Hamptons trains are on the Montauk line, but from Penn Station, you'll have to transfer at Jamaica, which means the train you need to get on at Penn Station will be on another line (usually to Hempstead or Babylon) and the Montauk connection will be listed on the screen alongside the track assignment. Listen for and look for the word Montauk, and when in doubt, ask the conductor or other passengers. It's about 20 minutes from Penn Station to Jamaica, where you'll transfer to the Montauk line. The Montauk train is almost always on track 8. Trains on the Montauk line stop at Westhampton, Hampton Bays, Southampton, Bridgehampton, East Hampton, Amagansett, and Montauk. Visitors going to Sag Harbor can get off in Bridgehampton and take a taxi. The train ride from Penn Station to Southampton usually takes about 2.5 hours, and the ride to Montauk usually takes 3 hours and 15 minutes.

On Friday afternoons, there's a special "bullet" train that leaves Penn Station at 4:06 p.m. and does not require a transfer at Jamaica. The trip is significantly faster, arriving in Southampton in under 2 hours.

Coming back to the city, there are daily trains that depart Montauk and pick up at Amagansett, East Hampton, Bridgehampton, Southampton, Hampton Bays, and Westhampton before continuing on to Jamaica, where you'll need to change trains to go to Penn Station. There's an extra train on Monday morning and additional trains all day on Sunday.

Peak tickets cost $29.25 one-way and off-peak tickets cost $21.25 one-way.

On arrival, there's always a line of taxis waiting at Hamptons train stations. The taxi inventory in town is limited, so they'll often pair you with other passengers heading in the same general direction and charge a flat rate of $30 per person, cash only.

SAVE ME A SEAT!

There are no assigned seats on the Long Island Railroad—these commuter trains are first-come, first-served. On Fridays in the summer, it's a common occurrence for the train to be standing-room only for the entire 2+ hour duration of the ride. Plan ahead, pack light, and remember to bring plenty of snacks. Beer and wine is sold in Penn Station and on train platforms at Jamaica. There are no dining cars on the trains, but it's legal to drink on board. The best plan of attack is to have your rudest friend leave their bags with you and worm their way into the train, saving a set of seats. The entitlement is palpable during the tense train scramble, so try not to get into a fight with anybody.

Schedules change frequently depending on the seasons and track maintenance, so check online for the most up-to-date information: mta.info/lirr.

Getting Around Town

Once you've arrived out east, it can be a bit tricky to get around—the Hamptons are not as close together as it may seem, and traffic between towns can be horrendous. It can take almost an hour to get from Southampton to Montauk in a car, even without traffic. East Hampton is the most central of the Hamptons: 35 minutes to Southampton, 15 minutes to Bridgehampton, 15 minutes to Sag Harbor, 5 minutes to Amagansett, and 20 minutes to Montauk. Each of these small towns is easily navigable by foot or bike—ask your hotel or rental if there are bikes available for guests. Some hotels also offer shuttle service to the beach or in to town. Taxis and Ubers are available, but the supply can't always keep up with the demand—especially on Friday and Saturday nights, and the prices can be exorbitant. If you can, it's a good idea to bring your own wheels, but it's perfectly easy to visit without a car. Either way, don't plan on too much driving, especially during the summer when traffic slows to a crawl. During holiday weekends, beware of drunk drivers. Drink responsibly, or designate a driver—even if you're not drunk, law enforcement is extra strict.

THE NORTH FORK

Getting There

BY CAR | On a good day with no traffic, it's possible to make the trip to Orient, at the far Northern tip of Long Island, in 2 hours, but it's a good idea to factor in at least 2.5 hours of driving time. Even if there's no traffic on Long Island, there will always be traffic leaving New York City. The fastest way to drive to Montauk is by taking I-495 (Long Island Expressway) East from either the BQE in Brooklyn or the Queens-Midtown tunnel from Manhattan. Those coming from the Bronx can access I-495 East from the Throgs Neck Bridge and I-295.

Take I-495 all the way to Riverhead, where you'll transfer to Highway 25, which takes you through Jamesport, Mattituck, Cutchogue, Southold, Greenport, and Orient.

Avoid making the drive on Fridays between 10 a.m. and 7 p.m. If you can't leave early (or ideally, the night before) wait until after dinner, when most of the commuter traffic has died down.

BY BUS | The Hampton Jitney is the best option for reaching Greenport and the North Fork by bus. Coach buses leave from multiple departure points in Manhattan, and make an airport connection stop (for both JFK and LGA) before heading to Long Island's North Fork. Schedules change depending on seasons and days of the week, but buses stop at Calverton, Mattituck, Cutchogue, Peconic, Southold, and Greenport. Some buses make additional stops at Riverhead, Aquebogue, Jamesport, and Laurel and continue past Greenport on to East Marion, Orient Village, and Orient Point. There's a bus around every 2 hours starting at

8 a.m. until 10 p.m. Regular coaches cost $24 per one-way ticket. Unlike in the Hamptons, there is no Ambassador line to the North Fork. Advance reservations are recommended, as these buses usually sell out during the high season. If you pay ahead of time, you can save $5 on your fare. Water and snacks are served on board, and there's supposedly free Wi-Fi, but it's often broken. The trip to Greenport usually last about 2 hours and 45 minutes.

See the website for up-to-date schedules and to make a reservation: hamptonjitney.com.

BY TRAIN | The most popular way of getting to the North Fork is on the Long Island Railroad. Trains on the Greenport line stop at Riverhead, Mattituck, Southold, and Greenport, which is the final stop on the train, located walking distance from town and directly next to the North Ferry to Shelter Island.

There's usually only one departure from Penn Station every evening, so plan accordingly. Trains are assigned a track at Penn Station about 8 minutes before departure, and this assignment is broadcast over the loudspeaker and on schedule screens throughout the LIRR waiting areas. All North Fork trains are on the Greenport line, but from Penn Station, you'll have to transfer at Jamaica, which means the train you need to get on from Penn Station will be on another line (usually to Hempstead or Babylon) and the Greenport connection will be listed on the screen alongside the track assignment. The ride takes about 2 hours and 45 minutes from Penn Station to Greenport.

Peak tickets cost $29.25 one-way and off-peak tickets cost $21.25 one-way.

Getting Around Town

Greenport is easily navigable by bike or on foot, but you'll need a car to explore the rest of the farm stands and wineries in the region, unless you plan to join an organized wine tour.

SHELTER ISLAND

Getting There

BY CAR, BUS, AND TRAIN | Shelter Island is situated between the Hamptons and the North Fork, making it easily accessible from both Greenport in the north and Sag Harbor in the south.

From the North Fork

If you're without your own car, the best option is to travel to Greenport. From there, the North Ferry to Shelter Island is right in town, steps from the train station. Purchase tokens at the little booth on the dock (cash only) for the $2 trip across the ferry on foot ($3 if you're bringing a bike).

If you're in a car, the crossing is more expensive. A car and driver is $11, with $2 for each additional passenger. There are no reservations, but during peak hours you might have to wait around 20 minutes. The North Ferry runs continuously every 10 minutes from 6 a.m. to 11:45 p.m. Check the website for special holiday and seasonal schedules: northferry.com.

From the Hamptons

Shelter Island is also accessible from the Hamptons, but it's a little bit trickier by foot. From Sag Harbor or Bridgehampton, you'll have to take a taxi to the ferry in North Haven (about 15 minutes and $30). Tickets for those on foot are $1, and a vehicle costs $14, plus $1 for each addition passenger. There are no reservations, so during peak hours you might have to wait about 20 minutes. The South Ferry runs continuously from 5:45 a.m. to 11:45 p.m. During the summer and on weekends, the ferry runs until 1:45 a.m. (southferry.com).

BY PLANE AND HELICOPTER | The most glamorous way to arrive on Shelter Island is by seaplane. Planes leave from East 23rd Street on Fridays and land on the water in front of Sunset Beach. Flights cost around $700 and last about 30 minutes. If you're staying at Sunset Beach for the weekend, ask about any flight and room packages they offer (shorelineaviation.com).

Getting Around Town

Having a car will help you get around faster, but all of Shelter Island is accessible by bike. Check with your hotel or rental to see if they provide bikes, or rent one on your own from the bike shop in town. There is also a limited supply of taxis available on the island, and the occasional Uber. Many hotels will provide transportation for their guests.

FIRE ISLAND

Getting There

BY BOAT | The only way to get to car-free Fire Island is by boat.

To get to Ocean Beach and the communities on the western part of the island, you'll need to get on the **Fire Island Ferries**, located in the town of Bay Shore. During the summer, ferries run about once an hour on Fridays, Saturdays, and Sundays from 7 a.m. to 9 p.m., with later ferries available on Friday and Saturday nights. One-way tickets cost $10 and there are very strict luggage restrictions. Passengers are limited to two pieces of hand-held luggage each, and anything extra (coolers, rolling luggage, etc.) is charged at $5 per piece. No bikes are allowed on the ferry. Check the website for seasonal schedules and exact times: fireislandferries.com.

To access Cherry Grove and Fire Island Pines, use the **Sayville Ferry Service**, located in the town of Sayville. To The Pines, the ferry runs about once every 2 hours on Friday and Saturday, and once an hour on Sundays from 8 a.m. to 8 p.m. To Cherry Grove, the ferry runs once an hour on Saturdays and Sundays and once every 2 hours on Friday. One-way tickets cost $9.50 and coolers and luggage cost $5. No bikes are allowed on the ferry. Check the schedule for seasonal schedules and exact times: sayvilleferry.com.

To get to Watch Hill and the National Seashore, take the ferry at Davis Park. There are limited departures about every 2 hours from 10 a.m. to 7 p.m. One-way tickets cost $9, and there's an extra charge for suitcases, bikes, and surfboards. Check the website for seasonal schedules: davisparkferry.com.

If you've missed the ferry or if you're trying to get to a place that doesn't offer ferry service, you can always call a water taxi: fireislandwatertaxi.com; 631.665.8885.

BY CAR | Robert Moses beach is the only part of Fire Island that is accessible by car. If you plan on driving to reach the car-free communities on Fire Island, you'll have to ditch your car on the mainland and hop on a ferry. Parking costs $50 per weekend at the ferry.

BY TRAIN | The train is the best way to access the Fire Island ferries. In Bayshore, the ferry terminal is 1 mile from the train station and there's usually a shuttle bus.

To get to Bayshore, which is on the Montauk line, you'll have to board at Penn Station and transfer at either Jamaica or Babylon. There are frequent departures about once per hour throughout the afternoon and evening. It's about an hour and 15 minutes to get to Bayshore from Penn Station. Peak tickets cost $19 and off-peak tickets cost $13.75.

For the ferries in Sayville, which is also on the Montauk line, you'll board at Penn Station and transfer at Jamaica or Babylon, depending on your departure time. There are frequent departures about once per hour throughout the afternoon and evening. In Sayville, the ferry terminal is 1.5 miles from the train station and there's usually a shuttle bus. The trip to Sayville takes about 1.5 hours from Penn Station. Peak tickets cost $19 and off-peak tickets cost $13.75.

Getting Around Town

There are no cars allowed on Fire Island, so the only way to get around is by bike or by foot. There's a continuous path that connects the western communities of Kismet, Saltaire, and Ocean Beach with Cherry Grove and the Pines. It's also possible to walk along the beach the whole length of the island. To walk from Ocean Beach to Cherry grove would take about 1.5 hours.

For distances that might be too far to walk, you can call a water taxi. Check with your hotel or rental to see if there are bikes available for rent.

GREATER LONG ISLAND

Getting There

BY CAR | A car isn't essential to a weekend on Long Island, but it will definitely make your life easier and give you the opportunity to explore more than you could otherwise. Long Island is home to a sprawling metropolis of suburban communities, so it's a good idea to expect traffic, especially during rush hour when commuters are on the road. I-495 is the main highway on Long Island, running from Queens to Riverhead. This main artery is the fastest way to get out east, but it's also the least charming (and sometimes backed up with bumper-to-bumper traffic). If you have the time, driving on the smaller surface roads will give you a better sense of what Long Island is really like.

BY TRAIN | Much of Long Island is considered the suburbs of New York, with an extensive commuter rail that can get you within a few miles of where you want to be for around $15–$30 one way. Download the MTA app or visit the Long Island Rail Road website to check train stations, schedules, and fees: mta.info/lirr.

Getting Around Town

There are a few towns on Long Island that you can visit without a car for the weekend and find plenty of things to see and eat, along with a nice place to stay. For places like Long Beach, Oyster Bay, and Port Jefferson, you can have a nice weekend exploring the town without a car. However, if you'd like to do a bit of exploring—to parks, vineyards, or historic estates, you'll need some wheels to get around.

// For those without a car, bikes are the best way to get around

THE JERSEY SHORE

Getting There

BY CAR | The great Garden State Parkway is the main artery of the Jersey Shore, getting you to the Northernmost beaches in the state in just over an hour from Manhattan. The fastest way to get on the Parkway is through Brooklyn and Staten Island, from I-278 to I-95. Once you're on the shore, Ocean Avenue takes you along the shore from Seabright to Sea Girt and everywhere in between. Driving to Asbury Park will take about one hour and 45 minutes.

BY TAXI OR UBER | A taxi, Uber, or private car to Asbury Park will cost around $200–$300.

BY TRAIN | New Jersey Transit takes passengers from Penn Station to the Jersey Shore on the North Jersey Coast Line. Trains depart once an hour from morning to evening, with stops in Long Branch, Elberon, Allenhurst, Asbury Park, Bradley Beach, Belmar, Spring Lake, Manasquan, Point Pleasant, and Bay Head, which is the furthest stop on New Jersey Transit. It's about an hour and 25 minutes to Long Branch, an hour and 45 minutes to Asbury Park, and two hours to Bay Head. One-way tickets cost $16.25.

There's no direct train route from New York to Atlantic City, but there is a train from Philadelphia to Atlantic City.

On the way home, keep in mind that there are two Penn Stations—Newark Penn Station and New York Penn Station. New York Penn Station will be the last stop on the train, so don't get off early.

BY FERRY | The fastest and most pleasant way to reach the Jersey Shore from Manhattan is by boat. **The Seastreak Ferry** leaves lower Manhattan and cruises under the Verrazano Bridge to Atlantic Highlands, New Jersey and Sandy Hook. Primarily a commuter ferry servicing the chichi suburbs of Northern New Jersey, Seastreak has 13 daily departures from New York to Highlands and/or Atlantic Highlands. From there, passengers can take a taxi down the coast to Long Branch, about 20 minutes away, or Asbury Park, about 30 minutes away.

On the weekends, Seastreak takes pleasure seekers from East 35th Street and Pier 11 on Wall Street to the beaches at Sandy Hook. There are three daily departures from New York and the last boat back to the city is at 7:45 p.m.

The ferry takes 50 minutes and costs $27 for a one-way tickCheck online for seasonal and holiday schedule changes: seastreak.com.

Getting Around Town

In Asbury Park, you don't want or need a car to get around. The town, the beach, the bars, and the hotels are all within walking distance. If you're staying in Long Branch, you might want a car to be able to drive to Asbury Park, but Uber is plentiful and affordable.

NEW YORK CITY BEACHES

Getting There

BY CAR | If you live in Brooklyn and have a car, driving is the fastest way to get to the beach—but Jacob Riis is the only option with easy parking ($10). For Coney Island or the Rockaways, it might be easier to take public transportation.

BY TRAIN | Coney Island is steps away from the Q and D trains. Rockaway Beach is accessible from Far Rockaway-bound A trains. To get to the 90th Street, 98th Street, 105th Street, and 116th Street stops, you'll have to transfer to the shuttle at Broad Channel.

BY BOAT | The Rockaway Ferry leaves from Pier 11 on Wall Street and brings passengers to the Rockaway Ferry Terminal at Beach 108th Street. From there, free shuttles bring passengers to Fort Tilden, Jacob Riis, and the Rockaway Beaches a few short blocks away. Check routes and schedules on their website: ferry.nyc/routes-and-schedules/route/rockaway/.

≡ *Where to Stay*

The first step in planning a trip to the Hamptons and Long Island or the Jersey Shore is figuring out where you're going to stay. From campsites to rentals to hotels, you'll find something for every budget, but you have to be willing to plan ahead or visit in the off season.

The best way to experience a weekend at the beach is in a house, where you won't be subjected to the crowds and traffic and where you can take advantage of the excellent local produce to cook yourself a lovely dinner rather than battling bank executives and former models for a table at an overpriced and overhyped restaurant. One of the best things about the Hamptons is the people who come here, but one of the worst things about the Hamptons is also the people who come here.

Sites like airbnb.com, vrbo.com, and onefinestay.com have rental options for something as simple as a room in a shared house to private palatial estates (with a palatial price tag). For the best deals, book as early as humanly possible. If you're looking to do an extended month-long or summer-long stay, check with local realtors or even the classified section of the local newspaper to see what's available for the summer. Renting a house for the whole summer is a popular option in places like the Hamptons and Fire Island.

Enterprising groups of young people can be known to rent a whole house for a month and split it between a group of friends. If 20 people go in on a five-bedroom house for one month, each person gets the room for one week (or, they can invest in a few inflatable mattresses or sleeping bags and sleep four people to a room). This is known as a "sharehouse" and is considered blasphemy in the local community. If you decide to go with this option, be cool, don't tell anybody, and try not to throw any ragers.

Out East, Montauk has the biggest inventory of hotel rooms—probably more than all the other Hamptons combined. In Montauk, there are two types of hotels: beachy mid-century hotels that have gotten a chic renovation, and beachy mid-century hotels that haven't gotten a chic renovation. While the stylishly renovated hotels can charge upwards of $1000/night on summer weekends (with a three-night minimum), even the divey places can be close to $400/night, frequently with a two- or three-night minimum, especially on holiday weekends.

BEST HAMPTONS HOTELS FOR THE OFF-SEASON

GURNEY'S MONTAUK RESORT & SEAWATER SPA · gurneysresorts.com /montauk

THE MAIDSTONE HOTEL · themaidstone.com   ★ *AUTHOR'S PICK*

TOPPING ROSE HOUSE · toppingrosehouse.com

THE AMERICAN HOTEL · theamericanhotel.com

THE CHEQUIT · thechequit.com

// The cozy-chic lobby at Ruschmeyer's

Hotels elsewhere in the Hamptons, Shelter Island, and the North Fork tend to be converted homes and mansions with an occasional chic motel or resort. These vary from reasonable mom-and-pop shops to uber-stylish celebrity hangouts. The rest of Long Island has everything from literal palaces to high-rise chain hotels and everything in between.

On the Jersey Shore, hotels are surprisingly few and far between, and there's truly only one chic place to stay—The Asbury in Asbury Park. With a huge demand for hotel rooms on the Jersey Shore, the prices there are similar to what you'll find in the Hamptons, although the cost of food and drinks once you're there tends to be a bit more modest.

While weekend hotels rates can be absolutely astronomical throughout the Jersey Shore and Long Island, mid-week prices plummet—sometimes by more than 75 percent in places like Montauk. If your schedule allows, aim for a mid-week visit to save some serious cash.

Many hotels, especially in Montauk and Fire Island, close during the off-season. Elsewhere, prices drop dramatically after Labor Day, known as "Tumbleweed Tuesday." September is one of the loveliest times to visit, with great weather, warm oceans, and fewer crowds.

ROUGHING IT: CAMPSITES ON LONG ISLAND AND THE JERSEY SHORE

Keep in mind that spending a month's rent getting a hotel room or renting a house are not the only options. In the Jersey Shore, the Hamptons, and Fire Island, there are a couple of campsites in beautiful natural settings. If you come prepared, you can have a memorable (and inexpensive) night on the beach, sleeping under the stars. Between April and October, most campgrounds require a 4-night stay between Thursday and Sunday. The website hipcamp.com lists private and public campsites and glamping stays, although there aren't very many options on Long Island or in New Jersey (yet).

Here are the best campgrounds on Long Island and in New Jersey, from east to west.

HITHER HILLS CAMPGROUND • parks.ny.gov • 164 Old Montauk Highway, Montauk, New York 11954 • 631.668.2554

CEDAR POINT COUNTY PARK CAMPGROUND • Suffolkcountyny.gov • 5 Cedar Point Road, East Hampton, New York 11937 • 631.852.7620

SHINNECOCK EAST • Suffolkcountyny.gov • Dune Road, Southampton, New York 11968 • 631.852.8839

CUPSOGUE CAMPGROUND • Suffolkcountyny.gov • 906 Dune Road, Westhampton Beach, New York 11978 • 631.852.8111

SMITH POINT COUNTY PARK CAMPGROUND • suffolkcountyny.gov • Mastic Beach, New York 11951 • 631.852.1313

WATCH HILL CAMPGROUND • Watch Hill, Fire Island National Seashore, New York, 11772 • nps.gov/fiis • 631.597.6074

INDIAN ISLAND • Suffolkcountyny.gov • Indian Point Road, Riverhead, New York 11901 • 631.852.3232

WILDWOOD STATE PARK • nysparks.com • 790 Hulse Landing Road, Wading River, New York 11792 • 631.929.4314

CAMP GATEWAY • nps.gov/gate • 26 Hudson Road, Highlands, New Jersey 07732 • 347.630.1124

// Sunset in the Hamptons

2

Escapes for Beach Bums

Where to Find the Best Beaches on Long Island and the Jersey Shore

Summer on the East Coast is synonymous with melting popsicles, umbrella-dotted beaches, and icy blue water. Whether you're hopping on the subway to spend an afternoon in the sand or packing your bags for a weekend away at one of the most beautiful beaches in the country, New York is a hub for Insta-worthy beach trips.

Though New York City is not renowned as a beach destination, what you'll find here may surprise you.

If you don't have the time or the money to pack up the car and spend a few days at the beach, you can still get some sand and sun on a short day-trip from New York City. Beaches in New Jersey, Long Island, and even Brooklyn and Queens offer a breezy break from sweltering summer temps—and in many cases, you don't even need a car to get there.

≡ *Montauk and the Hamptons*

Long Island is home to some of the country's most gorgeous and least-crowded beaches, from the gorgeous white sands of the Fire Island National Seashore to the pristine blue waters backed by mansions in East Hampton and the surfer hangouts of Montauk. With so much going on in the Hamptons, it's sometimes easy to forget that this is first and foremost a beach destination. There are plenty of beaches all along the Hamptons coastline, and they're all public property—there's no such thing as a private beach here, and beaches are always free for pedestrians. Parking passes are available for some beaches during the week, and a select few on weekends. Unless otherwise noted, all beaches require resident beach permits to park. Many of the beaches listed are walking distance from the nearest town, and those that aren't are within biking distance. Check with your rental or hotel to see if there are bikes available. Some hotels even offer complimentary shuttle service to the beach.

MONTAUK | *Laidback Surfer Vibes*

UMBRELLA BEACH (KIRK PARK BEACH)

95 South Emerson Avenue, Montauk, New York 11954

Just a few blocks from Montauk's main street, this is the most popular beach in town for swimming, sunbathing, beach games, and people watching. Flanked by restaurants, bars, and hotels, there's no need to bring much more than a swimsuit and a towel here. Seasonal lifeguards are on duty, and there are shower and toilet facilities, too. Wooden staircases leading onto the beach are especially photogenic.

DITCH PLAINS ⭐ *AUTHOR'S PICK*

18 Ditch Plains Road, Montauk, New York 11954

If you're planning to surf, head to Ditch Plains in Montauk. Located 2 miles outside of town, this beach is all about the break—it's perfect for veteran and newbie surfers and during the summer, you can sign up for surf camps or surf lessons here. On the western part of the beach, there are dramatic sand cliffs which look like a drip castle, and create a beautiful and eerie backdrop. There are seasonal lifeguards on duty, and food trucks on-site during summer weekends. At the far eastern point of the beach, there's a snack shop called Ditch Witch, serving coffee and sandwiches.

// Montauk is one of the only parts of Long Island where you'll find hotels right on the beach

Where Beach Lovers Should Eat

HOOKED

34 South Etna Avenue, Montauk, New York
11954 • 631.668.2111 • hookedmtk.com

Steps from the beach, Hooked might just
have the cheapest lobster roll in town.
Opened in 2018 by longtime local chefs, the
restaurant sources products directly from the
local fishermen, so you can guarantee you're
dining on fresh fish. The grab-and-go restaurant is open for lunch and dinner seven days
a week and has a wide-ranging menu that
serves more than just fried fish—you'll also
find a kale caesar, grilled fish tacos, and poke
bowls. Take your meal to the beach, or post
up at one of the picnic tables outside.

// The ever-popular lobster roll at Hooked

JOHN'S DRIVE IN

677 Montauk Highway, Montauk, New York 11954 • 631.668.5515 • johnsdriveinmontauk.com

One of those quintessential American fast-food restaurants, John's is a true vintage gem,
serving up burgers, fried chicken, and milkshakes. Stop here for an afternoon snack on your
way home from the beach—the soft serve is legendary.

JOHN'S PANCAKE HOUSE

721 Montauk Highway, Montauk, New York 11954 • 631.668.2383

John's Pancake House is a Montauk landmark, and one summer weekends, you'll see a line out
the door for brunch. Get an order of pancakes or crepes for the table, and stuff your face with
diner classics like omelettes, French toast, waffles, and fried chicken.

Where Beach Lovers Should Stay

BREAKERS MONTAUK

769 Old Montauk Highway, Montauk, New York 11954 • 631.668.2525 • beakersmtk.com

Breakers might be the cutest of the renovated motels along the Montauk highway, with cute
cabins surrounding a kidney-shaped pool. Rooms are cozy and bright, with white wood paneling, white duvets, and minimalist furniture. It's certainly more upscale than your average
beach motel, with chic design and Malin+Goetz amenities in the bathrooms, but Breakers
comes without the hefty price tag of some of Montauk's more fashionable hotels. From $169.

AMAGANSETT, SAG HARBOR, AND THE HAMPTONS | *Classic and Preppy*

Amagansett

ATLANTIC AVENUE BEACH

169 Atlantic Avenue, Amagansett, New York 11930

One of the most popular beaches in the Hamptons, Atlantic Avenue Beach is home to a permanent snack shop—a rarity in Amagansett and East Hampton. If you want to spend all day at the beach but don't want to pack a picnic, this is the best place to go. A surf chair is also available for those with mobility issues, along with seasonal lifeguards and restrooms. Parking passes are available for $25 Monday through Friday, but weekends are reserved for those with permits.

INDIAN WELLS BEACH

Indian Wells Highway, Amagansett, New York 11930

Frequented by locals and "sharehouse" bros, this wide beach is where you'll see families decked out in head-to-toe Lily Pulitzer alongside a boozy game of ladder golf. Like much of the Hamptons beaches, the ocean here can be quite rough, and the icy temperatures don't warm up until mid-July. Still, it's a quintessential beach, with grassy dunes, expansive views, and deep blue water. There are lifeguards on duty Memorial Day through Labor Day, and no dogs allowed from 9 a.m. to 6 p.m. The Hamptons are known for their windswept and undeveloped beaches, and this is one without food or drinks available for sale. While you need a resident sticker to park, Indian Wells is walkable from the train station in town, so no car is needed for this adventure.

East Hampton

EGYPT BEACH

Old Beach Lane, East Hampton, New York 11937 • easthamptonvillage.org/181/Beaches

This quiet beach with no facilities is one of the closest beaches to the town of East Hampton, but it's still at least a 30-minute walk from town. The most interesting thing about this beach

HAMPTONS BEACH RULES

1. No dogs on the beach from 9 a.m. to 6 p.m. from April 1 to October 1.
2. Fires must be in metal containers and all fire debris must be removed from the beach. No fires on the beach from 9 a.m. to 6 p.m.
3. No glass on the beach.
4. No alcoholic beverages (nobody actually follows this rule—just be cool).

1 The early bird catches the tan in the Hamptons

2 Lifeguards on duty at Georgica Beach

3 Waves crash into the jetty near Georgica Pond

is its proximity to the exclusive Maidstone Club, a private golf and tennis club that's hosted celebrities and politicians on its famous links course. There's not much to see from the beach, but you can catch a glimpse of the club as you approach Egypt Beach on the road.

GEORGICA BEACH ★ AUTHOR'S PICK

Lily Pond Lane, East Hampton, New York 11937 • easthamptonvillage.org/181/Beaches

Popular with families, Georgica Beach on Lily Pond Lane has seasonal lifeguards and restrooms with showers. Even at its most crowded, there's still plenty of room on this wide strand, and you'll see groups playing kadima, frisbee, and spikeball. The beach is located in a residential part of town that's home to some of East Hamptons grandest mansions. Hillary and Bill Clinton once rented a house on the beach here, and just next to the parking lot is the notorious Grey Gardens, once home to Big Edie and Little Edie Beale of documentary film fame.

MAIN BEACH

101 Ocean Avenue, East Hampton, New York 11937 • easthamptonvillage.org/181/Beaches

Main Beach is East Hampton's most accessible beach, with parking permits for $30. The picturesque wooden pavilion here is home to a snack bar, making this a great option for those who aren't interested in lugging their own picnic to the beach. There are also restrooms with showers.

Bridgehampton

MECOX BEACH

Jobs Lane, Bridgehampton, New York 11932

Mecox Beach, between Bridgehampton and Watermill, is located next to the prestigious (and private) Bridgehampton Tennis & Surf Club. The beach is popular with families because it offers two options for swimming: the ocean and the bay. About a 20-minute walk from the entrance, the beach narrows as the ocean meets Mecox Bay, and the shallow waters here are a good place for beginner swimmers to splash around. A seasonal lifeguard on is on duty and there are bathroom facilities on site. During the summer, food trucks can be found in the parking lot. Parking permits can be purchased for $25 every day.

SAGG MAIN BEACH

315 Sagg Main Street, Sagaponack, New York 11962

Sagg Main Beach in Bridgehampton is popular with day-trippers from Sag Harbor, Shelter Island, and the North Fork. Despite its popularity, the beach never feels overly crowded. There are seasonal lifeguards on duty and the shingled beach cottage at the entrance has restrooms with showers. During the summer, food trucks are parked on site. Monday through Friday, parking permits can be purchased for $25, but weekends are reserved for residents.

Southampton

COOPER'S BEACH

268 Meadow Lane, Southampton, New York 11968

Cooper's Beach is one of the loveliest beaches in New York, with a wide stretch of white sand flanked by (usually) mellow waves. It's one of the only beaches in the Hamptons that has chair and umbrella rentals on site ($10), as well as a permanent snack bar serving run-of-the-mill hamburgers and ice cream. For those staying in town, the beach is a long walk, but there's a free beach shuttle that runs regularly. There are seasonal lifeguards on duty. Parking passes are available daily for $50.

FLYING POINT BEACH

1055 Flying Point Road, Southampton, New York 11968

Known for celeb sightings, Flying Point Beach offers a little bit of peace and quiet compared to other Southampton beaches. There are restrooms and a seasonal lifeguard on duty. While there's no permanent restaurant, you might chance upon a food truck.

Westhampton

LASHLEY BEACH

385 Dune Road, Westhampton Beach, New York 11978

Separated from the town of Westhampton by Moriches Bay, this beach is a low-key local hangout. Facilities are limited, with no snack bar or food trucks on-site. There are seasonal lifeguards on duty.

PIKE'S BEACH

765 Dune Road, Westhampton Beach, New York 11978

In the tiny seaside community of Westhampton Dunes, Pike's Beach feels a bit like Fire Island. Being the farthest beach from the town of Westhampton, it's the least crowded option in town, with a sprawling strand of white sand. The beach borders Cupsogue Beach County Park, which is the tip of the peninsula. Parking permits can be purchased for $40 on weekdays. Weekends are reserved for residents.

ROGERS BEACH

105 Dune Road, Westhampton Beach, New York 11978

Rogers Beach is the closest beach to the town of Westhampton and the most convenient option for a beach day. There's a permanent snack bar on the premises, as well as restroom facilities and showers in the beach pavilion. Seasonal lifeguards are on duty.

Where Beach Lovers Should Eat

VILLA ITALIAN SPECIALTIES

7 Railroad Avenue, East Hampton, New York 11937 • 631.324.5110 • villaitalianspecialties.com

Villa is the best Italian deli in the Hamptons, serving sandwiches and a few pre-made meals like eggplant parm and pasta salad. Come here for monster subs to keep you sated for a long day at the beach, and a great selection of salads and desserts. For those who are planning to cook, this small shop also sells the essentials: cheese, olive oil, and pasta. Bonus—it's one of the only dining options in the area that has prices cheaper than New York City's.

Where Beach Lovers Should Stay

GANSETT GREEN MANOR

273 Main Street, Amagansett • 631.267.3133 • gansettgreenmanor.com

This cozy little hotel located on Main Street has rooms in a historic converted barn and four little cottages scattered throughout the property, ranging from studios to three-bedroom houses. The individually decorated rooms have a shabby-chic flair, with over-stuffed couches and block-printed textiles. Each accommodation has a private entrance and the property is dog-friendly. Although there's no pool, the hotel provides bikes and everything you'll need for a day at the beach, including towels, chairs, umbrellas, and parking passes. From $475.

SHARK SPOTTING

Sharks are incredible creatures and a vital part of the ocean ecosystem. Shark attacks are rare on Long Island and New Jersey, but not unheard of. In 2018, two separate incidents involving sharks attacking children (don't worry, they're okay) happened in July, freaking people out all over the Tri-State Area. If you'd like to scare yourself out even more, download the app sharktivity, where you can see shark sightings, shark attacks, and GPS locations of tracked sharks in your area (atlanticwhiteshark.org).

1 Sunset in East Hampton
2 Signs of life on the beach
3 Pastel hues at sunset in the Hamptons

☰ Shelter Island and the North Fork

While the Hamptons and Fire Island are known for their beaches, the rest of Long Island is not. On Shelter Island, beaches are small and rocky, but perfect for watersports, like kayaking, paddleboarding, jet skiing, or fishing. You won't find monster waves or soft white sand, but it's not impossible to have a traditional beach experience here. Many rentals and hotels are on the water, and although they don't always have a sandy beach, they'll usually have a dock where you can jump into the water or launch your kayaks.

On the North Fork, you'll find two types of beaches: rocky beaches similar to those on Shelter Island, that border Peconic Bay, and nicer sandy(ish) beaches that border the Long Island Sound. Beaches on the Long Island Sound aren't as nice as the South Fork beaches, but they offer a more traditional beach experience than the bay beaches.

SHELTER ISLAND | Watersports and Beachcombing

SHELL BEACH

Oak Tree Lane, Shelter Island Heights, New York 11964

Compared to the Hamptons, Shelter Island is not exactly a beach destination. However, that doesn't mean there aren't places to go where you can lay in the sun, bring a picnic, and go for a refreshing swim. On a narrow spit of land on West Neck Point, shell beach is directly along the road and has a narrow sandy area covered with shells (hence the name) where you can set up chairs or a blanket. Bring a floatie to bob in the calm waters of West Neck Harbor, or go beachcombing to the end of the peninsula, where you'll be rewarded with panoramic water views. There's no official parking lot, so park along the road.

SUNSET BEACH (CRESCENT BEACH)

Shore Road Shelter Island Heights, New York 11965

Named for the swanky hotel across the street, this beach is where Shelter Island's beautiful people go to mingle. Boats dock for the day in the harbor and rosé pours freely in this swanky corner of the island. The beach extends from Sunset Beach Hotel along shore road to The Pridwin Hotel. Come here for a lazy afternoon, and if you don't feel like packing a picnic, you can pop into one of the hotel restaurants for something to eat. It truly is the best place on the island to watch the sunset. There are seasonal lifeguards on duty.

>> Insider Tip: If you have a boat, the bay in front of Sunset Beach is a fun place to drop anchor, people watch, and swim to shore to stock up on rosé

THE NORTH FORK | *Rocky Bays and the Long Island Sound*

Greenport

GULL POND BEACH (NORMAN E. KLIPP MARINE PARK)

Manhanset Avenue, Greenport, New York 11944

This rocky shoreline is the best beach in the town of Greenport. Located next to Gull Pond, the beach has views of Shelter Island and Gardiner's Bay. There are no facilities or concessions, but there are seasonal lifeguards on duty, and parking permits can be purchased daily for $25.

Southold

GOLDSMITH'S INLET PARK

Soundview Avenue, Southold, New York 11971

Goldsmith's Inlet Park is about as beautiful a beach as you can find on Long Island's North Fork, with a long stretch of sand and small pebbles flanked by clear blue water. There are no facilities or dining options here, but the peace and quiet is what makes this place special. The inlet from the bay feeds a small salt pond, and depending on the tide, this can be a fun place to splash around.

TOWN BEACH

Southold Route 48, Southold, New York 11971

The busiest beach in the area, Town Beach is popular with families. The beach offers a play-ground and picnic area, as well as seasonal lifeguards on duty. Located on the Long Island sound, the beach is wider and longer than most North Fork beaches, making this an ideal place to swim and sunbathe. Parking permits can be purchased daily for $25.

// Shelter Island and the North Fork are home to rocky beaches

Where Beach Lovers Should Eat

BILLY'S BY THE BAY

2530 Manhasset Avenue, Greenport, New York 11944 • 631.477.8300 • billysbythebayrestaurant.com

The quintessential North Fork fish shack, Billy's waterfront location near Gull Pond Beach makes this an ideal dining option for those wanting to spend a day at the beach. Casual and fun, with decor that can only be defined as "WASPy tiki bar," Billy's serves surprisingly good seafood with a focus on the local. Dine on raw oysters, steamed clams, or fried shrimp, and wash it all down with a Bloody Mary or local beer. There's live yacht rock on weekends. Billy's is open from late spring to early fall.

Where Beach Lovers Should Stay

RAM'S HEAD INN

108 South Ram Island Drive, Shelter Island Heights, New York 11965 • 631.749.0811 • theramsheadinn.com

Ram's Head Inn is the epitome of Shelter Island style. This historic shingled hotel is homey and welcoming, with simple rooms and decor. The property is the most amazing thing about this hotel, with an expansive, sloping lawn that looks out across the water to Little Ram Island. It's an idyllic waterfront location with a small sandy beach where you can relax in the sun, swim out to the dock, or borrow a kayak and paddle around. Although it's elegant, this inn is truly vintage, so not all the rooms have a private bathroom. From $315.

FIRE ISLAND | *Quintessential Summer Seashore*

Fire Island is a 32-mile long barrier island, home to one long, gorgeous stretch of beach. The entire sandy coast is public land, and it's all available for swimming and sunbathing. Throughout the island, only a few beaches are staffed with lifeguards, and public facilities are rare. For safety and convenience, swim on the beaches directly in front of the oceanfront communities, where lifeguards are on duty. This carless island community thrives in the summertime, when New Yorkers make haste for one of the country's best beaches.

SAILOR'S HAVEN BEACH

631.597.6183 • nps.gov/fiis/plaNew Yorkourvisit/sailorshaven.htm

Accessible by ferry from Sayville, Sailor's Haven beach is a pristine natural landscape. In addition to the Sunken Forest boardwalk trail, Sailor's Haven has a beach with seasonal lifeguards. There are snacks and water available at the snack bar and gift shop. Facilities at Sailor's Haven are only open May–October, when the ferry from Sayville is running.

WATCH HILL BEACH

631.597.6455 • nps.gov/fiis

The beach at Watch Hill is open during the summer, with lifeguards, restrooms, and a snack bar. Accessible by ferry from Davis Park, the beach is part of the Fire Island National Seashore. There's a public marina where you can dock your boat and a picnic area near the visitor center.

Where Beach Lovers Should Eat

THE SAND CASTLE

106 Lewis Walk, Cherry Grove, New York 11782 • 631.597.4174 • fireislandsandcastle.com

Sand Castle is one of the only (if not *the* only) beachfront dining establishments on Fire Island. Open for breakfast, lunch, and dinner, Sand Castle is hard to resist. It may look like any old beach shack from the outside, but inside, the food is more upscale than you'd expect—ricotta French toast for breakfast, kale salad for lunch, and filet mignon for dinner. As with most restaurants on Fire Island, the prices may seem eye-popping, but you're paying for the view, the location, and the ambience. Nothing can compare to a drink with a view, and Friday and Saturday nights during the summer, there's a piano bar. Breakfast is served on Sundays only, and the kitchen is closed on Wednesdays (but the bar is open every day).

Where Beach Lovers Should Stay

DUNE POINT

134 Lewis Walk, Cherry Grove, New York 11782 • 631.597.6261 • dunepointfireisland.com

In a mostly residential community with few hotels, this is by far the chicest house-turned-hotel in all of Fire Island. Located directly on the beach and consisting of various apartments (some with ocean views and private decks), the recently updated guest house has exposed beams in some rooms and cozy and comfortable furnishings. From $149.

OCEAN SAFETY

Even when there's a lifeguard on duty, the ocean can be a dangerous place. Rip tides are a common occurrence at the beach, and it's always a good idea to know what the conditions are like before you go swimming. Even if it looks like calm water, you could get caught in a rip tide. Green flags mean it's safe to swim, yellow flags mean rough (but swimmable) water, and red flags mean that it's too dangerous to swim—which is usually when the surfers are out in full force.

// Gentle waves lap the shore on a sunny day

≡ *Greater Long Island*

Greater Long Island lacks the beautiful beaches of Fire Island and the Hamptons, but there's still plenty of shoreline to discover. Most beaches in the area are small, with pebbles or rough sand fronting the Long Island Sound. It's a warmer (and safer) place to swim, making the beaches here popular with families.

LONG ISLAND | *Rocky Inlets along the Long Island Sound*

North Shore (From East to West)

SUNKEN MEADOW STATE PARK

Sunken Meadow Parkway, Kings Park, New York 11754 • 631.269.4333

This park comprises a beach, a golf course, and lawns that are popular with frisbee players and picnickers. On holiday weekends, the park is packed with people grilling and playing music, and it's generally a festive atmosphere. Throughout the week, it's a quiet and rocky beach and a great place to swim in the Long Island Sound.

CRAB MEADOW BEACH

Waterview St W, Fort Salonga, New York 11768 • 631.261.7574

Crab Meadow Beach is located on the Long Island Sound. The beach is a good choice for timid swimmers and children, with calm waters and occasional tide pools that are fun to splash around in. You'll also find a playground and basketball court, making this beach extra family-friendly. There's a seasonal lifeguard on duty, and pizza and ice cream for sale at nearby Casa Cafe. Or, if you'd rather DIY your meals, there are grills and picnic tables.

// Beaches on the North Fork are often strewn with tiny shells and other ocean treasures

FLEETS COVE BEACH PARK

Fleets Cove Road, Centerport, New York 11721 • 631.351.3000

Situated on Northport Bay, Fleets Cove Beach is a popular picnic spot, with a shaded grassy lawn and boardwalk. There are grills and picnic tables, along with a playground area. The beach is great for swimming, fishing, and kayaking. Seasonal lifeguards are on duty.

CENTRE ISLAND BEACH

Bayville Avenue, Oyster Bay, New York 11717 • 516.624.6124

Centre Island beach is a narrow strip of land connecting Centre Island to the rest of Long Island. One side of the beach faces Oyster Bay, while the other side faces the Long Island Sound and Connecticut. It's a small and low-key beach with a peaceful setting. There's a small snack bar on-site.

South Shore (From East to West)

SMITH POINT COUNTY PARK

William Floyd Parkway, Shirley, New York 11967 • 631.852.1313

Part of the Fire Island National Seashore, Smith Point County Park is its own island, not accessible from the rest of Fire Island. The beach is a sweeping white sand strand backed by grassy dunes. Unlike the other beaches in the Fire Island National Seashore, there's no ferry service here—a bridge connects the beach to the mainland, and there's a parking lot on-site ($18), along with a snack bar. Those who are interested in exploring can check out the park visitor center or stay overnight at the campsites.

There's a solemn memorial near the beach for the 230 people who died during a 1996 TWA plane crash just offshore (twaflight800memorial.org).

ROBERT MOSES BEACH

Robert Moses Causeway, Babylon, New York 11702 • 631.669.0470 • parks.New York.gov/parks/7

This is one of the most beautiful—and the—most popular—beaches on Long Island, with over 3 million yearly visitors to this 875-acre beachfront locale. This is the only part of Fire Island you can drive to, with a parking lot next to the beach ($10). With almost 5 miles of shoreline, this massive seaside playground doesn't feel overly crowded, as long as you're willing to make a long trek from your car. Expect massive traffic delays all day Saturday and Sunday—parking here can be a nightmare. In addition to a beach, the park has a pitch and putt golf course, volleyball nets, and a gazebo with picnic tables. A snack bar on site will feed the unprepared, but it's a good idea to bring your own lunch. Those arriving by boat can use the public day-use marina, and you can purchase fishing and surfing permits for the beach. There are multiple lifeguards stationed throughout the beach. This is the far western end of Fire Island, so if you'd like to do a little exploring on foot, you can check out the lighthouse and the tiny villages of Saltair and Kismet, about an hour away.

JONES BEACH

Ocean Parkway, Wantagh, New York 11793 • 516.785.1600

With over 6 million yearly visitors, this is the most popular beach in New York—and for good reason. Just under an hour from the city by car (parking is $10), Jones Beach is equally popular with city folks and suburbanites. The beach and ocean are perfect for swimming, with lifeguards stationed throughout. When you're sick of the beach, you can stroll the boardwalk,

FOURTH OF JULY FIREWORKS

The Fourth of July means that summer is finally in full swing. Here's where to catch the best firework displays throughout Long Island and the North Jersey Coast. While many of the firework shows happen on July Fourth, some happen up to a week before the Fourth or a week later, depending on what day of the week the Fourth falls on.

JONES BEACH, NY	MASSAPEQUA, NY
MONTAUK, NY	GLEN COVE, NY
OAKDALE, NY	ATLANTIC HIGHLANDS, NJ
ASHAROKE, NY	ATLANTIC CITY, NJ
RIVERHEAD, NY	MANASQUAN, NJ
SHELTER ISLAND, NY	POINT PLEASANT, NJ
EAST HAMPTON, NY	

// Beach plums and other vegetation help keep the dunes healthy and thwart erosion

eat at a snack bar, play mini-golf or shuffleboard, or attend one of the concerts at the famous Jones Beach Theater. There are surf chairs for those with mobility issues, and calm waters near Zach's bay for beginner swimmers.

LONG BEACH

Long Beach, New York 11561 • 516-431-1021

The closest Long Island beach to New York City, Long Beach is accessible by the Long Island Railroad. Like Fire Island, Long Beach and neighboring Lido Beach are part of a narrow barrier island, but unlike Fire Island, Long Beach is open to vehicles. A boardwalk runs the length of the beach, with a few shops, restaurants, and hotels—and lots of apartment buildings. Life-guards are on duty during the summer, and nonresident entry fees are a whopping $15 per person (children under 12 are free).

Where Beach Lovers Should Eat

GROTTA DI FUOCO

960 West Beech Street, Long Beach, New York 11561 • 516.544.2400 • grottalbny.com

Grotta serves classic Italian-American fare at a higher notch, with high-quality fresh ingredients cooked over an open flame. The decor is industrial-chic, with reclaimed wood and metal chairs. Opt for wood-fired pizza with ricotta and pecorino, or get a heaping plate of fresh pasta topped with rabbit ragu or local little neck clams. It's a trendier scene than you might expect, with live music on the weekends and craft cocktails.

Where Beach Lovers Should Stay

ALLEGRIA

80 West Broadway, Long Beach, New York 11561 • 516.889.1300 • allegriahotelny.com

This upscale high-rise hotel is directly on the boardwalk, with sweeping views of the ocean. The decor is flashy and modern, with light fixtures and artworks that feel a little bit like they might belong in Vegas. The on-site restaurant, Atlantica, serves artfully plated, globally inspired seafood in a setting that wouldn't be out of place on an episode of *Real Housewives*. Everything about this hotel is indulgent and fabulous, and it brings a little bit of the Miami Beach experience to Long Island. Hang out at the rooftop pool, or head to the beach, where the hotel provides umbrellas, chairs, and towels, along with surfboard and bike rentals. From $495.

☰ *The Jersey Shore*

In New Jersey, mobs of people head to the beach every weekend to work on their tans. Beaches with boardwalks abound in New Jersey, some with a carnivalesque atmosphere. Beach towns all along the coast have boardwalks filled with bars, restaurants, and shops selling neon souvenirs. It's prime people watching territory, but the beach isn't too bad either. Just a couple of hours south of New York City, the ocean warms up and turns vividly blue.

JERSEY SHORE (FROM NORTH TO SOUTH) | *Colorful Beaches Full of Characters*

SANDY HOOK

732.872.5970 • nps.gov/gate/planyourvisit/sandy-hook-hours.htm

Easily accessible via a 45-minute ferry ride (seastreak.com) or a 1.5-hour drive from New York City, Sandy Hook is a slightly spooky former US Army base that has been turned into a park. The narrow peninsula of abandoned buildings and fort structures is surrounded by surprisingly pristine beaches on both the bay side and the ocean side, along with bird-filled trees and bushes. On a clear day, you can see New York from here, but it feels like a world away. There are bikes available for rent, or you can bring your own, to cruise the 7 miles of bike paths winding through the park. History buffs can wander the ruins of the army base and check out the Sandy Hook lighthouse.

>> Insider Tip: Gunnison, at the north end of Sandy Hook, is New Jersey's only nude beach.

// The abandoned structures at Sandy Hook

SEVEN PRESIDENTS OCEANFRONT PARK ⭐ *AUTHOR'S PICK*

221 Ocean Avenue, Long Branch, New Jersey 07740 • 732.229.0924 • monmouthcountyparks.com

Halfway between Sandy Hook and Asbury Park, Seven Presidents Oceanfront Park is an idyllic New Jersey beach, with grassy dunes and clear blue water, along with a snack bar, restrooms, and lifeguards on duty during the summer. The beach can get extremely crowded, particularly on holiday weekends, so come early or come late to grab a spot. A skatepark and epic playground will keep kids happy all day. Parking is $8 per vehicle, and admission is an additional $8 per person for those 18 and over.

LONG BRANCH

Ocean Avenue, Long Branch, New Jersey 07740

Easily accessible by train on New Jersey Transit, Long Branch is the beginning of boardwalk territory in New Jersey, with a wide wooden boardwalk overlooking the white sand beach. The boardwalk, part of Pier Village, is full of restaurants and bars. A daily parking pass is $7, and it costs $7 per person to access the beach. Children 17 and under are free.

ASBURY PARK

Ocean Avenue, Asbury Park, New Jersey 07712

Asbury Park's funky boardwalk has made this into one of the most popular beaches in New Jersey. There's a definite party atmosphere here, with beachside bars serving drinks and blasting music. The beach is packed, but it's fun and the water is surprisingly clean. Daily beach passes cost $7 and parking is $10.

>> Insider Tip: The boardwalk here is one of the coolest in the country—you'll find taco stands, an antique pinball museum, street art, and shops.

// New Jersey's beaches are just one hour from New York City via high-speed ferry

// The crowded and colorful beach at Asbury Park

ISLAND BEACH STATE PARK

Lanoka Harbor, New Jersey 08734 • islandbeachnj.org

South of Seaside Heights, Island Beach State Park is a barrier island that's one of the most beautiful beaches in New Jersey. On the south end of the beach, there's a view of Barnegat Lighthouse and Long Beach Island. The beach is only accessible by car, and the entrance fee is $20 per vehicle.

Where Beach Lovers Should Eat

MOBY'S

2 Bay Avenue, Highlands, New Jersey 07732 • 732.872.1245 • mobyslobsterdeck.com

If you have a car, head to nearby Atlantic Highlands and gorge on lobster, steamed clams, and baskets of fried seafood on the deck at Moby's. There are beer and cocktails for sale (served in plastic cups) and a view of the Atlantic Highlands harbor. You'll be able to see Sandy Hook across the water and fishing boats puttering around.

Where Beach Lovers Should Stay

CAMPING AT SANDY HOOK

nps.gov/gate/planyourvisit/sandy-hook-hours.htm

Bring your tents and sleeping bags and set up camp at Camp Gateway. Rates are $30 per night, and each campground sleeps up to six people. No alcohol or glass containers allowed, but dogs are okay, as long as they are on a leash no longer than 6 feet.

OCEAN PLACE

1 Ocean Boulevard, Long Branch, New Jersey 07740 • 800.411.6493 • oceanplace.com

Long Branch's Ocean Place is one of the only resort-style hotels on the North Jersey Coast. This clean and modern hotel has simple but comfortable rooms with a slightly sterile decor. But while the rooms may feel commonplace, the view does not. Ocean View guest rooms have balconies that face the Atlantic Ocean, offering epic ocean views. The best part of the hotel is the pool and spa—something many hotels in the area don't have. Book a massage or an herbal soak after a long day on the beach. Rooms from $269.

≡ New York City

Just a few subway stops from some of Brooklyn's trendiest neighborhoods, you can hit the beach and check out the up-and-coming surf scene in the Rockaways, or get your freak on in Coney Island.

BEACHY DAY TRIPPING FROM NEW YORK CITY (FROM WEST TO EAST) | *A Snapshot of New York City's Subway-Accessible Beaches*

CONEY ISLAND ⭐ AUTHOR'S PICK

Surf Avenue, Brooklyn, New York 11224 • coneyisland.com

Many New Yorkers discount the beach at Coney Island, but there's something amazing about this place. The carnival vibes feel like a step back in time, and the people watching is unmatched anywhere else on earth—nothing brings New Yorkers to the beach like a sweltering summer heat wave. There are tons of kids and families here, but that doesn't mean you can't

1 The water in the Rockaways is surprisingly clean
2 Bikes are the best mode of transportation in the Rockaways
3 Fort Tilden is a hipster haven

have some adult fun. Get a pina colada in a plastic cup from one of the boardwalk bars and head down to the beach. The water quality is not great here, so you might not be inspired to take a long swim, but it's refreshing enough for a quick dip.

Closest Subway: D, Q at Coney Island Stillwell Avenue Station; B at Brighton Beach Station.

FORT TILDEN ★ AUTHOR'S PICK

Breezy Point, New York 11697

Fort Tilden is hipster beach mecca, and this is where you'll find half of Bushwick on a Sunday afternoon, drinking, smoking, and topless sunbathing. Fort Tilden is full of beautiful people covered in tattoos, and spotting a local celebrity or two is not unheard-of. There aren't any facilities at this beach, but there are a couple porta-potties and a few beach vendors selling homemade rum punch. The beach is part of an abandoned army fort that's become somewhat of an arts destination. Each summer, MoMA presents Rockaway! with a different artist's installation. In 2018, Yayoi Kusama's highly Instagrammed Narcissus Garden took over the space.

Closest Subway: A at Rockaway Park Station—Beach 116 Street.

JACOB RIIS BEACH

Rockaway Park, New York 11694

Jacob Riis is where Brooklyn comes to the beach, with a huge expanse of sand absolutely covered in bodies. There's always a lively atmosphere here on weekends, with large speakers set up on the beach for impromptu dance parties and families making use of the grills. There are a few different snack bar options, as well as restrooms. The complex used to be a public bathhouse, and the funky art deco buildings are still standing. During the summer, glamping tents are set up just steps from the beach—one of the coolest urban glamping experiences out there (camprockaway.com). The Jacob Riis Beach Bazaar has managed to turn this into the most happening place in the Rockaways, with live music, shopping, pop-ups, and of course, food and drinks. Parking costs $10. riisparkbeachbazaar.com/

Closest Subway: A at Rockaway Park Station—Beach 116 Street.

ROCKAWAY BEACH

Queens, New York 11693

Rockaway Beach is slightly mellowed compared to Jacob Riis, but it's still a happening time, with crowds of people. Popular with the hipster set, the boardwalk has a couple of options for snack bars. It's easily accessible by subway or ferry, making this the simplest (and most affordable!) beach option for New Yorkers in need. Check out the current ferry schedule at ferry .nyc/routes-and-schedules/route/rockaway/.

Closest Subway: A at Beach 90 St Ferry to Beach 108 St and Ocean Channel.

Where Beach Lovers Should Eat

ROCKAWAY BEACH SURF CLUB

302 Beach 87th Street, Far Rockaway, New York 11693 • rockawaybeachsurfclub.com

This Rockaway staple is famous for its tacos: fish, chorizo, tofu, and black bean, served with guac or pickled veggies. The menu is simple, rounded out by chips and guacamole, cucumber salad, and corn. Come for the tacos, but stay for the cocktails and the hipster-surfer atmosphere. Eat at the bar or grab a picnic table outside, where there are murals on the walls and Christmas lights strung overhead.

Where Beach Lovers Should Stay

THE HIGH TIDE HOTEL

9720 Rockaway Beach Boulevard, Rockaway Beach, New York 11693 • 347.433.7905 • hightiderockaway.com

This unbelievably hip boutique hotel is far and away the coolest place to stay if you want to turn your day at the beach into an overnight. Artist-designed rooms are individually decorated. Some are classic and cool, while others offer an immersive art experience with murals on the walls, ceiling, and floor. From $250.

3

Escapes for Art Lovers

Where to Find the Coolest Art on Long Island and the Jersey Shore

Long Island has long been a playground for artists of all kinds, from writers and photographers to sculptors and painters.

With music venues, art spaces, bookstores, and historical points of interest, Long Island and the Jersey Shore make for a rich tapestry of multimedia arts—it only makes sense, since this is the weekend destination for New York, one of the greatest cities for art in the world. Much like New York City, Long Island has something for every kind of art lover, from classic historical mansions filled with impeccable antiques to edgy pop-up galleries and gritty urban decay.

Keep your eye on the events calendar at local institutions and if you plan to be a regular, sign up for the newsletters for your favorite galleries and organizations. That way, you'll be the first to know about insider events and openings worth planning a trip around.

☰ *Montauk and the Hamptons*

Before the billionaires priced everybody out of the Hamptons, the area was an idyllic place for artists—and it's easy to see why: the natural beauty here is breathtaking, and the quality of life is downright inspiring.

Now the arts scene has much more star power, with famous musicians and actors making a home for themselves here. You'll quickly find that even the regular people who call this place home (at least for part of the year) tend toward the creative class: chefs, interior decorators, boat builders, florists, stylists, designers, curators, editors, and anybody who likes to be seen brushing elbows with the aforementioned artistic elite.

The arts scene is strong here; there are world-class galleries and museums, along with local non-profits, historic homes, and even workshops and events designed to indulge your creative side. During the summer, there's something happening every day of the week. After Labor Day the pace slows down, but opportunities to create or witness artistic expression still abound, especially if you know where to look. While Montauk's year-round art scene isn't very robust, look out for seasonal pop-ups from some of the coolest names in the art world.

MONTAUK | *Hipster Pop-Ups*

BOO-HOORAY SUMMER RENTAL

277 Grand Street, Third Floor, New York, New York 10002 • 805 Main Street, Montauk, New York, 11954 • 212.641.0692 • Boo-hooray.com

The excruciatingly hip Boo-Hooray is a summer outpost of the downtown New York gallery dedicated to preserving social movements and cultural ephemera of the 20th and 21st century. Part gallery, part museum, it's a love letter to vintage pop-culture, showcasing zines, photos, rare books, records, manuscripts, and other cultural relics. The Montauk space is quickly becoming one of the see-and-be-seen destinations in town.

Where Art Lovers Should Eat

SCARPETTA BEACH

290 Old Montauk Highway, Montauk, New York 11954 • 631.668.1771 • scarpettarestaurants.com/montauk

Located in Gurney's Resort and only open for dinner, Scarpetta Beach serves perfectly executed artful Italian fare in an over-the-top setting. While the sleek chairs, velvet booths, and glass chandeliers dangling from high ceilings might feel a bit out of place in Montauk, the whole restaurant feels a bit like a work of art, and so does the food. Seafood crudo, decadent pastas, and fresh salads are served in carefully plated arrangements. If you're not interested in dropping the cash for an expensive dinner here, stop in for dessert and a craft cocktail at the bar.

// Local artist Isabel Bacon displays her work at an outdoor show

Where Art Lovers Should Stay

THE SURF LODGE

183 Edgemere Street, Montauk, New York 11954 • 631.483.5037 • thesurflodge.com

Hands-down the most star-studded hotel in Montauk for over 10 years, the Surf Lodge is a local institution. Besides being a bar and concert venue, the Surf Lodge is also, well, a lodge, with impeccably designed, bright rooms with natural accents like rattan basket chairs hanging from the ceiling and sinks made from carved wooden bowls. It's hard to get a room here, so book far in advance and expect a three-night minimum during summer weekends. From $375.

AMAGANSETT, SAG HARBOR, AND THE HAMPTONS | *The Land of Famous Artists, Curators, and Collectors*

Amagansett

THE ART BARGE: THE VICTOR D'AMICO INSTITUTE OF ART

Napeague Meadow Road, Amagansett, New York 11930 • 631.267.3172 • theartbarge.org

Located out in the middle of a grassy field on Napeague Harbor, the art barge (yes, it's an actual barge) looks more like a shipwreck than an art studio. But drive up the sandy road and you'll find a gallery, workshop, and studio offering classes for all skill levels and ages. Students can opt for season-long classes or weeklong immersive workshops focusing on everything from painting and drawing to ceramics, printmaking, and writing. There's also a children's studio that offers summer-long or week-long art camps for kids. Check the calendar online for special events like artist lectures and art exhibits—if you're not interested in creating art yourself, it's the best way to get a glimpse of this one-of-a-kind space.

GRAIN SURFBOARDS 🌟 AUTHOR'S PICK

11 Indian Wells Highway, Amagansett, New York 11930 • 631.267.9283 • grainsurfboards.com

Yes, it's a super-groovy shop where you can make your own custom surfboards, but that's not why you should visit Grain Surfboards. Throughout the year, Grain hosts art shows and sells handmade art prints and crafts (along with surf wax and other practical surf stuff) at this outpost in Amagansett. Check the website for a schedule of art openings, or stop by on a weekend to see what's new. For those interested in making their own surfboard, Grain offers classes and workshops.

KARMA GALLERY

249 Montauk Highway, Amagansett, New York 11930 • 631.267.7728 • karmakarma.org

An outpost of New York City's Karma, this gallery/bookstore exhibits contemporary art and rare art books in a beautiful, bright space. The store is only open occasionally.

THE POLLOCK-KRASNER HOUSE AND STUDY CENTER

830 Springs Fireplace Road, East Hampton, New York 11937 • 631.324.4929 • stonybrook.edu/pkhouse

The original house that Jackson Pollock and his wife Lee Krasner moved into in 1945, the Pollock-Krasner house is a museum, studio, and educational center. Showcasing temporary exhibits from other artists along with a permanent collection of some of Krasner and Pollock's works, a visit here is interesting because what seems like an unassuming cottage on Accabonac

1 Grain Surfboards frequently displays local artwork, like this driftwood piece by Jane Parkes
2 The signature Pollock splatter at the Pollock-Krasner House and Study Center
3 The Pollock-Krasner House and Study Center in Springs

Harbor is where some of the most famous abstract expressionist works of the 20th century were created. Perhaps the most stunning artwork of all is the floor of the barn, which Pollock and later Krasner used for their studios, as it's covered in splattered paint. Visitors can only see the house and barn studio during guided tours on Thursday, Friday, and Saturday. Reservations are required, and tours cost $10.

Sag Harbor
BAY STREET THEATER

1 Bay Street, Sag Harbor, New York 11963 • 631.725.9500 • baystreet.org

With kids' programming, theater classes, and musical performances, Bay Street Theater is more than just your average small-town theater. While music and comedy performances are usually one-night-only shows featuring touring guests, the theater also puts on a big summer production with multiple performances throughout the week. It's a small theater, but you'll be swept away by the talent, set design, and production value of these shows.

CANIO'S BOOKS

290 Main Street, Sag Harbor, New York 11963 • 631.725.4926 • caniosbooks.com

More than just a bookstore, Canio's is the hub of Sag Harbor's literary community, often hosting readings, signings, lectures, and events.

GRENNING GALLERY

17 Washington Street, Sag Harbor, New York 11963 • 631.725.8469 • grenninggallery.com

Specializing mostly in paintings with a seaside slant, this gallery in historic downtown has openings throughout the summer that focus on both established and up-and-coming artists.

EASTVILLE COMMUNITY HISTORICAL SOCIETY

139 Hampton Street, Sag Harbor, New York 11963 • 631.725.4711 • eastvillehistorical.org

The Eastville Community Historical Society is dedicated to preserving the culture of Eastville, a traditionally African American area of Sag Harbor. The museum has art, photographs, and artifacts, as well as rotating exhibits that highlight cultural diversity. The Historical Society also owns the Street. David A.M.E. Zion Church, thought to be a stop on the Underground Railroad.

ROMANY KRAMORIS GALLERY

41 Main Street, Sag Harbor, New York 11963 • 631.725.2499 • kramorisgallery.com

Romany Kramoris exhibits a mix of local and international painters. Exhibits tend toward the abstract, but it's more than a gallery here; there's also a shop selling blown glass, stationery, fragrances, and gifts.

TULLA BOOTH GALLERY

66 Main Street, Sag Harbor, New York 11963 • 631.725.3100 • tullaboothgallery.com

Tulla Booth gallery focuses on fine art photography. With subjects ranging from celebrities to the natural world, you'll find works from renowned photographers as well as emerging artists.

East Hampton

CLOTHESLINE ARTS SALE

631.324.0806 • guildhall.org

With over 400 participating artists, the Clothesline Arts Sale brings art to the masses; artists here sell directly to consumers. It's only $15 to enter as an artist, and the event is free for visitors to browse, chat, and buy works ranging in price from $75 to $2,500, making art truly accessible. For young collectors, it's a great place to make genuine connections with artists while shopping for prints, paintings, and drawings.

EAST HAMPTON LIBRARY

159 Main Street, East Hampton, New York 11937 • 631.324.0222 • easthamptonlibrary.org

While it might look like a regular house on the outside, this small-town library in an historic building is bright and cheery on the inside, with tall ceilings, exposed beams, and a life-size windmill that serves as the reference desk. While you must be a resident to get a library card and check out books, it's a nice place to visit on a rainy day.

EAST HAMPTON SHED

30 Blue Jay Way, East Hampton, New York 11937 • 631.741.8462 • easthamptonshed.com

Quite literally an East Hampton shed, this gallery space in the backyard of the Vogel book bindery provides an "only in the Hamptons" viewing experience, with up-and-coming artists exhibited in a small (and surprisingly clean!) backyard shed.

ERIC FIRESTONE GALLERY
⭐ AUTHOR'S PICK

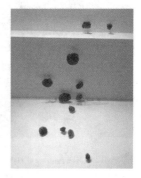

4 Newtown Lane, East Hampton, New York 11937 • 631.604.2386 • ericfirestonegallery.com

Arguably the most zeitgeist-y gallery in the Hamptons, Eric Firestone is an intimate space to discover art by well-known artists as well as The Next Big Thing. Always edgy, sometimes astonishingly expensive, the space and the art here have a wow-factor that's unmatched at any other local galleries. This is the kind of gallery where you'll find historically significant modern art alongside Instagram-worthy structures that are big, bright, and colorful.

// Gilded beehives adorn the walls of a gallery

1 A psychedelic painting at Halsey McKay Gallery

2 The Hamptons are home to some surprisingly hip galleries, like Halsey McKay

3 Galleries and community centers often feature local artists

THE FIREPLACE PROJECT

851 Springs Fireplace Road, East Hampton, New York 11937 • 631.324.4666 • thefireplaceproject.com

This garage gallery in Springs presents solo and salon-style shows in a non-traditional gallery setting. There's little pomp and circumstance here, and past shows have been themed toward accessibility, like the 9999 show, which only featured works under $10,000. The gallery is only open on Saturdays and Sundays, or by appointment.

GOLDEN EAGLE ARTIST SUPPLY

144 North Main Street, East Hampton, New York 11937 • 631.324.0603 • goldeneagleart.com

One step inside this little house will spark your creativity. Catering to both serious artists and amateur hobbyists, Golden Eagle Artist supply sells everything from watercolor pencils to scissors to vellum and craft paper—almost everything you need to fulfill your dream of quitting your job, moving to the Hamptons, and becoming an artist like so many before you. Even if you're not artistically inclined, it's hard to resist the gorgeous tools of the trade here, from leather-bound notebooks to gel pens and handmade pencil cases.

// Upcycled bottles create a colorful hanging lamp

GUILD HALL

158 Main Street, East Hampton, New York 11937 • 631.324.0806 • guildhall.org

East Hampton's Guild Hall is the epicenter of the Performing Arts scene in the Hamptons, showcasing acts both big and small. Apart from theater and musical performances, there are also indie film screenings and lectures, along with classes, workshops, and a children's program. Guild Hall is also home to a museum whose permanent collection includes works by mid-19th century East End artists like Jackson Pollock and Cindy Sherman. Notable performers in 2018 included Tig Notaro, the New York City Ballet, David Sedaris, Questlove, chef Masaharu Morimoto, and more. Tickets to events at this non-profit range from free to hundreds of dollars, but most fall in the $15–$50 range.

HALSEY MCKAY GALLERY

79 Newtown Lane, East Hampton, New York 11937 • 631.604.5770 • halseymckay.com

One of the newest galleries in East Hampton, Halsey McKay is full of edgy and experimental art from up-and-coming artists, which means this might be the perfect place to snag an affordable piece of art from somebody before they become Somebody.

// Local art on display in Springs

HAMPTONS INTERNATIONAL FILM FESTIVAL

hamptonsfilmfest.org

Held every October, the Hamptons International Film Festival is—unsurprisingly—a star-studded event that's a great excuse to visit during the off season. For over 25 years, the festival has brought both big names and indie films to Hamptons theaters with a weekend of films, lectures, and of course, parties.

HARPER'S BOOKS

87 Newtown Lane, East Hampton, New York 11937 • 631.324.1131 • harpersbooks.com

This gallery/bookstore in the town of East Hampton showcases an astonishing collection of rare books, art and architecture coffee table tomes, and fine art exhibitions.

THE LONGHOUSE RESERVE ⭐ AUTHOR'S PICK

133 Hands Creek Road, East Hampton, New York 11937 • 631.329.3568 • longhouse.org

A Dr. Seuss-meets-Dali playground of art installations, sculptures, and nature, this under-the-radar outdoor museum is one of the best-kept-secrets on Long Island. The vibe here is quirky, but with and undercurrent of star power; you'll find works by Yoko Ono, Buckminster Fuller, and Dale Chihuly amongst the fairytale-like discoveries here. With over 16 acres to explore, this sprawling sculpture garden is full of secret pathways and hidden art-filled nooks. It would

// Glass sculptures at the incredible Longhouse Reserve

be impossible to discover everything in just one visit. For the best viewing experience, visit in the height of summer, when the grounds are lush and green.

MULFORD FARM AND HOME SWEET HOME

10 James Lane, East Hampton, New York 11937 • 631.324.6869 • easthamptonhistory.org/museums

Located right before the town of East Hampton, this museum comprises a homestead, barn, and a windmill that dates to the 1700s. While opening hours are few and far between, tours are given on Saturdays at 10 a.m. and cost $5. Besides that, it's worth a visit here for a stroll around the grounds and a peek in the windows at the preserved historical furnishings. This may or may not be considered trespassing, so if somebody yells at you, you didn't get that advice here.

RENTAL GALLERY

87 Newtown Lane, East Hampton, New York 11937 • 631.527.5524 • rentalgallery.us

Sometimes provocative and always cutting-edge, the works at Rental Gallery are not just catering to the "something nice for my vacation home" crowd. However, the edgy paintings, drawings, and collages exhibited here would certainly make for conversation-starters in any home.

1 A Lego-like sculture at The Longhouse Reserve
2 A Seussian swirl of color at The Longhouse Reserve
3 The garden and fountain at The Longhouse Reserve

Bridgehampton and Sagaponack

DAN FLAVIN ART INSTITUTE 🌟 *AUTHOR'S PICK*

23 Corwith Avenue, Bridgehampton, New York 11932 • 631.537.1476 • diaart.org/visit/visit/the-dan-flavin-art-institute-bridgehampton-united-states

This place will turn any social media Luddite into a selfie-taking influencer. Housed in a converted firehouse in Bridgehampton, the seemingly simple neon light installations play tricks with your eyes, creating an otherworldly glow that will confuse your depth perception. Admission is free and the installation is open Thursday-Sunday afternoons May through October and Saturday and Sunday afternoons November through April.

MADOO CONSERVANCY 🌟 *AUTHOR'S PICK*

618 Sagg Main Street, Sagaponack, New York 1196 • 631.537.8200 • maddoo.org

Madoo is one of those "only in the Hamptons" places—a seemingly run-down former artist residence that will remind you of the good old days on Long Island's East End. While it's open to the public, it's not necessarily the kind of place where you can just drop by, as it's only open on Friday and Saturday afternoons. However, there are classes, events, lectures, and workshops hosted throughout the summer. Admission is free, and the real reason to visit is a stroll around the whimsical gardens, an epic mix-up of styles eschewing the perfectly manicured hedges that are ubiquitous in the Hamptons. Time your visit during the lush early summer for maximum photo ops.

THE WATERMILL CENTER

39 Water Mill Town Road, Water Mill, New York 11976 • 631.726.4628 • watermillcenter.org

This innovative and experimental multi-disciplinary space holds workshops, farm-to-table dinners, and yoga classes in an unbelievable modern space with a library, a sculpture garden, and an art museum. Stop by for a weekend tour (reservations required) or check the calendar for special events and performances.

THE WHITE ROOM GALLERY

2415 Main Street, Bridgehampton, New York 11932 • 631.237.1481 • thewhiteroom.gallery

With vibrant mixed media and paintings, the White Room Gallery is a Bridgehampton staple, showcasing contemporary abstract and graphic art with new exhibits every three to five weeks during the summer season. There's a distinct rock-and-roll vibe here, with graffiti art alongside creative pop-culture portraits.

// In summer, The Longhouse Reserve is swathed in green

Southampton

COLLECTIVE ART + DESIGN

200 North Sea Road, Southampton, New York 11968 • 631.353.3445 • collectiveartdesign.com

This gallery in a converted power station in East Hampton combines art and design in a modern and evocative showroom. With both functional and decorative pieces, everything here is a work of art, even if it's meant to be sat on instead of hung on your wall. It is a decorator's dream come true, with funky, exquisite, and one-offed furniture, art, and decor.

THE PARRISH ART MUSEUM

279 Montauk Highway, Water Mill, New York 11976 • 631.283.2118 • parrishart.org

By far the most traditional art museum experience on Long Island's East End, the Parrish Art Museum is a work of art to behold. The modern barn building with retractable walls is an architectural marvel that creates a welcome setting for the well-established modern and contemporary artists exhibited inside. Widely considered one of the best small-town art museums in America, the Parrish Art Museum is a must-see for any art lovers planning a trip to Long Island. In addition to thought-provoking temporary exhibits, the museum is home to a permanent collection of local and international artists including Roy Lichtenstein, Chuck Close, William Merritt Chase, and Fairfield Porter. Make sure to check the website for special events and performances.

ROGERS MANSION/SOUTHAMPTON HISTORY MUSEUM

4911, 17 Meeting House Lane, Southampton, New York 11968 • 631.283.2494 • southamptonhistory.org

The Southampton History Museum is comprised of twelve historic buildings, including the Rogers Mansion, a pristine white Gilded Age estate from 1834. While the mansion hosts rotating exhibits, the other structures, including a carriage house and one-room-schoolhouse, are more educational in nature, with archival materials. The museum has over 8,000 volumes of photographs, books, maps, and memorabilia.

SOUTHAMPTON ARTS CENTER

25 Jobs Lane, Southampton, New York 11968 • 631.283.0967

With film screenings, lectures, and art exhibits, the Southampton Arts Center is a community hub for visual arts. The nonprofit center frequently partners with film festivals, concerts, and art schools to bring world-class programming to Southampton.

SOUTHAMPTON CULTURAL CENTER

25 Pond Lane, Southampton, New York 11968 • 631.287.4377 • scc-arts.org

In a brick building in Southampton, this performing arts center hosts dance, music, and theater performances throughout the year, in addition to lectures and special events. The space is also home to a gallery with rotating exhibits, including paintings, photography, and other multimedia art. The center also offers workshops and one-off music and dance classes for all ages, from babies to adults.

TRIPOLI GALLERY

30 Jobs Lane, Southampton, New York 11968 • 631.377.3715 • tripoligallery.com

This sleek and innovative Southampton gallery showcases well-curated contemporary art in a beautiful downtown location. Working with both local and international artists, the gallery strives to create and cultivate a community of artists and art collectors on Long Island.

Westhampton and Quogue

THE QUOGUE GALLERY

44 Quogue Street, Quogue, New York 11959 • 631.653.6236 • quoguegallery.com

Part gallery, part community space, The Quogue Gallery is a hub for artists, curators, and collectors. Along with exhibiting a diverse range of artwork, the gallery hosts lectures and events on contemporary art in a modern barn-like space.

WESTHAMPTON BEACH PERFORMING ARTS CENTER

76 Main Street, Westhampton Beach, New York 11978 • 631.288.1500 • whbpac.org

Focusing on film and live music and theater performances, the Westhampton Beach Performing Arts Center is more than just a performance space. The center also serves as an arts academy for the year-round community, putting on various local productions throughout the year—even in the winter.

Where Art Lovers Should Eat

THE MAIDSTONE ★ *AUTHOR'S PICK*

207 Main Street, East Hampton, New York 11937 • 631.324.5006 • themaidstone.com/dine

Cozy, chic, and impeccably decorated with a combination of vintage and modern furnishings, the dining room at the Maidstone Hotel should be on the itinerary for any design-oriented foodies. The menu is upscale and modern, with deconstructed dishes and the occasional foam, all with a focus on local ingredients. Opt for seafood like the seared scallops with kohlrabi and pancetta, and don't miss out on the decadent house-made desserts. Open year-round, the prices here are reflective of the Hamptons price point, but surprisingly decent given the quality of the food and the beautiful setting.

FAMOUS HAMPTONS ARTISTS

ROBERT RAUSCHENBERG 1925–2008

A graphic pop artist of the 1950s, Rauschenberg is most famous for his collages.

JACKSON POLLOCK 1912–1956

Pollock ushered in a new era of Abstract Expressionism with his iconic splatter paintings.

LEE KRASNER 1908–1984

Pollock's wife Krasner was one of the most important figures of the Abstract Expressionism movement.

DAN FLAVIN 1933–1996

Flavin's trippy light installations are minimalist neon creations.

ROY LICHTENSTEIN 1923–1997

One of the most famous pop artists, Lichtenstein used a comic-book–like approach to art.

ELAINE DE KOONING 1918–1989

Married to Willem de Kooning, Elaine is most famous for her figurative expressionism.

Shelter Island and the North Fork

SHELTER ISLAND | *Hidden Studios and Quaint Galleries*

ARTISTS OF SHELTER ISLAND

artsi.info

This collective hosts an annual open studio, where visitors can visit the artists' studios (usually located in their homes) to meet artists and purchase works directly from the local community.

BLACK CAT BOOKS

54 North Ferry Road, Shelter Island, New York 11964 • 631.725.8654 • blackcatbooks.com

Selling used and rare books, Black Cat is the perfect place to spend a rainy afternoon on Shelter Island, with well-curated bookshelves holding first editions, signed copies, and rare manuscripts.

HANDWERKLAB ART GALLERY

36 NorthFerry Road, Shelter Island, New York 11964 • 631.294.2765

This art gallery and boutique sells one-of-a-kind jewelry and homewares inspired by natural surroundings—go here for woven lamps, quartz necklaces, stones, and ceramics.

THE NORTH FORK | *Funky, Cutting-Edge Art*

CAROUSEL

115 Front Street, Greenport, New York 11944 • 631.477.2200

This antique carousel next to Greenport Harbor is a work of art with wooden floors, hand-painted ponies, and old-timey music to boot. Housed in a glass building in the harborfront park, it's worth a photograph (or a ride), even if you don't have any kids in tow.

// Greenport's antique carousel will delight vintage lovers (and kids)

NORTH FORK ART COLLECTIVE

15 Front Street, Greenport, New York 11944 • northforkartcollective.com

This collective of local artists has turned a temporary pop-up gallery into a permanent space in a Greenport storefront. The workspace and exhibition space features contemporary art created by its community members.

THE SOUTH STREET GALLERY

18 South Street, Greenport, New York 11944 • 631.477.0021 • thesouthstreetgallery.com

Open by chance or by appointment, check the website for openings and exhibits of local, regional, and national artists.

VSOP ART + DESIGN PROJECTS

311 Front Street, Greenport, New York 11944 • 631.603.7736 • vsopprojects.com

The coolest gallery in town, VSOP exhibits contemporary and colorful multimedia pieces that pop. From sculptures to drawings to paints, the works here are always interesting, and the opening receptions are well-attended by a hip crowd. With year-round shows, the gallery space in a historic home in Greenport aims to be a gathering place for the growing community of artists, curators, and designers on the North Fork.

Where Art Lovers Should Eat

VINE STREET. CAFÉ

41 South Ferry Road, Shelter Island, New York 11964 • 631.749.3210 • vinestreetcafe.com

Shelter Island's legendary Vine Street. Cafe has a homey-chic vibe, with white tablecloths and wood-paneled walls in a cozy cottage setting. Serving internationally inspired fare made with local ingredients, people trek here from all over Long Island for dishes like crispy duck confit, local oysters, or wild striped bass. The menu is always changing depending on what's in season, and reservations are essential. Book far in advance or come on a weeknight to get a table.

Where Art Lovers Should Stay

AMERICAN BEECH

300 Main Street, Greenport, New York 11944 • 631.477.5939 • americanbeech.com

The courtyard at American Beech is the epicenter of Greenport's artsy community, with restaurants, shops, and a hotel with a handful of bright white rooms. Individually decorated rooms are large and comfortable, with grey wooden floors and whitewashed wood-paneled walls, along with fluffy white beds and cool artwork.

FIRE ISLAND | *Creative Performances and Seasonal Galleries*

Fire Island's long history as an LGTBQ community has provided a backdrop for several arts organizations to create summer-long programming like residencies, exhibits, and performances. While Fire Island does not have the star power, year-round community, or physical land to support any kind of significant art galleries and museums, what you'll find out here is still cutting-edge, just as it was in the 1960s. The art scene on Fire Island is, admittedly, a bit harder to crack for visitors, but keep an eye on the websites we've listed for special events.

ARTS PROJECT OF CHERRY GROVE

180 Bayview Walk, Cherry Grove, New York 11782 • 631.597.3192 • artsprojectcg.org

The oldest gay and lesbian theater in America, APCG is the heart of Fire Island's performing arts community, showcasing concerts, theater performances, and community programs, along with special events.

BOFFO

347.603.6956 • boffo-ny.org

With an artist residency and an annual performance festival, BOFFO is a cutting-edge cultural organization for Fire Island and New York City. With events throughout the summer, including an irreverent art camp for adults along with movie nights, lectures, and exhibitions, BOFFO is continuing Fire Island's legacy as a hub for radical creative expression.

FIRE ISLAND ARTIST RESIDENCY

fireislandartistresidency.org

True to Fire Island's roots as a thriving LGBTQ community, this is the country's first artist residency exclusively for LGBTQ artists. Each year, five resident artists are chosen to work and live on Fire Island, and community members are invited to lectures, exhibits, and open studios.

FIRE ISLAND PINES ARTS PROJECT

fipap.org

This non-profit organization on Fire Island aims to bring the community together with performances and a biennial art exhibit featuring works by local residents. Check the website for performance schedules and dates for the biennial.

Where Art Lovers Should Eat

THE PINES BISTRO AND MARTINI BAR

36 Fire Island Boulevard, The Pines, New York 11782 • 631.597.6862 • pinesfi.com/pinesbistro

Possibly the most upscale restaurant in an area that generally follows a "no shirt, no shoes, no problem" philosophy, The Pines Bistro is a sophisticated eatery serving New American dishes with an Italian bent—fried calamari and fresh seafood entrees alongside decadent pasta dishes like spaghetti bolognese. Order a bottle of wine with dinner, or stick with a martini.

Where Art Lovers Should Stay

CHERRY GROVE HOTEL

1 Ocean Walk, Cherry Grove, New York 11782 • 631.597.6600 • grovehotel.com

Cherry Grove is the artistic hub of Fire Island, and the hotel is just steps away from the historic Cherry Grove theater. Clean and simple (although far from stylish) rooms all have private bathrooms, and some have balconies.

≡ *Greater Long Island*

GREATER LONG ISLAND | *Gold Coast Mansions Full of Antiques*

Throughout Greater Long Island, there are historical mansions to explore, art museums and galleries, and a plethora of performing arts venues ranging from intimate jazz clubs to enormous concert stadiums.

Centerport

VANDERBILT MUSEUM AND PLANETARIUM

180 Little Neck Road, Centerport, New York 11721 • 631.854.5579 • vanderbiltmuseum.org

This Spanish Baroque mansion may seem a little out of place on Long Island, but the architecture makes sense once you consider that the estate was the summer home of William K. Vanderbilt II, one of America's original jet-setters. The mansion and museum are home to natural and cultural artifacts from around the world, as well as a dazzling art collection. The planetarium is cutting-edge, with a 60-foot dome for sky shows and an observatory. General admission for a guided tour, access to the grounds, and a planetarium show is $22. Open weekends and Tuesdays September through April, the museum is open Tuesday through Sunday during the summer season.

WHAT TO READ AND WATCH BEFORE YOUR BEACHY WEEKEND

PHILISTINES AT THE HEDGEROW: PASSION AND PROPERTY IN THE HAMPTONS by Steven Gaines • A juicy and entertaining non-fiction portrayal of the Hamptons elite.

SOMETHING'S GOTTA GIVE • A classic Nancy Meyer rom-com starring Jack Nicholson and Diane Keaton, set in the Hamptons.

ETERNAL SUNSHINE OF THE SPOTLESS MIND • Montauk features heavily in in this quirky and cerebral love story.

THE WOLF OF WALL STREET • One of Leonardo diCaprio's best roles, this is the debauched story of how one Long Island man won (and lost) millions on the stock market.

STRONG ISLAND • A stunning and heartbreaking documentary about the death of an unarmed black man in 1992.

GREY GARDENS • The infamous documentary (and later remake) that introduced the world to Big Edie and Little Edie Beale, Jackie O's cousins living in squalor in the Hamptons.

JERSEY SHORE • A guilty-pleasure reality TV show that follows the lives of young adults spending the summer in Seaside Heights, New Jersey.

A SPECK IN THE SEA • The incredible true story of a Montauk fisherman lost at sea, this story was first a New York Times article, then a book, with possible plans to turn the story into a movie starring Ben Affleck and Matt Damon.

THE AMITYVILLE HORROR • There are multiple book and film versions of this classic (possibly true) story of a Long Island house plagued by malicious spirits.

CHERRY GROVE, FIRE ISLAND: SIXTY YEARS IN AMERICA'S FIRST GAY AND LESBIAN TOWN by Esther Newton • An award-winning story about Long Island's thriving LGBTQ community.

THE GREAT GATSBY by F. Scott Fitzgerald • An iconic story of wealth and privilege set in a fictional town on Long Island's Gold Coast, later made into a spectacular Baz Luhrmann production

SAG HARBOR by Colson Whitehead • A coming-of-age memoir about the author's childhood and preteen years growing up in the African American community of Sag Harbor.

THE AFFAIR • A sexy and soapy Showtime series set in Montauk.

REAL HOUSEWIVES OF NEW YORK CITY • A reality television show about New York City's rich and tacky, featuring frequent escapades Out East.

STRANGER THINGS • This hit Netflix show was supposedly inspired by Camp Hero, the abandoned Montauk military base.

THE HIGH SEASON by Judy Blundell • A juicy beach read about the secret lives of the North Fork's artistic elite.

Hempstead

NASSAU COUNTY MUSEUM OF ART

One Museum Drive, Roslyn, New York 11576 • 516.484.9338 • nassaumuseum.org

The Nassau County Museum of Art is housed in the historic Frick Mansion, and it comprises a permanent collection and a sprawling sculpture park. The museum has big-name artists like Frank Stella and Mark Rothko alongside significant local artists. The sculpture park, a 145-acre outdoor museum, has works by Marco Remec and Alexander Calder.

SANDS POINT PRESERVE (MANSIONS)
⭐ *AUTHOR'S PICK*

127 Middle Neck Road, Sands Point, New York 11050 • 516.571.7901 • sandspointpreserveconservancy.org

Formerly a Guggenheim estate, Sands Point Preserve is home to three different mansions set on over 200 acres. Hempstead House might be the star of the show, a classic granite castle that looks like it's been flown over straight from Britain. In reality, the 40-room mansion was designed by New York City-based architects and built in 1912. The setting is absolutely jaw-dropping, and the mansion is frequently used for private events and film shoots. When it's not in use, tours are available at 11 a.m. and 2 p.m.

// Hydrangeas in bloom

on Saturdays and Sundays. Castle Gould, which served as the carriage house, stables, and maid's quarters, is not open for tours, but check the calendar for any public events. Falaise, a brick mansion built in the style of a 13th-century Norman manor house, is open Thursday through Sunday. The landscaped grounds are worth a wander, especially the rose garden, with over 1,500 red rose bushes. Admission to the grounds is $10 per car, and tours cost an additional $15 per person.

Oyster Bay and Cold Spring Harbor

PLANTING FIELDS ARBORETUM STATE HISTORIC PARK

1395 Planting Fields Road, Oyster Bay, New York 11771 • 516.922.9200 • plantingfields.org

With a Tudor-style manor and over 400 acres of woodlands, gardens, and lawns, Planting Fields is a stunning public estate. There are two greenhouses on-site with seasonal plant exhibits, as well as formal gardens and hiking trails throughout the property. The manor, Coe Hall, contains decadent original furnishings, and a cafe and museum shop are on-site. Admission costs $8 per car, and visits to Coe Hall cost $5.

SAGAMORE HILL NATIONAL HISTORIC SITE

20 Sagamore Hill Road, Oyster Bay, New York 11771 • 516.922.4788 • nps.gov/sahi

Known as "The Summer White House," Sagamore Hill was the Long Island home of President Theodore Roosevelt. Unsurprisingly, the home is filled with trophies and taxidermy, including bison heads, cheetah skins, and elephant tusks. Part of the National Park Service, the home is only accessible on a guided tour, which costs $10. Reservations are recommended. The adjacent Sanctuary and Audubon Center, where Roosevelt is buried, is a 12-acre sanctuary for more than 125 species of birds.

Islip

ISLIP ART MUSEUM

50 Irish Lane, East Islip, New York 11730-2098 • 631.224.5402 • islipartmuseum.org

Showcasing contemporary art in a landmark brick estate on Long Island, Islip Art Museum presents exhibits, lectures, classes, and a fabulous museum store with one-of-a-kind artworks, jewelry, and gifts.

LOCAL MAGAZINES

Long Island's East End has a plethora of glossy mags. During the summer, you'll see stacks of magazines outside businesses, usually with a celebrity on the cover. While those magazines full of yoga poses and beautiful houses are great eye candy, there are a few that stand out for stellar reporting, local features, and great design.

Part of East Hampton Star newspaper, *East Magazine* publishes a diverse selection of local lore, food features, and fascinating history. easthamptonstar.com

Whalebone is a Montauk-based publication covering all things water-related. With gorgeous design and incredible photography, the magazine features stories from the East End and beyond. whalebonemag.com

Food-focused *Edible East End* has thoughtful features and farm-fresh recipes (edibleeastend.com).

// *East Magazine* is one of the best local magazines

Stony Brook

THE JAZZ LOFT

275 Christian Avenue, Stony Brook, New York 11790 • 631.751.1895 • thejazzloft.org

This historic and intimate venue hosts jazz performances on Thursday, Friday, and Saturday nights. The non-profit also serves as an educational center and community resource, with sensory-friendly events, swing dance classes, and a young artists program.

Port Washington and Surrounds

ANTIQUE SHOPS

Main Street, Port Washington, New York 11050

Main Street in Port Washington is home to several antique shops with everything from kitschy to elegant treasures salvaged from local Long Island estates. Among the best are Stam Gallery, Old Port Antiques, Bubba Brown's Treasures, and House of Crystal.

OLD WESTBURY GARDENS ⭐ *AUTHOR'S PICK*

71 Old Westbury Road, Old Westbury, New York 11568 • 516.333.0048 • oldwestburygardens.org

The former estate and gardens of John Shaffer Phipps is one of the finest examples of an intact Gold Coast Mansion. The 200-acre property is landscaped with formal gardens, ponds, and

// Long Island's estates are known for lavishly lush gardens

woodlands. The house is filled with art and antiques belonging to the heir to a steel fortune; it offers tours, lectures, classic car shows, concerts, and art exhibits. Closed from January 1 to March 30, Old Westbury Gardens is only open on weekends in November and December. Open Wednesday through Monday from April through October. Admission costs $10.

Huntington

THE HECKSCHER MUSEUM OF ART

2 Prime Avenue, Huntington, New York 11743 • 631.423.2145 • heckscher.org

From kids' festivals to free sketching classes, the Heckscher Museum of Art is a multidisciplinary museum bringing art to the community. The museum hosts lectures and educational programs, and it's the host of the Long Island Biennial, a juried exhibit showcasing local artists. Highlights from the permanent collection include works by Georgia O'Keefe and Man Ray.

Jones Beach

NIKON THEATER AT JONES BEACH

895 Bay Parkway, Wantagh, New York 11793 • 866.558.8468 • jonesbeach.com

This popular outdoor amphitheater at Jones Beach has hosted some of the biggest musical acts in the world. Popular with the boomer crowd, check the schedule for artists like Neil Young and Jimmy Buffett.

Where Art Lovers Should Eat

TULLULAH'S

12 4th Avenue, Bay Shore, New York 11706 • 631.969.9800 • tullulahs.com

This speakeasy-themed restaurant is as hip as anything you'll find in the city, with exposed brick, Edison bulbs, and craft cocktails. The menu has spiffed-up Long Island classics like clams casino alongside varied international dishes like pork belly tacos, Niçoise salad, and truffle arancini.

Where Art Lovers Should Stay

GARDEN CITY HOTEL

45 7th Street, Garden City, New York 11530 • 516.747.3000 • gardencityhotel.com

Classic, cozy, and old-school, with an "is this place haunted?" vibe, this is arguably the coolest non-beach hotel on Long Island. Close to the Belmont racetrack, it's said that the bar and restaurant here are a popular watering hole for the jockeys. It's not exactly chic, but the leather sofas, crystal chandeliers, and sometimes decadent decor make this place feel like a New York City hotel.

☰ *The Jersey Shore*

On the Jersey Shore, the most significant arts destination is Asbury Park, a town that was once well past its glory days but has had a renaissance, with a new generation of artists and musicians calling this place home. While there are a few galleries in town, the real draw for art-lovers here is the boardwalk, where the skeletal remains of Asbury Park's glorious Beaux-Arts 1920s pleasure palaces still stand.

JERSEY SHORE | *Street Art and Urban Decay*

Ocean Grove

JERSEY SHORE ARTS CENTER

66 South Main Street, Ocean Grove, New Jersey 07756 • 732.502.0050

The Jersey Shore Arts Center is the Jersey Shore's premier performing arts organization, putting on year-round theater performances, classical music showcases, and an annual 5k race.

Asbury Park

ASBURY PARK BAZAAR ⭐ AUTHOR'S PICK

Asbury Park, New Jersey 07712 • asburyparkbazaar.com

This is a recurring night market in the convention center on the Asbury Park Boardwalk. Vendors set up throughout the site are a highly curated selection of artists, jewelers, artisans, designers, and vintage collectors.

ASBURY PARK BOARDWALK STREET ART

Asbury Park, New Jersey 07712 • apboardwalk.com

A gritty reminder of the glamorous 1920s, the Asbury Park Boardwalk's Beaux-Arts structures are a photographer's dream. The ruins of the casino, carousel, and steam power plant are worth exploring, especially as they've been brightened by street art. Throughout the boardwalk, artists have left their mark with sweeping, colorful murals.

// Asbury Park's boardwalk is filled with street art

EXHIBIT NO. 9

550-102 Cookman Avenue, Asbury Park, New Jersey 07712 • 908.818.8970 • exhibitnumber9.com

In downtown Asbury Park, this multidisciplinary gallery hosts exhibitions of contemporary fine art. Apart from the well-curated exhibits, the space is also a printing and framing shop, and the gallery has restored and enlarged a series of vintage Asbury Park postcards showcasing the golden age of the glamorous boardwalk: the perfect souvenir.

HOT SAND

550 Cookman Avenue #103, Asbury Park, New Jersey 07712 • 732.927.5475 • hotsandap.com

While some might not consider glass-blowing fine art, there's no denying the sense of wonder and spectacle of a glass-blowing demonstration. At Hot Glass, visitors can sign up for glass blowing classes, where you get to take home a work of art you made yourself. There's also a gallery of blown glass crafts for sale.

PARAMOUNT THEATER

1200 Ocean Avenue, Asbury Park, New Jersey 07712 • 732.897.6500 • apboardwalk.com/the-paramount-theater

Asbury Park's Paramount Theater, located in the Asbury Convention Hall directly on the boardwalk, is a gorgeous restored theater from 1927. Part of the National Register of Historic Places, the 1600-seat theater hosts live shows, screenings, and musical performances.

PARLOR GALLERY

717 Cookman Avenue, Asbury Park, New Jersey 07712 • 732.869.0606 • parlor-gallery.com

Distilling the essence of Asbury Park's cool cachet, Parlor Gallery curates a community of emerging and established contemporary artists. As part of the New Jersey art scene for 10 years, Parlor features local and international artists in this downtown gallery as well as in art fairs and pop-ups around the country.

SILVERBALL MUSEUM

1000 Ocean Avenue, Asbury Park, New Jersey 07712 • 732.774.4994 • silverballmuseum.com/asbury-park

Who doesn't love a bit of nostalgia? This museum and arcade, located directly on the boardwalk in Asbury Park, has over 100 pinball machines, many of them from the 1950s and 1960s. Museum passes are sold by the hour or day, ranging from $10 for a half-hour of admission up to $25 for all-day play on the free machines inside. For those who only want to browse and not play, admission is $2.50.

// Reyla is one of Asbury Park's many design-forward dining experiences

Where Art Lovers Should Eat

REYLA

603 Mattison Avenue, Asbury Park, New Jersey 07712 • 732.455.8333 • heyreyla.com

This super-stylish restaurant serves craft cocktails and modern Mediterranean fare in a minimalist Scandinavian-chic setting. It's one of Asbury's busiest restaurants, with well-heeled groups and couples coming in for complicated takes on falafel, shawarma, and shakshuka. While the food is complex, flavorful, and satisfying, it might actually be the cocktails that steal the show here, like the Hips Don't Lie, with rosehip-infused mezcal, coconut yogurt, lychee, violet liqueur, and lemon.

Where Art Lovers Should Stay

ASBURY OCEAN CLUB

1101 Ocean Avenue, Asbury Park, New Jersey 07712 • 732.705.1100 • asburyoceanclub.com

Set to open in summer 2019, this super-sophisticated luxury residential project and hotel has modern rooms with floor-to-ceiling windows, a private beach club, and an absolutely unrivaled ocean view—it's the only high-rise hotel in town, and it's located right on the boardwalk.

4

Escapes for Foodies

Where to Find the Best Restaurants, Vineyards, and Farm Stands on Long Island and the Jersey Shore

For New Yorkers, it can be easy to forget that Long Island is, actually, an island. A robust year-round fishing community means that seafood is the name of the game here, from roadside clam shacks serving fried seafood in paper plates to heavenly lobster dishes dreamed up by James-Beard–Awarded and Michelin-starred chefs. There's actually little middle ground here when it comes to seafood, and our advice is to check out both the dives and the gourmet kitchens.

In the summer, fresh produce abounds at farm stands throughout Long Island. Specifically, corn, tomatoes, peaches, and squash seem to taste better here than anywhere else.

At restaurants throughout Long Island and the Jersey Shore, you might be shocked at the prices—even coming from New York. While there are some low-key hangouts and top-notch fine dining establishments, most of the options listed here fall into the same price point (kind of expensive). Many of the restaurants barely break even during the year, and summer is when they make most of their money. Don't be surprised to see $30 lobster rolls, $20 burgers, $15 salads, and $45 entrees on the menu. When it comes to drinks, you'll rarely find a cocktail for under $10, and anything remotely crafty will likely be in the $14–$18 range, especially at trendy nightlife spots in Montauk. It's possible to find a bottle of wine for under $50 on the menu at most places, but they'll be listed next to wines that cost upwards of $1,500.

≡ Montauk and the Hamptons

The best way to eat in Montauk and the Hamptons is to do a mix of high and low. Fancy places are often cheaper at lunch (especially since you probably won't be drinking as much) and farm stands and organic markets and bakeries are a great place to gather ingredients for a simple and stylish picnic.

Most of the bougie restaurants worth your time in the Hamptons have relationships with local farms and purveyors, and if they don't, then don't eat there. You'll find that in The Hamptons, a lot of the menus look the same. Some of the dishes you can find almost everywhere are local oysters and clams, lobster rolls, watermelon and feta salads, striped bass, and Long Island duck.

MONTAUK | *Hook-to-Table Local Seafood*

ARBOR

240 Fort Pond Road, Montauk, New York 11954 • 631.238.5430 • arbormontauk.com

With communal tables, farm-fresh food, and romantic lighting, Arbor is a beachy and elegant restaurant. Start your meal with local oysters and seasonal salads before moving on to dishes like bouillabaisse, seared scallops, or grilled octopus. The menu is simple and unfussy, serving high-quality food that's expensive but not overpriced. Arbor is only open during the summer.

CLAM AND CHOWDER HOUSE AT SALIVAR'S DOCK

470 West Lake Drive, Montauk, New York 11954 • 631.668.6252 • clamandchowderhouse.com

This family-run seafood spot on the water is just like Montauk itself—stylish and hip, but staying true to its roots as a community of fishermen. Checkerboard floors, a long wooden bar, trophy fish, and a neon sign perfect the hipster fisherman vibe, while the menu is a mashup of old meets new: clams casino, buffalo wings, lobster, and garlic bread alongside a sushi bar that serves standard and specialty rolls. You will find a restaurant and bar inside, along with an upstairs deck that looks out over the harbor.

DURYEA'S LOBSTER DECK

5460, 65 Tuthill Road, Montauk, New York 11954 • 631.668.2410 • duryealobsters.com

Duryea's is an old-school joint that's gotten a spiffy makeover, bringing the fashion set to this waterside cottage (with a dock) for fresh seafood with a view. Drop in for a boozy lunch with lobster rolls and rosé, and ask to sit out on the deck. For dinner, try the heirloom tomato salad (in season), the steamers, or the mussels mariniere. The raw bar has local oysters and clams, along with jumbo shrimp, snow crab, and chilled lobster. If you're with a group, order one of the raw bar towers to sample everything.

EAST BY NORTHEAST

51 Edgemere Street, Montauk, New York 11954 • 631.668.2872 • eastbynortheast.com

This Asian-fusion restaurant serves Far East cuisine made with Northeast ingredients. Over-looking Fort Pond, the wood-paneled dining room has an upscale yacht club vibe. The menu is unique, with dishes like kung pao calamari, duck tacos, and pork and kimchi dumplings as well as those that are a bit more standard for this neck of the woods: clam chowder, raw oysters, burgers, and steamed lobster.

HARVEST ON FORT POND

11 South Emery Street, Montauk, New York 11954 • 631.668.5574 • harvestfortpond.com

Part restaurant, part garden, Harvest on Fort Pond brings organic ingredients right to your table. The setting is beautiful, especially on the back patio, where you're surrounded by green-ery and overlooking the pond. Start with charbroiled oysters or marinated lamb ribs for the table, and continue on to grilled pizza, handmade pasta, or main dishes like salmon with lemon beurre blanc or skirt steak with arugula, manchego, and roasted garlic tomato butter. Reserva-tions can be tricky to come by—call at least a week in advance, especially for a weekend night.

SOLE EAST

90 2nd House Road, Montauk, New York 11954 • 631.668.2105 • soleeast.com

The backyard at Sole East resort has a simple menu for breakfast, lunch, and dinner. The focus is on healthy, local cuisine, with veggie-centric dishes alongside fresh seafood. Brunch is pop-ular here, where you can get a slightly healthier take on hangover food, like avocado toast, an asparagus omelet, or a Mediterranean plate with fava bean hummus, crema di pecorino, grilled cipollini onion, grilled pita bread, spicy eggplant, and marinated olives.

Where Foodies Should Stay

HERO BEACH CLUB

626 Montauk Highway, Montauk, New York 11954 • 631.668.9825 • herobeachclub.com

One of the cutest new hotels on the Montauk scene, Hero Beach Club is located steps from the beach and the town of Montauk, making this the perfect landing place to experience everything Montauk has to offer: the great outdoors, and an amazing dining and nightlife scene. The hotel is a converted motel, with a pool surrounded by Balinese-style furniture and a spacious backyard with ample room to mingle or sunbathe. The decor is simple, but chic, with wooden accents, white walls and beds, and water-themed artwork.

AMAGANSETT, SAG HARBOR, AND THE HAMPTONS | *Organic Farms and Fancy Feasts*

Amagansett

AMBER WAVES FARM

375 Main Street, Amagansett, New York 11930 • 631.267.5664 • amberwavesfarm.org

With a market in Amagansett, Amber Waves brings organic, local produce to the community. And if you've rented a house with a kitchen, this is a great place to go for seasonal ingredients (and it's not a bad idea to haul some groceries back to the city, either). The farm also has workshops and events, and there's a food education program for kids. Every year, Amber Waves hosts an Outstanding in the Field Dinner, a touring pop-up dinner party on the farm. Visit outstandinginthefield.com for dates and tickets.

// A perfectly ripe Long Island peach tastes a little bit like heaven

EDIBLE SOUVENIRS

The best souvenirs aren't always something you're going to cherish forever, or something that's going to languish in a linen closet, waiting to be regifted. Sometimes, the best way to rekindle fond memories of a trip is with your taste buds—by bringing home a gastronomic specialty you can't find anywhere else. No one dislikes food, and if you're shopping for presents to bring back home, the best are those that can be shared. Long Island is foodie heaven, with locavore restaurants and organic farm stands dotted all over the island. Many of these restaurants, wineries, bakeries, and farm stands have created their own products for you to take home, ranging from honey and preserves to hot sauce and gin. While some of these foodie finds have gone mainstream (if you've never had a Tate's cookie, you're living under a rock!), some are small-batch items that are only sold on site. The list below is just a small fraction of what you'll find on the East End, so keep your eyes peeled (especially at farmers' markets!) for anything local, organic, and perfectly packaged for you to take home.

Sweet and Salty Snacks

THE HAMPTON POPCORN COMPANY · hamptonpopcorn.com

NOFO GRANOLA · nofocrunch.com

NORTH FORK CHOCOLATE · northforkchocolate.com

NORTH FORK POTATO CHIPS · northforkchips.com

TATE'S COOKIES AND PIES · tatesbakeshop.com

Preserves and Condiments

EAST END APIARIES HONEY · eastendapiaries.com

AMAGANSETT SEA SALT · amagansettseasalt.com

IACONO FARM BBQ SAUCE · iaconofarm.com

SANG LEE FARMS CHERRY BOMB HOT SAUCE · sangleefarms.com

BALSAM FARMS RELISH · balsamfarms.com

SMOKED GREEN SRIRACHA FROM KIMCHI JEWS · kimchijews.com

Boozy Treats

WÖLFFER SUMMER IN A BOTTLE · wolffer.com

SAG HARBOR RUM · sagharborrum.com

PINE BARRENS GIN · lispirits.com

LIV VODKA · lispirits.com

BALSAM FARMS ✹ *AUTHOR'S PICK*

293 Town Lane, Amagansett, New York 11930 • 631.267.5635

662 Montauk Highway, Montauk, New York 11954 • 631.238.5119 • Balsamfarms.com

One of Long Island's most plentiful farm stands, Balsam is a perennial local favorite for everything from fresh produce and flowers to a curated selection of locally produced breads, cheese, desserts, and preserves. While it can be slim pickings in May and June, July through October Balsam is a cornucopia of spicy arugula, juicy heirloom tomatoes, sweet corn, and delectable peaches. It's hard to cook a bad meal when you're cooking with ingredients from Balsam.

In October, this place becomes a pumpkin paradise, with crates and trucks full of exotic decorative gourds in trendy colors like millennial pink and seafoam green. Make your city friends jealous with your epic seasonal tablescape. In 2018, Balsam opened a brick-and-mortar store in Montauk, selling a wider selection of fresh produce, baked goods, canned and refrigerated items, and florals.

// Stop at a farm stand to stock up on Long Island produce like tomatoes and corn

THE CLAM BAR

2025 Montauk Highway, Amagansett, New York 11930 • 631.267.6348 • clambarhamptons.com

Across from the Lobster Roll on the Montauk highway between Amagansett and Montauk, this seafood shack is a local favorite. There's much dispute over which restaurant is better, but you'll find that those in the know prefer the Clam Bar. Serving baskets of fried seafood, some of the best clam chowder on Long Island, and a surprisingly upscale menu (this is the Hamptons, after all) of fish tacos, salads, and raw oysters, this outdoor restaurant is a quintessential Hamptons destination—not to mention a restaurant worthy of a photo op.

HAMPTON CHUTNEY

12 Amagansett Square, Amagansett, New York 11930 • 631.267.3131 • hamptonchutney.com

Hampton Chutney is Amagansett's most popular restaurant and the place of many minor celebrity sightings. Famous for their dosas (eggy Indian crepes) stuffed with all manner of fresh ingredients (some Indian-inspired, others not so much), this is the place where everybody goes to cure their hangover. Number 9 is a local favorite, stuffed with curried chicken, chutney, roasted onions, and spinach. Round out your morning with a cardamom coffee, chai, and mango lassi.

JACK'S STIR-BREW COFFEE

146 Montauk Highway, Amagansett, New York 11930 • 631.267.5555 • jacksstirbrew.com/amagansett

Jack's is Amagansett's unofficial community hub, where the line is out the door on the weekends. You never know who you might run into here, so keep your eyes peeled for celebrities in their "off duty" weekend looks. Celebs—they're just like us! They have caffeine addictions, too. In addition to 100-percent organic coffee and vegan treats, Jack's has a selection of eye-wateringly expensive cold-pressed juices that really hit the spot on a hot summer day.

LA FONDITA

74 Montauk Highway • 631.267.8800 • lafondita.net

Don't let the unassuming digs at this roadside taqueria fool you—this is still the Hamptons, with the prices to prove it. But don't worry; you'll be happy to spend $13 on delicious homemade chips and guac if it means getting to relax in this hip indoor/outdoor restaurant with mismatched tables and Adirondack chairs. The cuisine is inspired by Mexican street food stalls, with a distinctly upmarket twist. You'll find all the basics here, like tacos, tortas, burritos, and tostadas. Leave room for dessert—Mexican wedding cookies and tres leches cake.

// La Fondita and The Hideaway are the best Mexican restaurants in the Hamptons

THE LOBSTER ROLL

1980 Montauk Highway, Amagansett, New York 11930 • 631.267.3740 • lobsterroll.com

On the highway between Amagansett and Montauk, there are two seafood restaurants across the street from each other. One is the Lobster Roll, a more sit-down-style place with indoor seating and waiters. The food here may not be as good as it's counterpart across the street, but there's a certain mid-century charm here that makes it popular with families. And fans of the hit TV show *The Affair* will recognize this restaurant as the place where the main character works.

SOTTO SOPRA

231 Main Street, Amagansett, New York 11930 • 631.267.3695 • restaurantsottosopra.com

Sotto Sopra is as swank as it gets in laid-back Amagansett, serving upscale Tuscan cuisine in an elegant yet modern setting. Come here for authentic Italian crowd-pleasers like clams oreganata, risotto, and veal Milanese. The restaurant also offers wood-fired pizza and some serious grilled meats: lamb chops, sirloin, filet mignon, and porterhouse. This buzzy spot can be popular on weekends, so plan ahead.

STUART'S SEAFOOD MARKET

41 Oak Lane, Amagansett, New York 11930 • 631.267.6700 • stuartsseafood.com

Hidden on a residential side street, Stuart's is a favorite with locals looking for some of the best variety of seafood, including clams, lobster, and striped bass. If you're renting a house for the weekend and don't want to get your hands dirty cooking a seafood feast, you can also call ahead to order cracked steamed lobsters. There's an entire menu of prepared items perfect for your beach picnic, like various seafood salads. There are a few shelves of essentials to round out your perfect seafood meal, like herbs, pasta, olive oil, and lemons, making this a one-stop-shop for a simple dinner.

WÖLFFER KITCHEN

4 Amagansett Square, Amagansett, New York 11930 • 631.267.2764 • amagansett.wolfferkitchen.com

In Amagansett Square, this vineyard-to-table restaurant is the second Wölffer restaurant to open in the Hamptons (the first is in Sag Harbor). Serving breakfast, lunch, and dinner, the Amagansett outpost has a slightly more casual and family-friendly approach to their coastal-inspired cuisine. The healthy and sophisticated menu has California vibes, with crab tacos, zucchini noodles, and a tofu bowl with spinach and tamari. Stop by for dinner or a rosé-fueled weekend brunch.

Sag Harbor

THE BEACON

4454, 8 West Water Street, Sag Harbor, New York 11963 • 631.725.7088 • beaconsagharbor.com

The Beacon is like a combination of a yacht club dining room, your favorite neighborhood restaurant, and a trendy French bistro. The bar and dining area feel classic but not stuffy, with wood-paneled walls and windows looking out onto the marina. The menu is decidedly International-American, with menu items like pork belly buns and shellfish bouillabaisse along-side crispy fish tacos and steamed mussels. Good food doesn't come cheap in the Hamptons, and this is no exception—but considering the ambiance and the view, it's a small price to pay.

DOCKSIDE BAR & GRILL

26 Bay Street, Sag Harbor, New York 11963 • 631.725.7100 • docksidesagharbor.com

Restaurants on the water are sought-after in the Hamptons, and surprisingly rare for such a water-logged destination. Dockside will satisfy your craving for a fancy lunch with a water view, with a big wooden deck overlooking the Sag Harbor Yacht Club and the bay across the street. Stop by for burgers, lobster rolls, or BLTs—don't forget to order a side of onion rings. Wash it all down with a local draft beer.

CAVANIOLA'S GOURMET

89 Division Street, Sag Harbor, New York 11963 • 631.725.0095 • cavaniolas.com

This cheese shop, wine store, and restaurant should be the first stop for anybody planning a fancy picnic or cocktail party. With a well-curated selection of imported and domes-tic cheeses, Cavaniola's is the perfect place to go to create an impressive antipasto plate with cheese, olives, spreads, salumi, dried fruit, and crackers. The wine cellar has a great selection of organic and biodynamic wines—all displayed in the cellar of a beautiful historic home. The kitchen here is simple, but you won't be disappointed with one of the paninis—all made with ingredients from the cheese shop, of course! There's also a location in Amagansett Square.

LULU KITCHEN & BAR

126 Main Street, Sag Harbor, New York 11963 • 631.725.0900 • lulusagharbor.com

Serving elevated Mediterranean fare, Lulu is the place to go for whole grilled branzino, wood-fired lamb skewers, or wood-fired pizza. The setting is both homey and modern, with leather banquettes, an exposed brick wall, and a gleaming hardwood floor. The open-format kitchen lets you watch some of the cooking, and the food is always prepared fresh. Make sure to order something from the "farm stand" section of the menu, featuring salads and veggie dishes made with local produce.

PAGE AT 63 MAIN

63 Main Street, Sag Harbor, New York 11963 • 631.725.1810 • page63main.com

Page has one of the most beautiful restaurant settings in the Hamptons, with a stylish dining room filled with hanging plants. Plants are a big part of the theme here at the Hamptons' first "seed to table" restaurant—the restaurant uses sustainable aquaponics in their seasonal rooftop garden, vertical garden wall, and indoor grow room. It's a fascinating hi-tech approach to local, organic, and sustainable cuisine, and the restaurant is worth a visit for that alone (call ahead to ask about scheduling a garden tour before your meal). But what makes this restaurant worth returning to is the quality of the food. While you might expect a restaurant like this to serve only quinoa bowls, that's not the case—at brunch you can feast on eggs benedict and home fries, or you can stop by for dinner for taste local duck confit with celery root puree and baby purple brussels sprouts. (There's also a quinoa bowl on the menu, of course.)

PROVISIONS MARKET

7 Main Street, Sag Harbor, New York 11963 • 631.725.3636 • provisionsnaturalfoods.com

Part health food store and part cafe, Provisions is the place to go for organic groceries, eco-friendly products, and kombucha. The cafe here is one of the only places in the Hamptons with a made-to-order juice bar, serving baked goods, prepared items, and a few vegan- and vegetarian-friendly dishes like the vegan quesadilla and huevos rancheros.

SAG PIZZA

103 Main Street, Sag Harbor, New York 11963 • 631.725.3167 • sagpizza.com

Serving wood-fired pizza everybody in the Hamptons craves, newcomer Sag Pizza might be the best place to get a high-quality pie on the South Fork. The decor is super simple and purposefully un-stylish, which only serves to highlight the pizza masterpieces. Pizzas tend toward the traditional rather than the bougie, with toppings like pancetta, taleggio, and Sicilian oregano on pies with perfectly charred crusts. Do not under any circumstances leave without trying the vongole pizza, topped with clams, garlic scallion butter, guanciale, oregano, and lemon.

SEN

23 Main Street, Sag Harbor, New York 11963 • 631.725.1774 • senrestaurant.com

Sag Harbor has the Hampton's most diverse dining options, and Sen goes beyond the standard "coastal New American" theme with high-quality sushi. The setting is upscale but not overly snazzy, and so are the rolls. You'll find classic favorites here (rainbow, spicy tuna) along with local scallop sashimi and creative twists like the bagel roll, with smoked salmon, cream cheese, cucumber, and scallion. Sen also offers tempura and teriyaki for the raw-fish-averse, in addition to dumplings and steamed buns for appetizers.

East Hampton

BAY KITCHEN & BAR

39 Gann Road, East Hampton, New York 11937 • 631.329.3663

On the water overlooking Three Mile Harbor, Bay Kitchen & Bar is an off-the-beaten-path preppy-chic eatery. It's decorated like a fashionable yacht club, with whitewashed wood and fun printed textiles. It's all about local seafood and lobster here, with harbor fluke, Montauk tuna, and local oysters on the menu. The restaurant is only open in the summer.

BHUMI FARMS

131 Pantigo Road, East Hampton, New York 11937 • 646.496.8364 • bhumifarms.com

This picture-perfect roadside farmstand is almost too cute for words. Selling home-grown organic produce along with a few items sourced from local purveyors on the East End, this is a great place to stop on your way home from the beach, to see what's fresh.

EMP SUMMER HOUSE

341 Pantigo Road, East Hampton, New York 11937 • empsummerhouse.com

This seasonal pop-up began in 2017 while New York City's Eleven Madison Park—voted the best restaurant in the world—closed for renovations. EMP sent their staff to the Hamptons for the summer, opening up a sprawling restaurant inside a mansion on the road between East Hampton and Amagansett. The restaurant is more casual than the New York City version, but it's still the best fine-dining experience in the Hamptons and one of the most sought-after tables in town. There are two dining options here—the inside, which is a bit more serious, serving lobster, caviar, and steak for two at prices that are astonishingly high (but a bargain compared to the New York City restaurant). The food here is inventive, taking fresh local ingredients and giving them an elevated spin, like the striped bass seared with zucchini and green curry. On the patio, walk-ins are welcome for more casual fare and craft cocktails. You'll find bougie fast food, like double fried chicken with chili-lime mayo and soft-serve ice cream with honey brittle, shortbread, milk meringue, and salt. The lobster roll here might be the best one in town, and it's only a few dollars more than the lobster rolls elsewhere.

>> Insider Tip: Reservations can be made online, but only with an American Express card—if you don't show up, you'll be charged. The patio is first-come, first-served. The restaurant is only open during the summer.

FRESNO

8 Fresno Place, East Hampton, New York 11937 • 631.324.8700 • fresnorestaurant.com

Craft cocktails, local seafood, and a low-key vibe make this stylish restaurant a neighborhood favorite. Sit at the bar or out under the string lights on the covered patio and choose from starters like crispy bay shrimp, burrata salad with local tomatoes, or smoked local bluefish rillette with pickled onion and crostini. For a main course, try the black bean falafel or the local tilefish. You can't go wrong with the burger, served with crispy pommes frites. Fresno works with local purveyors to obtain super-fresh ingredients, with produce and seafood sourced from farms and fishermen throughout the East End.

HIGHWAY RESTAURANT

290 Montauk Highway, East Hampton, New York 11937 • 631.527.5372 • highwayrestaurant.com

Highway Restaurant is the perfect place to welcome you to the weekend after the long drive out to the Hamptons. It's homey and unpretentious, serving craveable comfort food with global influences: steamed pork buns, fish tacos, miso-glazed salmon, and eggplant parmigiana. It's the sort of food you'd cook at home, but probably better. The restaurant also has a sushi bar that's an outpost of New York City's Shuko, serving omakase-style sushi. Reservations are recommended for the sushi bar.

RED HORSE MARKET

74 Montauk Highway, East Hampton, New York 11937 • 631.324.9500 • redhorsemarket.com

This unassuming grocery store has a secret: in the back, behind the cheese counter in the produce department, is a man named Pasquale who makes the world's best mozzarella. Locals swear by it and show up early to make sure they don't miss out on this fluffy, salty, and melt-in-your-mouth piece of perfection. Eat it plain straight from the container, put it in a salad, or melt it onto a pizza.

>> Insider Tip: If you ask nicely, they'll sell you raw pizza dough to take home and bake yourself (but you didn't hear that here).

ROUND SWAMP FARM

184 Three Mile Harbor Road, East Hampton, New York 11937 • 631.324.4438 • roundswampfarm.com

With everything you could possibly need for a beach picnic, Round Swamp Farm is much more than a farm stand. Focusing on local, healthy, and gourmet snack items, this tiny grocery shack is where you'll find handmade gluten-free crackers and local spreads. With locations in both East Hampton and Bridgehampton, it's a great stop for snacks on your way to the beach or a great stop on your way home to pick up some essentials for dinner—such as fresh produce, seafood, and baked goods.

THE QUIET CLAM

100 Montauk Highway, East Hampton, New York 11937 • 631.324.4447

One of the most casual sit-down restaurants in East Hampton (although don't expect low prices). The Quiet Clam, unsurprisingly, serves local little neck clams with a plethora of options: steamed, fried, baked, raw, and in a chowder. The setting is a sort of upscale fisherman's shack, and the rest of the menu is heavy on the fried fish, but with sophisticated touches like Panko breading and hand-cut French fries. Occasionally, steamed lobsters are on the menu, for the best price you'll find in the Hamptons, served with local corn and a side of slaw.

Bridgehampton, Water Mill, and Sagaponack

CALISSA

1020 Montauk Highway, Water Mill, New York 11976 • 631.500.9292 • calissahamptons.com

Bringing a little bit of the Greek Isles to the East End, Calissa serves local fare with Mediterranean flair. The vibe here is fun, and the decor is reminiscent of a beachside grill in Mykonos, with whitewashed walls, driftwood accents, and woven rattan light fixtures. The outside patio is the perfect place to enjoy cocktails and a mezze platter. There's an emphasis on seafood here, with items like fluke crudo, grilled octopus, calamari, and branzino rounding out the menu.

CANDY KITCHEN

Montauk Highway, Bridgehampton, New York 11932 • 631.537.9885

The ultimate American diner, Candy Kitchen has been serving the East End for nearly 100 years. The old-fashioned diner is the place to go for greasy-spoon style hungover breakfasts or a simple hamburger, French fries, and milkshake on a Saturday night. The vintage interior has leather padded bar stools, a red countertop, and white tiles. It's perfect here.

GOLDBERG'S FAMOUS BAGELS

358 Montauk Highway, Wainscott, New York 11975 • 631.537.5553 • goldbergsbagels.com

On a Saturday morning in the summer, you'll see a line out the door at Goldberg's, an old-school bagel shop that's been serving the East End for decades. Come here for a hangover-curing egg sandwich, or stock up on a dozen bagels (or flagels, flat bagels!) and cream cheese (plain and scallion) to bring back to your rental. There's another location in Amagansett.

HAMPTON COFFEE COMPANY

869 Montauk Highway, Water Mill, New York 11976 • 631.726.2633 • hamptoncoffeecompany.com

Hampton Coffee Company has locations all over the East End: Southampton, Westhampton Beach, Riverhead, and the original location in Water Mill, which has a bakery, espresso bar, and juice bar in addition to a full-service restaurant that's open for breakfast and lunch. Stop by any of the locations for a quick grab-and-go cappuccino (or a bag of coffee to bring home) or go here for eggs, sandwiches, and soups.

LOAVES AND FISHES

50 Sagg Main Street, Sagaponack, New York 11962 • 631.537.0555 • landffoodstore.com

Loaves and Fishes is a gourmet grocery store with a huge selection of prepared foods for takeout. This is where you can stock up for a sophisticated picnic or grab some canapes and appetizers to garnish your cocktail party. If you're somebody who loves to cook, stop by the cookshop down the road for elegant cookware and table settings.

MECOX BAY DAIRY

855 Mecox Road, Bridgehampton, New York 11932 • 631.537.0335 • mecoxbaydairy.com

One of the only local dairy farms in the Hamptons selling farm-fresh cheese and milk, the farm store at Mecox Bay Dairy is the perfect place to stock up on souvenirs. Everything sold at the store is made at the farm, from artisan cheeses to raw milk, fresh eggs, and cut-flower arrangements.

Southampton

BLUE DUCK BAKERY & CAFÉ

30 New York-27A, Southampton, New York 11968 • 631.204.1701 • blueduckbakerycafe.com

With locations in Southampton, Greenport, and Riverhead, Blue Duck has become a staple in the world of East End pies. The café in Southampton serves cakes, cookies, pastries, and pies along with coffee and juice. You can also pick up a huge range of desserts, from cannolis to cupcakes, as well as artisan breads.

LE CHEF

75 Jobs Lane, Southampton, New York 11968 • 631.283.8581 • lechefbistro.com

With white tablecloths, a happening bar scene, and a popular prix fixe menu, Le Chef has been entertaining Southamptonites since 1980. Le Chef serves consistently good food that makes it a local favorite, with dishes like Long Island duck with sweet cherry glaze and potato galette and local flounder crusted with nuts and served with sundried tomato.

RED BAR BRASSERIE

210 New York-27A, Southampton, New York 11968 • 631.283.0704 • redbarbrasserie.com

Serving Frenchified local food, Red Bar has been a Southampton staple for over 20 years. It's a classic American brasserie, serving oysters and foie gras to start and entrees like truffled chicken breast with mushroom risotto and braised boneless beef short ribs with creamy polenta and broccoli rabe. With white tablecloths, leather banquettes, and bistro chairs, the vibe here is definitely old-school. Check out the sister restaurant, Little Red (littlered southampton.com), for a more casual version of the same great experience.

WINERIES OF LONG ISLAND

CHANNING DAUGHTERS VINEYARDS · 1927 Scuttle Hole Road,
Bridgehampton, New York 11932 · 631.537.7224 · channingdaughters.com

Channing Daughters has leaned hard into the rosé trend, with over six varietals of the Hamptons' favorite summer beverage. The tasting room here isn't as grand as some others, but it's still a fun experience. For some reason, lingering seems to be discouraged, with a glass of wine costing a whopping $16 (for reference, a bottle is only $24), with no food menu and no picnicking allowed. Still, it's one of the finest wine producers on Long Island, so you can't go wrong with a bottle or two.

DUCK WALK VINEYARDS · 231 Montauk Highway, Water Mill, New York 11976 ·
631.726.7555 · duckwalk.com

Duck Walk Vineyards should be a stop on any wine tour of the East End. The tasting room here charges just $10 for four wines, and you can buy bottles and cases directly from the winery. There are also snacks available, and a few tables and chairs have been set up outside for those who want to enjoy a picnic overlooking 30 acres of vines. Service is excellent, and it's a little more old-school than some of the trendy and stylish hot spots. As with most Long Island wineries, stick with white and rosé and you won't be disappointed. There's also a location in Southold on the North Fork, where Sauvignon Blanc grapes are grown.

WÖLFFER ESTATE ☆ AUTHOR'S PICK
139 Sagg Road, Sagaponack, New York 11962 · 631.537.5106 · wolffer.com

One of Long Island's most beautiful wineries, Wölffer encompasses acres of vines and an elegant tasting room that offers more than just wine—visitors can relax at tables and order from a small menu of light bites like cheese and charcuterie platters. In summer, the grounds are filled with picnicking groups on the patio looking out at the vibrant green vines. Wölffer is one of the most famous rosé producers and their affordable "summer in a bottle" is one of the best local souvenirs around. If you don't have time for the full winery experience, stop by the convenient "wine stand" on the adjacent property on Montauk Highway.

// Rosé in every shade of pink at Channing Daughters Vineyards

LONG ISLAND FARMERS' MARKETS

LONG BEACH FARMERS' MARKET • Saturdays 9 a.m.–2 p.m., May–November • ligreenmarket.org/long-beach

BAYSHORE FARMERS' MARKET • Fridays 3–7 p.m., June–August • facebook.com/BayShoreFarmersMarket

ISLIP FARMERS' MARKET • Saturdays, 7 a.m.–12 p.m., June–November

HUNTINGTON FARMERS' MARKET • Sundays 7 a.m.–12 p.m., June–November

PORT JEFFERSON FARMERS' MARKET • Sundays 9 a.m.–2 p.m., May–November • facebook.com/pjfarmersmarket

WESTHAMPTON BEACH FARMERS' MARKET • Saturdays 9 a.m.–1 p.m., May–October • facebook.com/WesthamptonBeachFarmersMarket

SOUTHAMPTON FARMERS' MARKET • Sundays 9 a.m.–2 p.m. • facebook.com/SouthamptonFarmersMarket

SAG HARBOR FARMERS' MARKET • Saturdays 9 a.m.–1 p.m. • facebook.com/sagharborfarmersmarket/

EAST HAMPTON FARMERS' MARKET • Fridays 9 a.m.–1 p.m., May–September • facebook.com/easthamptonfarmersmrkt

SPRINGS FARMERS' MARKET ⭐ *AUTHOR'S PICK* • Saturdays 9 a.m.–1 p.m., June–September • facebook.com/SpringsFarmersMarket

MONTAUK FARMERS' MARKET • Thursdays 9 a.m.–2 p.m., June–September • Fridays 9 a.m.–2 p.m., September–October • facebook.com/montaukfarmersmarket

SHELTER ISLAND FARMERS' MARKET • Saturdays 9 a.m.–12:30 p.m., May–September • facebook.com/ShelterIslandFarmersMarket

GREENPORT FARMERS' MARKET • Saturdays 10 a.m.–2 p.m., June–October • facebook.com/GreenportFarmersMarket

// Long Island farmers' markets are the best place to shop for souvenirs

TATE'S BAKE SHOP

43 NorthSea Road, Southampton, New York 11968 • 631.283.9830 • tatesbakeshop.com

Tate's cookies are a Hamptons institution, found in pantries across Long Island. While the cookies are now available for the mass market and found in gourmet grocery stores all over the country, the Southampton Bakery still creates handmade baked goods, like cupcakes, pies, and brownies.

Westhampton and Quogue

RENE'S CASA BASSO

59 Montauk Highway, Westhampton, New York 11977 • 631.288.1841 • casabasso.net

This old-school Italian joint serves heaping portions of Italian-American favorites in a one-of-a-kind setting. The restaurant is part of an actual castle on the side of the highway—a stucco building with turrets, a circular tower, and arched windows. Next door is where you'll find the restaurant and bar, which feels like a piece of the Hamptons that time forgot.

Where Foodies Should Stay

THE HUNTTING INN

94 Main Street, East Hampton, New York 11937 • 631.324.0410 • thepalm.com/huntting-inn/

On Main Street in East Hampton, The Huntting Inn is centrally located, making it the perfect home base to explore the culinary exploits of the Hamptons, Amagansett, and Sag Harbor. The elegant historic inn is cozy and homey—it sort of feels like staying in the guest room at a rich friend's house. Downstairs at the Inn, you'll find The Palm, a romantic old-school steakhouse popular with local celebrities. From $475.

☰ *Shelter Island and the North Fork*

Dotted with farms and wineries and surrounded by abundant sea life, the North Fork is, unsurprisingly, one of the best dining destinations in the country. It's honestly hard to find a bad meal out here, and towns like Greenport are chock-a-block with world-class restaurants that would give New York City's best chefs a run for their money.

SHELTER ISLAND | *Seafood Shacks and Five-Star Dining*

18 BAY

23 NorthFerry Road, Shelter Island, New York 11964 • 631.749.0053 • 18bayrestaurant.com

In one of Shelter Island's iconic Victorian houses, 18 Bay serves an Italian-inspired prix-fixe menu that changes weekly. Expect fresh and local ingredients, beautifully plated. Depending on the season, the seven-course tasting menu will include antipasti like striped bass crudo with fresh corn and peppers or fried oysters with chili and mint before moving on to a handmade ricotta ravioli with heirloom tomato sauce. There's usually a choice of a fish or land entree, like seafood stew or roasted duck breast. For $75 per person (not including drinks), it's a pricey night out, but incredibly reasonable compared to what you might find in the Hamptons or New York City—especially when you consider that the restaurant was nominated for a James Beard Award in 2018.

// Fresh herbs for sale

COMMANDER CODY'S SEAFOOD

41 Smith Street, Shelter Island, New York 11964 • 631.749.1851 • facebook.com/
ShelterIslandFishMarket

Eating at Commander Cody's feels a little bit like eating in somebody's backyard, and
that's because it is. At 5 p.m., Commander Cody starts cooking, and he doesn't stop until
the food runs out. The menu is always changing, depending on what's fresh and available,
but you can expect fried chicken, pulled pork, friend shrimp, and lobster. It's a hidden
gem among Shelter Island's pricey seafood restaurants and one of the most unique dining
experiences on the East End. It's cash only and there's no ATM on the premises, so come
prepared.

MARIE EIFFEL   *AUTHOR'S PICK*

184 NorthFerry Road, Shelter Island, New York 11964 • 631.749.0003 • marieeiffelmarket.com

The best place to get a cup of coffee on Shelter Island, Marie Eiffel is a popular cafe with a
line out the door most weekends. Along with high-quality espresso and coffee drinks, Marie
sells pastries and sandwiches behind the counter in the small shop, where you can stock up
on organic produce, artisanal bread, and fresh fish, meat, and cheese. There's also a made-to-
order juice bar in the back, and a lovely deck out the back door where you can sip your coffee
and eat your morning pastry with a view of the water.

THE NORTH FORK | *Farm-Fresh Produce and World-Class Chefs*

Orient

ORIENT COUNTRY STORE

950 Village Lane, Orient, New York 11957 • 631.323.2580

The sea salt oatmeal cookies are something of a local celebrity on Long Island's East End, and
for good reason: they are chewy, salty, sweet perfection. But the store sells more than just
cookies—there are sandwiches, cakes, muffins, and a blueberry pie that Sam Sifton of the *New
York Times* called "perfect."

Greenport

1943 PIZZA BAR   *AUTHOR'S PICK*

308 Main Street, Greenport, New York 11944 • 631.477.6984 • rollingindoughpizza.com

Hands-down the best pizza on the North Fork, 1943 serves brick oven pizza with perfect char.
In the courtyard of American Beech hotel and restaurant, this hip pizza place uses fresh ingre-

dients to create perfect pies with toppings like speck, arugula, burrata, and ricotta. Don't miss out on the clam pie, and the classic margarita is absolutely perfect. The name 1943 refers to the year when pizza became mainstream in America.

AMERICAN BEECH RESTAURANT

300 Main Street, Greenport, New York 11944 • 631.477.5939 • americanbeech.com/eat

Part of the hotel of the same name in Greenport's most happening courtyard, American Beech serves new American cuisine in a stark white setting with funky accents like striped floors and multicolor lighting. The courtyard in front is a popular place to gather for after-dinner drinks, with an outdoor bar and couches. Dine on small plates like watermelon gazpacho or spaghetti squash latkes before moving on to a shrimp curry bowl or the famous vegan Impossible Burger. There are also some East End standards like seared scallops and a lobster roll.

BARBA BIANCA

102 Main Street, Greenport, New York 11944 • 631.333.2600 • barbabiancany.com

This chic waterside eatery is only open in the summer, serving authentic Italian food on their stylish painted dock. The food here is as beautiful and photogenic as it is delicious, with dishes you won't find anywhere else on the North Fork, like frog legs, saffron arancini, whelk salad, and fried rabbit. Come here for creative food in a cool setting.

FORK & ANCHOR

8955 Main Road, East Marion, New York 11939 • 631.477.3277 • forkandanchor.com

A few miles east of Greenport in East Marion, Fork and Anchor is a gourmet deli and general store. This cute, vintage-chic spot will create the perfect picnic—call ahead and they'll have sandwiches, drinks, chips, a salad, and cookies ready to go for a day of exploring. If you'd rather not take your goodie to go, you can dine in on breakfast burritos, egg and cheese croissants, a BLT with basil mayonnaise, or a green goddess chicken salad.

NO LIMOS, PLEASE!

Hiring a limo is a fun way to explore the North Fork's wineries without having to worry about a designated driver. However, on busy weekends, some wineries have a "no limos" rule due to parking. If you're traveling in a group larger than four people, call ahead to make reservations, and nominate somebody to help herd the cats so you can stick to your schedule.

THE FRISKY OYSTER

27 Front Street, Greenport, New York 11944 • 631.477.4265

With funky paper lanterns and wildly patterned wallpaper, the Frisky Oyster feels a little bit out of place in low-key Greenport. But this bistro is one of the town's most happening spots, with craft cocktails like the Beaver Fever, made with blanco tequila, cucumber, cilantro, jalapeno, and lime. The menu changes daily, with starters like the grilled lobster quesadilla or duck confit spring rolls and entrees like charred octopus and seared sea scallops.

THE HALYARD

58775 County Rd 48, Greenport, New York 11944 • 631.477.0666

Part of the stylish Soundview Inn, The Halyard is one of the best new restaurants on the North Fork. The decor here feels like a hip, updated version of where a sea captain might hang out, and the menu matches that vibe, with simple, seafood-focused dishes that highlight the local bounty. Start with clam chowder or mussels in white wine and garlic broth before moving on to sea scallops with corn succotash, or the decadent surf and turf: half a poached lobster and a six-ounce filet.

// Don't leave Long Island without trying some Peconic Bay Oysters

LITTLE CREEK OYSTERS   🌟 AUTHOR'S PICK

37 Front Street, Greenport, New York 11944 • 631.477.6992 • littlecreekoysters.com

Everything this tiny restaurant has on the menu is the best version of that thing you'll find anywhere on Long Island: the best oysters, the best clams, and the best clam chowder—brothy, creamy, and utterly un-goopy, with thinly sliced tomatoes and the perfect proportion of clams. It's one of the places you'll want to go early on in your visit to the North Fork, because chances are, once you've been here, you'll want to go back. In the winter, sit at the cozy bar and chat with the shuckers, or grab a picnic table outside in the summer.

LUCHARITO

119 Main Street, Greenport, New York 11944 • 631.477.6666 • lucharitos.com

Cute and colorful Lucharito serves Mexican food in a fun and casual setting. Go for the tacos and burritos in a variety of flavors, like cilantro lime shrimp, grilled adobo chicken, al pastor, or veggies. There's also a location in Aquebogue.

// The tiny Little Creek Oysters is one of the best dining experiences on Long Island (or anywhere else, for that matter)

Southold

NORTH FORK TABLE & INN

57225 Main Road, Southold, New York 11971 • 631.765.0177 • northforktableandinn.com

Probably the most famous restaurant on Long Island, The North Fork Table has been hailed by critics across the country as a pioneer of the farm-to-table movement. The restaurant retains a commitment to fresh, seasonally inspired food with tasting menus and a la carte entrees that highlight the organic, local produce the North Fork is famous for. Despite the restaurant's fame, it's still a simple and low-key place with friendly service. The menu changes frequently, but expect to find local seafood options like Peconic Bay fluke crudo with rice cracker, peanut Sabayon, and Thai caramel, or entrees like day boat sword-fish with eggplant, harissa, and vanilla cashew butter. There's a well-curated wine and cock-tail list (with a separate menu just for whiskey), or you can order a wine pairing with your tasting menu. Reservations are essential and must be made one month in advance, to the date. If you can't get a table or don't want to splurge on a five-course tasting menu, you can stop by to sample something at their seasonal food truck, with options ranging from a $5 hot dog to a $20 lobster roll.

Peconic

GREENPORT HARBOR BREWERY AND RESTAURANT

42155 Main Road, Peconic, New York 11958 • 631.477.1100 • greenportharborbrewing.com

Greenport Harbor Brewery makes the North Fork's favorite beer: the nearly perfect Harbor Ale, an American-style pale ale. They also make Black Duck Porter, Otherside IPA, and Tidal Lager. Their Leaf Pile Ale and Antifreeze Ale are available seasonally. The brewery has tastings and events, along with a restaurant on site, serving Long Island pub fare like fish and chips and duck spring rolls. There's also a tasting room and brewery in downtown Greenport.

SANG LEE FARMS

25180 County Rd 48, Peconic, New York 11958 • 631.734.7001 • sangleefarms.com

Organic produce from Sang Lee Farms can be found at Farmers Markets on the East End, but it's worth a stop by this charming farmstand for fresh veggies and baked goods, along with jarred preserves and frozen soups.

// Fresh produce goes beyond tomatoes on Long Island

Cutchogue

8 HANDS FARM

4735 Cox Lane, Cutchogue, New York 11935 • 631.494.6155 • 8handsfarm.com

This photogenic farm with a red barn offers tours of their sustainable and organic operation. Stop by the farm store to purchase organic produce, eggs, meat, and dairy, along with some incredible yarn and knitted items—all made from wool from the farm's sheep.

Mattituck

LOVE LANE KITCHEN

240 Love Lane, Mattituck, New York 11952 • 631.298.8989 • lovelanekitchen.com

This homey cafe serves fresh comfort food in a cute diner setting. Stop by for lunch and order baja fish tacos or a cobb salad. There are also homemade soups and a regular and veggie burger. It's great food, made with love, in a welcoming setting.

// Bring home locally grown peppers from one of the many farm stands

Where Foodies Should Stay

NORTH FORK TABLE & INN

57225 Main Road, Southold, New York 11971 • 631.765.0177 • www.northforktableandinn.com

For the ultimate foodie vacation, what better place to stay than at Long Island's most famous farm-to-table restaurant? At the North Fork Table & Inn, all you have to do is roll upstairs after your meal and dive under the covers in one of four cozy farmhouse-style rooms. From $250.

FIRE ISLAND | *Fried Fish and Dockside Dining*

Fire Island has a year-round population of about 300 people. Unless otherwise noted, restaurants there are only open during the summer—although some open in spring and stay open in fall. If you plan to visit between Labor Day and Memorial Day, call ahead to check the hours (especially on a weekday). Because of the short season and the lack of access, it's not exactly a foodie destination, but you might be surprised at the quality of the ingredients and the care that goes into preparing them.

Kismet

KISMET INN

1 Oak Street, Kismet, New York 11706 • 631.583.5592 • thekismetinn.com

The quaint and historic Kismet Inn has been in operation for over 90 years—it's also one of only two restaurants in town. Come here to meet everyone in town and dine on classic dishes in an old-school setting. The menu has Italian-American seafood favorites, like linguine with clams, seafood fra diavolo, and shrimp scampi. The restaurant also offers steak, burgers, and a BLT. Wash it down with a cocktail as you swap stories with old-timers about the good ol' days.

Fair Harbor

LE DOCK

Bay Walk, Fair Harbor, New York 11706 • 631.583.5200 • ledockrestaurant.com

This upscale waterfront restaurant by Jean-Georges serves globally inspired seafood overlooking the bay in Fair Harbor. Starters like tuna tartare or spring pea guacamole give way to roasted hake with garlic broth, fava beans, and artichoke heart, or charred wagyu tenderloin with chimichurri and vegetables. With chic decor and beautifully presented foods, it's one of the most expensive places to eat in (the already pricy) Fire Island.

UNFRIENDLY'S ICE CREAM SHOP

21 Broadway Avenue, Fair Harbor, New York 11706 • 631.583.5600 • pioneermarket.net

Part of Pioneer Market, Unfriendly's Ice Cream Shop is a Fire Island landmark, serving ice cream cones, sundaes, and milkshakes, along with coffee and smoothies.

Ocean Beach

THE HIDEAWAY RESTAURANT

785 Evergreen Walk, Ocean Beach, New York 11770 • 631.583.5929 • facebook.com/hideawayob

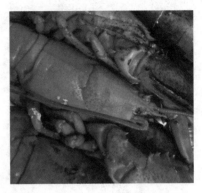

This bayside restaurant is a popular sunset spot. The back deck is usually packed in the evening, with diners sitting on plastic chairs sipping cocktails. There's a range of fried seafood on the menu here, along with some upscale options like a lobster roll, steamed mussels, and lobster mac and cheese.

// Lobster is almost always on the menu in the Hamptons

THE LANDING RESTAURANT OCEAN BEACH

620 Bay Walk, Ocean Beach, New York 11770 • 631.583.5800 • facebook.com/TheLandingOB

The Landing is one of the more slightly upscale restaurants in town, in a shingled building with an open porch. Open for lunch and dinner, the restaurant offers you a choice of cobb salad, fried calamari, or a cheeseburger on a brioche bun. The truffle mac and cheese is a favorite here, along with the decadent cocktails. Go here to drink a mudslide as an afternoon pick-me-up.

RACHEL'S RESTAURANT AND BAKERY

325 Bay Walk, Ocean Beach, New York 11770 • 631.583.9552 • rachelsfireisland.com

Famous for their Black Magic Cake and chocolate chip cookies, Rachel's has transformed from a bakery to a full-service restaurant, offering breakfast classics like omelets and benedicts along with a full lunch and dinner menu with buffalo wings, calamari, and grilled chicken. Just make sure to leave room for dessert. The bakery stays open until 4 a.m., satisfying the sweet tooth cravings of late-night partiers.

VINEYARDS IN THE NORTH FORK

OSPREY'S DOMINION VINEYARDS · 44075 Main Road, Peconic, New York 11958 · 631.765.6188 · ospreysdominion.com

This popular vineyard has a dog- and kid-friendly picnic area where you can bring your own food and buy a bottle of wine. There's live music on weekends, as well as lawn games and a food truck. Come here to hang out for an afternoon, sipping on one of their signature chardonnays, sauvignon blancs, or cabernet sauvignons.

PINDAR VINEYARDS · 37645 New York-25, Peconic, New York 11958 · 631.734.6200 · pindar.net

The gorgeous sunflower field at Pindar is almost as much of a reason to visit as the wine. The vineyard is known for great customer service and great value; tastings here happen in a huge wooden barn. There are weekly tours of the winery, or you can call to schedule a private tasting. You can also join one of their exclusive Champagne, Chopin, & Caviar tours, which takes you inside the traditional champagne process.

BEDELL CELLARS · 36225 New York-25, Cutchogue, New York 11935 · 631.734.7537 · bedellcellars.com

This beautiful farmhouse estate is home to 75 acres of sustainably grown grape vines. Since 1980, Bedell Cellars has created a surprising range of wines, from their $125 Musee to their $18 rosé. The tasting room experience is one of the best on Long Island, with expert sommeliers and an outdoor picnic area. Go online to book a reservation and keep in mind that it's a popular event space, so it might be closed on Saturdays during wedding season.

CASTELLO DI BORGHESE VINEYARD & WINERY · 17150 County Rd 48, Cutchogue, New York 11935 · 631.734.5111 · castellodiborghese.com

Castello di Borghese is where the North Fork's first vines were grown by Alex and Louisa Hargrave in 1973. Tastings at this vineyard are in the wood-paneled bar, led by an expert sommelier. Every glass has a story here, and although walk-ins are welcome, plan ahead and make a reservation for a private guided tour that will take you through the history of wine on Long Island and end with a wine and cheese tasting in the rustic barn.

PUGLIESE VINEYARDS · 34515 Main Road, Cutchogue, New York 11935 · 631.734.4057 · pugliesevineyards.com

At this quaint family-run vineyard, you can sip wine under a pergola or at picnic tables overlooking the pond. The winery is known for their Cabernet Sauvignon and Chardonnay Reserve, as well as sparkling and dessert wines—all at reasonable prices. Pugliese also makes Grey Gardens rosé, a tribute to Big and Little Edie Beale, made by a descendant of the Bouvier-Beale family.

SHINN ESTATE VINEYARDS · 2000 Oregon Road, Mattituck, New York 11952 · 631.804.0367 · shinnestatevineyards.com

At this vineyard, winery, and bed-and-breakfast, you can stop by for a tasting or vineyard tour. The 22-acre estate creates biodynamic wines at a reasonable price point. The back patio is a lovely place to split a bottle of wine, overlooking the vines.

HARMONY VINEYARDS · 169 Harbor Road, St James, New York 11780 · 631.804.0367 · monyvineyards.com

Harmony Vineyards is one of the westernmost Vineyards on the North Fork, and therefore one of the closest to New York City, making this almost doable as a day trip. The waterfront winery has a small selection of wines, the most notable of which is their chardonnay. Stop in for a tasting, or make a reservation for the farm-to-table brunch.

JAMESPORT VINEYARDS · 1216 Main Road, Jamesport, New York 11947 · 631.722.5256

Jamesport Vineyards, known for their riesling and merlot, is also a restaurant and inn. Stop by for a tasting, or plan your visit around one of their ticketed Jazz in the Vines events, where world-class jazz musicians play an open-air concert while you sip wine.

LONG ISLAND SPIRITS · 2182 Sound Avenue, Baiting Hollow, New York 11933 · 631.630.9322

Known for their LiV Vodka and Pine Barrens Gin, Long Island Spirits is Long Island's first craft distillery. The tasting room here has industrial charm, with metal stools and a long wooden bar. The tasting room is open seven days a week, year-round.

PAUMANOK VINEYARDS · 1074 Main Road, Aquebogue, New York 11931 · 631.722.8800

Paumanok is one of Long Island's most beautiful wineries, with a rustic barn and outdoor patio overlooking vines as far as the eye can see. The price point here is a bit higher than at other wineries in the area, but so is the quality. The selection is also bigger than at most wineries, with everything from a $19 rosé to an $85 merlot.

// The North Fork is known for its white wine varietals

Cherry Grove

TOP OF THE BAY BISTRO

159 Dock Walk, Cherry Grove, New York 11782 • 631.597.6028 • topofthebaycherrygrove.com

Overlooking the Cherry Grove Marina, Top of the Bay has a glossy wooden bar, black leather banquettes, and a wall of windows looking out over the water. The menu is a sophisticated take on Fire Island's ubiquitous fried seafood joints, with goat cheese bruschetta, arugula salad with radish, roasted chicken breast with whipped potatoes, and grilled brussels sprouts. Get the flourless chocolate cake for dessert, with whipped cream, cocoa, and blackberries.

Where Foodies Should Stay

PALMS HOTEL

168 Cottage Walk, Ocean Beach, New York 11770 • 631.583.8870 • palmshotelfireisland.com

The Palms Hotel is right in the middle of the action in Ocean Beach, walking distance from all the bars and restaurants. With suites, cottages, and bungalows on the property, there's something for everyone here. Fire Island is a quirky place, and that's reflected in this property, with odd decor choices like sexy boudoir photography and white leather couches. From $149.

LONG ISLAND (NORTH) | *Classic Steakhouses and Roadside Diners*

The Northfork and the Hamptons is where you'll find fine dining that rivals New York's restaurant scene, but the rest of the island shouldn't be overlooked just because it's suburbia. There are some classic finds here, like historic steakhouses, and old-school seafood joints. Long Island is full of hidden gems that are worth a road trip, so if you have your own car, that's the best way to explore the culinary offerings in off-the-beaten-track locations. Brooklyn is ever-expanding, both metaphorically and physically speaking, and if you have an open mind, you might be shocked at the cool, creative, and delicious restaurants we've found.

Garden City and Surrounds

RED SALT ROOM BY DAVID BURKE

45 7th Street, Garden City, New York 11530 • 516.877.9385 • gardencityhotel.com

In this historic Garden City Hotel, Red Salt Room by David Burke is a classic American steakhouse, complete with a raw bar and four different cuts of beef in varying sizes. A la carte sides like roasted asparagus, corn succotash, creamed spinach, and baked potato round out the meal. Have a drink in the hotel's King Bar, or visit during the outrageous Sunday brunch buffet, when you can visit the seafood bar, the meat carving station, or the sushi station.

WATERZOOI GARDEN CITY

850 Franklin Avenue, Garden City, New York 11530 • 516.877.2177 • waterzooi.com

This Belgian-style bistro is known for its steamed mussels and raw oysters (and of course—french fries and beer). The spacious restaurant has red leather banquettes and a long bar, with a wide selection of beer on tap. Try the lobster croquettes and Hudson Valley foie gras to start, before digging into entrees like steak frites or braised short rib. Mussels are the main event here, served with fries and mayo and the choice of twelve different broth styles, including Provencal, Thai, Calabrian, Creole, and more.

LONG ISLAND WINE TOURS

If you don't have a designated driver and you'd like to visit a few different wineries in one go, consider joining a tour. The tour companies below can put together custom wine tasting packages, complete with different transportation options. If you're planning a bachelor or bachelorette party, this is the way to go.

EAST END WINE TASTING TOURS • eastendwinetastingtours.com •

NORTH FORK WINE TOURS • northforkwinetours.com

WINE TASTING LONG ISLAND • winetastinglongisland.com

LIVINO TOURS • livinotours.com

LONG ISLAND WINE DIVAS • liwinedivas.com

NORTH FORK WINE WAGON • northforkwinewagon.com

On board the North Fork Wine Wagon, eight to fifteen people join a guide/bartender to pedal a giant bike to different wineries. There's music, and you can bring your own snacks as you propel the wine wagon to different wineries on a three-hour tour.

NORTH FORK TROLLEY • northforktrolley.com

Book online as a group or an individual for a wine tour aboard the old-school trolley.

// Long Island's vineyards are a great place to spend an afternoon

Port Washington and Surrounds

KYMA ROSLYN

1446 Old Northern Boulevard, Roslyn, New York 11576 • 516.621.3700 • kyma-roslyn.com

With an all-white-everything theme and stylish design, Kyma is the coolest restaurant in Roslyn. The Greek-chic decor translates to the menu, where you'll find spanakopita, halloumi, saganaki, and sardines. Kyma is known for their whole fish preparations, with branzino, sea bass, and snapper on the menu. Go for a fancy lunch to try the prix fixe menu, with three courses for $32.95.

LOUIE'S OYSTER BAR AND GRILL

395 Main Street, Port Washington, New York 11050 • 516.8834242 • louiessince1905.com

A Port Washington staple, this Main Street institution has been in business since 1905. Serving classics like fish and chips, burgers, and lobster rolls alongside upscale seafood dishes like miso black cod, monkfish pasta, and lobster cioppino, the mahogany and brass bar with a view of the harbor is one of the town's most upscale (read: pricey) dining destinations. Don't miss out on the extensive wine and cocktail list.

Huntington and Surrounds

OHEKA CASTLE

135 West Gate Drive, Huntington, New York 11743 • 631.659.1400 • oheka.com

Set on the grounds of a literal palace in the Long Island suburbs, Oheka Castle's bar and restaurant is a must-visit, even if you're not staying there. The setting is truly unbelievable—come for an early dinner while it's still light out so you can take a quick walk around the grounds before you sit down for an elegant (but not outrageously priced, considering the setting) meal of crab cakes, beet salad, and filet mignon. If you're interested in seeing more of the castle, you can book a mansion tour for $25.

PRIME

117 North New York Avenue, Huntington, New York 11743 • 631.385.1515 • restaurantprime.com/huntington

Overlooking the harbor, Prime is a stylish destination for surf and turf. The restaurant is massive, with plenty of outdoor seating—ask to sit out on the deck. At brunch, lunch, or dinner, you can choose from an extensive menu that includes steak, sushi, and a raw bar.

SANDBAR

55 Main Street, Cold Spring Harbor, New York 11724 • 631.498.6188 • sandbarcoldspringharbor.com

Sleek and stylish with a nautical vibe, Cold Spring Harbor's buzziest restaurant serves upscale pub food and seafood specialties. Start with appetizers like duck tacos and spicy grilled calamari before dining on roasted salmon, grilled lobster, and pan-seared swordfish.

SWALLOW

366 New York Avenue, Huntington, New York 11743 • 631.547.5388 • swallowrestaurant.com

Swallow serves a variety of small plates and craft cocktails to a hip crowd in one of Huntington's coolest spaces. Come here with a group to share dishes like charred beets with ricotta, arugula, almonds, and fresh horseradish, or shrimp and grits with pan-seared shrimp, andouille sausage, and tomato. It's also a popular brunch spot, where you can dine on avocado toast, pulled pork hash, or eggs Florentine. There's also a (slightly hipper) location in Montauk.

TIM'S SHIPWRECK DINER NORTHPORT

46 Main Street, Northport, New York 11768 • 631.754.1797 • shipwreckdiner.com

This charming vintage diner has been in business for over 50 years, bringing greasy-spoon classics to downtown Northport. You can have pancakes, French toast, and omelets for breakfast, or you can satisfy your craving for a Reuben. For dessert, there are egg creams, malts, shakes, and floats.

VAUXHALL

26 Clinton Avenue, Huntington, New York 11743 • 631.425.0222 • vauxhallhuntington.com

Vauxhall is a snazzy gastropub in a brick building downtown with a surprising selection of creative burgers. Keep it safe with bacon and cheddar, or go wild with ghost pepper marmalade, vinegar onion crisps, and Pepperjack cheese on a pretzel bun. Not into burgers? They also offer grilled cheese, fish tacos, and fried chicken.

Port Jefferson and Surrounds

EATMOSAIC

418 North Country Road, St. James, New York 11780 • 631.584.2058 • eatmosaic.com

At eatMOSAIC in St. James, you'll get artfully plated New American fare served in an upscale dining room. The five-course tasting menu changes daily depending on what's fresh, but you can expect dishes like asiago baked gnocchi with fennel, stewed tomato, and tuscan kale; or miso glazed salmon with barley, yoghurt, ponzu, and pickled beet.

TIGER LILY CAFÉ

156 East Main Street, Port Jefferson, New York 11777 • 631.476.7080 • tigerlilycafe.com

In the land of surf and turf, vegan options can be hard to come by. That's not the case at Tiger Lily Cafe, a veggie-focused casual lunch spot serving falafel, tofu wraps, and veggie burgers. There's some meat on the menu too, mostly in sandwich form.

Riverhead and Surrounds

BRIERMERE FARMS ⭐ *AUTHOR'S PICK*

4414 Sound Avenue, Riverhead, New York 11901 • 631.722.3931 • briermere.com

Famous for their pies (get the peach and blackberry), Briermere Farms is a cult favorite on Long Island. In addition to pies, this little farmhouse shop in Riverhead sells baked goods and preserves made from fruit from their Long Island orchard. If your trip takes you through Riverhead, buy a couple of pies to take home and freeze. They are perfect when reheated in the oven, especially in the dead of winter.

// Fresh berries make for excellent pies at Briermere Farms

LONG ISLAND (SOUTH SHORE)

Long Beach and Surrounds

APERITIF BISTRO

242 Sunrise Highway, Rockville Centre, New York 11570 • 516.594.3404 • aperitifbistro.com

This super-chic French bistro may look like a regular suburban restaurant on the outside, but inside, it's pure France. With red leather banquettes, a patterned tile floor, and mirrors on the wall, this restaurant wouldn't be out of place in New York City (or maybe even Paris, for that matter). The menu is extensive, serving everything from crepes and omelets for lunch to mussels, raw oysters, and coq au vin for dinner. Try a reasonably priced wine flight with your meal, or sip on a martini at the bar.

THE CABANA

1034 West Beech Street, Long Beach, New York 11561 • 516. 889.1345

A Tex-Mex surf shack and tiki bar, The Cabana is an oddly charming dive bar with great margaritas.

JIMMY HAYS STEAKHOUSE

4310 Austin Boulevard, Island Park, New York 11558 • 516.432.5155 • jimmyhayssteakhouse.com

This is the ultimate old-school steak house, with dark wood paneling, mirrored walls, and booths upholstered with plaid fabric. It's a trip back in time, with classic eats like baked clams, pork chops, and chicken cordon bleu. The selection of beef is huge, with filet mignon, chateaubriand, and even calves' liver on the menu.

POP'S SEAFOOD SHACK & GRILL

15 Railroad Pl, Island Park, New York 11558 • 516.432.7677 • popsseafoodshack.com

This multi-level seafood shack is the place to go for friends, seafood, and frozen drinks with a view of the water. Hang out in the Adirondack chairs on the sand and people watch. The atmosphere here is fun and lively, with decor that's the perfect amount of kitsch.

Massapequa

ALL-AMERICAN HAMBURGER DRIVE-IN

4286 Merrick Road, Massapequa, New York 11758 • 516.798.9574

This classic roadside fast-food restaurant is a throwback to the 1950s, serving burgers, fries, and shakes. It's a local favorite, with thin hamburgers, crispy fries, and thick milkshakes—the perfect retro pit stop on a Long Island road trip.

SALUMI MASSAPEQUA

5600 Merrick Road, Massapequa, New York 11758 • 516.620.0057 • salumibarli.com

Salumi is a Spanish tapas bar, serving decadent small plates in a cozy setting. Everything is for sharing here, like the pork ribs with black garlic sauce or the jamon iberico with pickled red onion, sundried tomatoes. Marcona almonds, and olive oil. If you're in the mood for wine and cheese, choose a rioja from the wine list and order the Spanish board, with a selection of meats and cheeses served with jam, almonds, dried fruit, and olives.

Sayville

SOUTH SHORE DIVE SAYVILLE

65 Main Street, West Sayville, New York 11796 • 631.218.6500 • southshoredive.com

This funky restaurant and bar has a fun atmosphere, with pressed tin ceilings, colorful lights, and reclaimed wood details inside and a back patio with cool hanging chairs and tons of plants. Dine on pub fare like baked mac and cheese or a pastrami reuben, or just hang out and have a cocktail. The Holy Lola is a popular choice, made with blanco tequila, local lavender, and fresh pressed lime.

Where Foodies Should Stay

JEDEDIAH HAWKINS INN AND RESTAURANT

400 South Jamesport Avenue, Riverhead, New York 11901 • 631.722.2900 • jedediahhawkinsinn.com

Riverhead's Jedediah Hawkins Inn and Restaurant is one of greater Long Island's best hotels for a foodie getaway. Located in the armpit of the North and South Forks, almost everything is doable in a day trip from Riverhead. The hotel, in a converted mansion, has individually decorated rooms that feel cozy and homey, with fireplaces, wood floors, and patchwork quilts in some. If you get hungry, the on-site restaurant is one of Riverhead's hidden gems. Don't miss the speakeasy, a hidden restaurant within a restaurant where you can sip wine and hear stories about the inn's namesake ghost. From $250.

≡ *The Jersey Shore*

Foodies shouldn't overlook New Jersey, whose moniker is "The Garden State." You haven't tasted a tomato until you've had a vine-ripened Jersey tomato, fresh from the garden. If you think New Jersey is all about pork rolls and subs, you're absolutely right, in one sense. However, there's so much more than that in Asbury Park, where you'll find everything from Asian fusion to (possibly) America's best pizza. New restaurants are opening every week in this ultra-hip town, so be on the lookout for newcomers in creative spaces.

JERSEY SHORE | *Hip New Restaurants and Classic Boardwalk Eats*

Highlands

BAHR'S LANDING

2 Bay Avenue, Highlands, New Jersey 07732 • 732.872.1245 • bahrslandingnj.com

This classic dockside restaurant is a Jersey Shore staple. Open year-round, it's cozy in the winter and breezy in the summer, with a wood-paneled dining room with huge windows that look out on to the water. The menu is old-school and slightly upscale, with a heavy emphasis on seafood. Start with steamers or a salad before cracking into a whole lobster (steamed or broiled), served with a side of coleslaw and homemade biscuits. Don't miss the cute souvenir shop on your way out for lobster-themed merch.

Long Branch

STROLLO'S LIGHTHOUSE

250 Ocean Avenue, Long Branch, New Jersey 07740 • 732.229.1222 • strolloslighthouse.com

Ask anyone who grew up on the Jersey Shore, and they'll tell you that summer is all about Italian Ice. This shaved ice with flavored syrup is a quintessential Jersey dessert, and Strollo's is the OG. Come here after a hot day at the beach and try to eat it all before it melts.

WINDMILL

200 Ocean Avenue, Long Branch, New Jersey 07740 • 732.870.6098 • windmillhotdogs.com

This old-school hot dog stand is as kitschy as it gets. In an actual (non-functioning) windmill, diners order at the counter for hot dogs, fries, burgers, and the incredibly delicious mushroom bites, a breaded and fried mushroom cap. Eat in if you can find space in the tiny restaurant, or eat outside on a hot summer night.

Asbury Park

ASBURY PARK DISTILLING CO.

527 Lake Avenue, Asbury Park, New Jersey 07712 • apdistilling.com

At Asbury Park's only distillery, you can get a behind-the-scenes look at the process as you sip on craft cocktails in their super-stylish bar. The cocktail menu is tailored to their spirits (the only alcohol they can legally serve) with housemade bitters, tonics, tinctures, and shrubs to complement their Double Barrel Bourbon, Barrel Finished Gin, and vodka.

// A New Jersey institution, Bahr's is the kind of seafood restaurant that never goes out of style

BARRIO COSTERO

610 Bangs Avenue, Asbury Park, New Jersey 07712 • 732.455.5544 • barriocostero.com

With funky lighting and craft cocktails, Barrio Costero is a chic setting for Mexican-inspired creative dining. You won't find traditional Mexican dishes on the menu here, but the innovative dishes are interesting, like vegetable huarache with mole roja, mushrooms, and avocado; or the fish tacos with gooseberry salsa, cabbage, and carrot crema. Stop by for brunch and try one of the special brunch cocktails, like the hibiscus mimosa or the green chile Bloody Mary.

CARDINAL PROVISIONS

513 Bangs Avenue, Asbury Park, New Jersey 07712 • 732.898.7194 • crdnal.com

Open for breakfast and lunch, Cardinal Provisions serves chef-y sandwiches in a hip counter service restaurant. Come here to cure your hangovers with a gravlax everything bagel or chicken and waffles, or you can get a to-go bag for the beach. Crafty sandwiches range from a cheesesteak to vegan avocado toast. The French picnic sandwich has Italian tuna in olive oil, marinated red peppers, oil cured olives, red onion, parsley, basil, capers, and aioli on a toasted baguette.

MOGO

632 Cookman Avenue, Asbury Park, New Jersey 07712 • 732.361.3684 • eatmogo.com

With locations on the boardwalk and in town, MOGO serves Korean fusion tacos. Choose your style (taco, burrito, or bowl) and then choose your protein: Korean BBQ marinated rib-eye, soy-ginger chicken thighs, fried cod, spicy pork belly, sweet and sour shrimp, or spicy glazed tofu. Don't forget a side of homemade kimchi and the Asian pear hot sauce. While the boardwalk location is a counter-service shack in a repurposed shipping container, the downtown location has room to actually sit and eat.

TOAST

516 Cookman Avenue, Asbury Park, New Jersey 07712 • 732.776.5900 • toastasburypark.com

Asbury Park is a party town, and every good party town needs a great breakfast place. At Toast, there's something for everyone; dishes range from pancakes to huevos rancheros to lobster rolls. The weekend waits can be brutal, but the service is fast and efficient, and you can order a drink and sit outside while you wait.

VINTAGE SUBS ASBURY PARK

729 Bangs Avenue, Asbury Park, New Jersey 07712 • 732.361.5839 • vintagesubsasburypark.com

New Jersey invited the Italian sub, and nobody does it better than Vintage Subs in Asbury Park. The Classic Italian has cappacola, ham, genoa salami, and provolone, topped with shredded lettuce, tomato, onion, oregano, and oil and vinegar.

// Lining up for tacos at MOGO

Sea Girt

THE PARKER HOUSE

290 1st Avenue, Sea Girt, New Jersey 08750 • 732.449.0442 • parkerhousenj.com

This restaurant in a seaside Victorian mansion has been serving seafood for 140 years. With legendary happy hours and an excellent raw bar, this sprawling restaurant with a wrap-around porch is a Jersey Shore must. It's upscale (no tank tops, dudes), but affordable, serving lobster, filet mignon, and crab cakes. The food is good, but you're here more for the ambiance—live entertainment, people watching, and being a part of the general jolly mayhem on a Saturday night.

Where Foodies Should Stay

BUNGALOW

50 Laird Street, Long Branch, New Jersey 07740 • 732.229.3700 • bungalowhotel.net

Bungalow is Long Branch's hippest place to stay, with bright rooms overlooking the promenade. The decor is funky and irreverent, with lucite furniture, colorful chandeliers, and black and white photography. The rooms are sleek and modern, and the downstairs bar is buzzing at night. The fluffy white beds are super-comfy and the suites (some with balcony) all have a bathtub in the room. From $175.

LONG ISLAND FOOD FESTIVALS

LONG ISLAND RESTAURANT WEEK · longislandrestaurantweek.com

During Long Island Restaurant Week, over 150 participating restaurants offer a three-course menu for $29.95. Held during the spring and fall, it offers a great way to try some of the fancier restaurants at an affordable price.

MATTITUCK STRAWBERRY FESTIVAL · mattituckstrawberryfestival.org

Sample strawberry shortcake and watch a new Strawberry Queen get crowned every June at the Mattituck Strawberry Festival on the North Fork.

ROSÉ SOIRÉE · danstasteofsummer.com

Southampton's 21+ Rosé Soirée lets you sample over 40 different wines from Long Island and beyond with one general admission ticket. Come dressed to impress and stay for the live music and dancing.

GRILLHAMPTON · danstasteofsummer.com

Grillhampton, held every year in Bridgehampton, brings together the best chefs of Long Island's East End to compete against NYC chefs in an epic cooking competition and tasting.

TASTE OF TWO FORKS · danstasteofsummer.com

Taste of Two Forks showcases the best cuisine of the North and South Forks, with specialty cocktails, a raw bar, and a celebrity host.

LONG ISLAND MARITIME MUSEUM SEAFOOD FESTIVAL · limmseafoodfestival.org

Come for live music and lobster at Sayville's seafood festival, held every August.

MONTAUK SEAFOOD FESTIVAL · montaukseafoodfestival.com

Montauk's seafood festival keeps it local with booths full of wine, beer, and shellfish. Family-friendly activities and live music make this popular with visitors and locals.

LONG ISLAND FALL FESTIVAL · lifallfestival.com

Huntington's fall festival brings the carnival to town, with rides, games, live music, and a food court full of food trucks and local vendors. Also included are a farmers' market and kid-friendly activities.

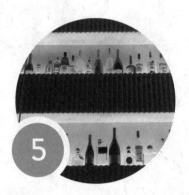

5

Escapes for Party Animals

How to Have a Good Time on Long Island and the Jersey Shore

Summer is a time to let loose and have fun, and we'll show you exactly where to do that. From the Jersey Shore's world-class music clubs to the hipster hangouts of Montauk, the summer's best parties are happening by the beach. When you add beautiful people to a beautiful place and throw in some locally produced rosé, the party never stops.

☰ *Montauk and the Hamptons*

In the winter, Montauk is a sleepy fishing town, but in the summer, every weekend is a party, from Friday afternoon to Sunday night. There are day parties, boat parties, beach parties, and pool parties. You can party from sunset to sunrise, at hipster summer camps, celebrity hideouts, and dockside dive bars. There's no shortage of excitement to be had in Montauk, where every bar is packed to the gills and cocktails are served by the pitcher. Party-centric hotels mean the fun never stops. As you head west towards the Hamptons, things tend to calm down a bit. As the mansions get bigger, the fun gets ever-so-slightly more sophisticated, relegated to private parties, artsy fundraisers, and overpriced restaurants. Amagansett's Stephen Talkhouse is the Hamptons Party place, with hundreds of people in line on a Saturday night to dance and drink.

MONTAUK | *Dive Bars and Exclusive Parties*

MONTAUK BREWERY

62 South Erie Avenue, Montauk, New York 11954 • 631.668.8471 • montaukbrewingco.com

With their simple and stylish cans, Montauk Brewery has exploded in popularity in the last few years. Their Montauk tasting room has all of their top-sellers (Double IPA, Driftwood Ale, Summer Ale, Session IPA, and Wave Chaser IPA) along with some seasonal brews, like the Watermelon Session Al and the Pumpkin Ale. The little red house right in town is a place to sip and mingle. Pick up some of the merch as a souvenir, or get some beer to go.

SWALLOW EAST

474 West Lake Drive, Montauk, New York 11954 • 631.668.8344 • swalloweastrestaurant.com

In a vintage-chic stylish setting with wood-paneled walls, framed black-and-white photographs, and long wooden tables with metal chairs, Swallow East serves shareable small plates and craft cocktails. There's live music every weekend in the summer for a super-hip crowd.

THE SURF LODGE

183 Edgemere Street, Montauk, New York 11954 • 631.483.5037 • thesurflodge.com

As the original Montauk party place, the Surf Lodge has been bringing world-class musical acts like Street. Lucia, Gary Clark Jr., and Janelle Monae to the East End of Long Island for over ten years. The hotel, restaurant, and bar make up an intimate outdoor venue overlooking Fort Pond. The decor is surf-chic, with lots of whitewashed wood, natural materials, and tropical prints. Outside there's a deck where concerts take place and a sandy beach area with sun loungers and low tables. While the concerts are a draw, sometimes the people in attendance are more famous than the musicians—this is the place to go for celeb-spotting. It's nearly impossible to get in here without a reservation, and you might encounter a little bit of snobbery, but if you go with a group on a low-key night, it's one of the best parties on Long Island.

MEMORY MOTEL

692 Montauk Highway, Montauk, New York 11954 • 631.668.2702 • memorymotel.com

Memory Motel is where the late-night parties happen in Montauk, on the sweaty dance floor of this iconic motel-turned-bar. Open until 4 a.m., it's usually the last place on any night out. And yes, it is that Memory Motel from the Rolling Stones song.

RUSCHMEYER'S

161 2nd House Road, Montauk, New York 11954 • 631.668.2877 • ruschmeyers.com

The recently updated hotel and restaurant is always a party scene on the weekend, with mobs of people dancing inside at the bar. Out on the lawn, groups drink pitchers of beer or cocktails at picnic tables or roast marshmallows by the fire pit. You can have a group dinner (lobster rolls! clam pizza!) before joining the dance party or taking the party outside for lawn games.

// The ping pong and party room at Ruschmeyer's in Montauk

NAVY BEACH

16 Navy Road, Montauk, New York 11954 • 631.668.6868 • navybeach.com

Montauk is one of the only places on the East End with an uninterrupted view of the sunset over the water to the west. Located directly on Fort Pond Bay, Navy Beach serves dinner with a sunset view. You might share small plates like ceviche, shishito peppers, or PEI mussels, or you could dine on entrees like grilled scallops, fried chicken, or roasted swordfish. The restaurant specializes in large parties, with themed prix fixe menus for groups. It's a popular spot for sunset cocktails, with rum drinks and pitchers.

SLOPPY TUNA

148 South Emerson Avenue, Montauk, New York 11954 • 631.647.8000 • lisloppytuna.com

Sloppy Tuna is a rarity in this part of Long Island: a bar that's located directly on the ocean. This notoriously wild beach bar has two floors to party on (plus the beach out front), both serving pub grub and fried seafood. The party gets started early here, so stop by in the afternoon for the full experience.

LIAR'S SALOON

401 West Lake Drive, Montauk, New York 11954 • 631.668.9597

One of the only late-night bars in Montauk, Liar's is somewhat of a secret, hidden away in a boatyard. It's open 365 nights a year, serving cold mudslides and cheap beer. It's completely and utterly un-hipsterfied, which is the best part about it.

668 THE GIG SHACK

782 Main Street, Montauk, New York 11954 • 631.668.2727 • 668thegigshack.com

Serving great seafood with a local vibe, the family-run Gig Shack is known for live music. Open for lunch and dinner right on Main Street, the menu has tacos, lobster rolls, baby back ribs, and fresh salads.

VIKING FLEET BOOZE CRUISE 5126

462 West Lake Drive, Montauk, New York 11954 • 631.668.5700 • vikingfleet.com/activities/sunset-cocktail-cruise

Hop on an organized sunset cruise with Viking, or charter your own booze cruise on one of their fishing boats. Sunset cocktail cruises are $35, and there's a full bar on board where you can buy drinks (cash only).

MONTAUK BEACH HOUSE POOL/BAR

55 South Elmwood Avenue, Montauk, New York 11954 • 631.668.2112 • thembh.com

When summer is in full swing, but the ocean's still too cold for swimming, the party is at Montauk Beach House. This hotel and restaurant has a happening daytime bar scene, with loungers by the pool filled with people sipping drinks. Try one of their signature cocktails, like the Cucaracha, made with mezcal, fresh ginger juice, organic cucumber puree, agave, lime, and chile salt.

SHAGWONG TAVERN

774 Montauk Highway, Montauk, New York 11954 • 631.668.3050 • shagwongtavern.com

Shagwong is a year-round treat in Montauk. This old-school bar and grill is where you'll find fishermen swapping stories over ice-cold beers. It's the anti-hipster antidote to places like the Surf Lodge; you can have an old-fashioned good time here, with some surprisingly good food. Stick with the classics like clams casino, fish and chips, or steamed lobster.

1 Cozy up to the bar at Shagwong to swap surfing stories with locals

2 At Ruschmeyer's, dinner turns into drinks, dancing, and lawn games

3 The sunset view from Montauket

MONTAUKET ⭐ *AUTHOR'S PICK*

88 Firestone Road, Montauk, New York 11954 • 631.668.5992

The best view of the sunset in Montauk is at Montauket, the unpretentious local bar on Fort Pond Bay. It's perfectly dated without being kitschy about it—just a bar, some bar stools, and windows looking out onto the back deck, where everyone gathers when the sun begins to set. There are no fancy drinks to be had here, just cold beer.

Where Party Animals Should Stay

RUSCHMEYER'S ⭐ *AUTHOR'S PICK*

161 2nd House Road, Montauk, New York 11954 • 631.668.2877 • ruschmeyers.com

Relive your summer camp days (only with more alcohol) at the woodsy-chic cabins at Ruschmeyer's. This super cute hotel, restaurant, and bar has small but cozy rooms with wood paneling and fluffy white beds. Set on three acres, the 13 cabins feel secluded and calm by day and like an outdoor music festival by night. The hotel is only open in the summer.

AMAGANSETT, SAG HARBOR, AND THE HAMPTONS | *Country Club Vibes and Private Parties*

Amagansett

STEPHEN TALKHOUSE

161 Main Street, Amagansett, New York 11930 • 631.267.3117 • Stephentalkhouse.com

Stephen Talkhouse is an OG Hamptons party destination—many of your favorite musicians have played here, and every local has a wild story about a night out here. On summer weekends, the line to get in can stretch down the block with frat bros in button downs, but on weeknights and the off-season, this is a local gem, and one of the most epic places to go people watching. Wednesday is karaoke night, when amateurs take the stage to sing their hearts out. The bar is a huge, winding venue with multiple buildings and an indoor/outdoor area.

Sag Harbor

MURF'S BACKSTREET TAVERN ⭐ *AUTHOR'S PICK*

64 Division Street, Sag Harbor, New York 11963 • 631.725.8355

The only dive bar left in the Hamptons, Murf's is a fun and unpretentious place for a late night out. The clientele here is the most mixed group you'll find, with hedge funders and celebrities alongside teachers and firemen. It's a storied place and not without controversy—police activity and drunken patrons frequently make the local newspaper.

THE AMERICAN HOTEL

3012, 45 Main Street, Sag Harbor, New York 11963 • 631.725.3535 • theamericanhotel.com

This is Sag Harbor's quintessential bar, and no visit to town is complete without stopping here for a strong drink. It's a historic place, in an old brick hotel on Main Street, where locals swap tales of the good old days. The bar was a popular hangout for the literary elite of the Hamptons; there are stories about Truman Capote and E. L. Doctorow drinking here. Now, the celebrity sightings range from Bono to Christie Brinkley, but the magic hasn't faded.

East Hampton

MOBY'S

295 Three Mile Harbor Hog Creek Road, East Hampton, New York 11937 • 631.329.2800 • mobysny.com

On the water overlooking Three-Mile Harbor at East Hampton Point, Moby's is one of only a handful of places with an after-dinner bar scene in East Hampton. Enjoy sunset views and live music inside or out on the deck while sipping on cocktails or dining on small plates like scallop crudo, burrata, and octopus. The restaurant and bar are only open in the summer.

THE CLUBHOUSE

174 Daniels Hole Road, East Hampton, New York 11937 • 631.537.2695 • ehitclubhouse.com

East Hampton's newest bowling alley has miniature golf and arcade games. Open until midnight, there's a bar on premises, making this a great place to go after dinner or on an afternoon when the weather's not great. In addition to a more robust wine, beer, and cocktail list than you might expect at a bowling alley, The Clubhouse also has a full restaurant, with late-night burgers, onion rings, wings, and artichoke dip.

Southampton

JUE LAN CLUB

268 Elm Street, Southampton, New York 11968 • 631.353.3610 • juelanclub.com

Jue Lan serves upscale Chinese dim sum in a gorgeous patio setting in Southampton. The interior is bright white, with a long bar that leads out onto a covered porch and brick patio. The menu here is almost like a standard Chinese food menu, only fancified (and quadruple the price): lobster fried rice, Grand Marnier jumbo prawns, Peking duck, and filet mignon with black pepper sauce. You can order a la carte or opt for the prix-fixe menu (not served on weekends). Come with a group and order a feast, because you won't want to miss out on any of the appetizers, satays, bao, or dumplings.

Westhampton

DOCKERS

94 Dune Road, East Quogue, New York 11942 • 631.653.0653 • dockerswaterside.com

This yacht club-chic waterside eatery serves oysters, sushi, and lobster in a beautiful location with live music on weekends. Order the crab cakes, calamari, or lobster mac and cheese for dinner, or just stop by for a drink with a view.

Where Party Animals Should Stay

THE AMERICAN HOTEL

45 Main Street, Sag Harbor, New York 11963 • 631.725.3535 • theamericanhotel.com

Sag Harbor's iconic American Hotel has only eight rooms in the historic brick building on Main Street. The decor in the individually decorated rooms is old school, with carpets, patterned wallpaper, and antique furniture. The real draw here is the legendary bar downstairs, where celebrities and whalers have been partying for over a century. From $240.

≡ *Shelter Island and the North Fork*

SHELTER ISLAND | *Quiet Local Bars and a Rocking Beach Party*

SUNSET BEACH

35 Shore Road, Shelter Island Heights, New York 11965 • 631.749.2001 • sunsetbeachli.com

Sunset Beach is the sceniest spot on Shelter Island. The hotel, restaurant, bar, and boutique on Crescent Beach is a popular hangout for the rich and famous, with a seaplane that brings in well-heeled clientele on Friday evenings. Come for the rosé and cocktails and stay for the chic design, fun ambiance, and excellent people watching.

THE DORY

185 NorthFerry Road, Shelter Island Heights, New York 11965 • 631.749.4300

Shelter Island's only dive bar, The Dory is a (mostly) low-key hangout with friendly bartenders, strong drinks, and cold beer. The Dory is also a restaurant, with simple seafood staples and pub food, open for dinner and lunch. The bar stays open until 1 a.m., which on sleepy Shelter Island is as late as it gets.

THE SHIPWRECK

63 Menantic Road, Shelter Island, New York 11964 • 631.749.5535 • www.islandboatyard.com/shelter -island-boat-bar

This outdoor bar on Menantic Creek is a literal shipwreck, with a bar built into the hull of a 1930 sailboat. There are a few barstools surrounding the boat, along with Adirondack chairs and picnic tables nearby. Sip a Dark and Stormy while watching boats enter the marina below.

THE NORTH FORK | Cozy Pubs and Waterfront Bars

Greenport

BRIX & RYE

308A Main Street, Greenport, New York 11944 • 631.477.6985 • brixandrye.com

This underground cocktail bar has a speakeasy vibe, located below the popular American Beech courtyard. Along with crafty whiskey-focused cocktails like Sazeracs and sours, the bar serves a few snacks like olives, burrata, and crostini.

WHISKEY WIND

30 Front Street, Greenport, New York 11944 • 631.477.6179 • whiskeywindtavern.com

The Whiskey Wind is Greenport's favorite dive bar, a spacious place with cheap drinks, cold beer, and pub food.

CLAUDIO'S

111 Front Street, Greenport, New York 11944 • 631.477.1889 • claudios.com

Claudio's has a few different establishments in town, including the Clam Bar and Crabby Jerry's, a dockside restaurant with a tiki bar and stage. Come on a weekend night when there's live music.

PORT WATERFRONT BAR & GRILL

104 3rd Street, Greenport, New York 11944 • 631.333.250 • portbarandgrill.com

Sort of a hipster yacht club, Port serves tasty seafood standards on their large outdoor patio. It's the perfect place to go with a group, with menu items like the $500 lobster roll—a two-foot-long overstuffed roll topped with foie gras and caviar and served with a bottle of Dom Perignon. Don't worry—the rest of the menu is reasonably priced, with burgers, mussels, tacos, and a lobster grilled cheese. If the weather is nice, grab some friend and order a pitcher of margaritas or one of the other large-format cocktails, like the fishbowl punch with vodka, coconut rum, blue curacao, pineapple, lime, and Swedish Fish.

// Greenport is one of the best places for year-round dining on Long Island

Where Party Animals Should Stay

SUNSET BEACH

35 Shore Road, Shelter Island Heights, New York 11965 • 631.749.2001 • sunsetbeachli.com

From the creators of New York City's Mercer Hotel and L.A.'s Chateau Marmont, this is the most stylish place to stay (and party) on Shelter Island. All 20 rooms here have water views and private decks, and the Street. Tropez-meets-Shelter Island decor is simple, with bright white walls, white furniture, and colorful accents in the hotel's signature yellow. The restaurant and bar here are the best place to be when the sun gets low in the sky, with seafood, cocktails, and excellent sunset views. From $300.

FIRE ISLAND | *Raucous All-Night Beach Parties*

Fire Island's parties are legendary, especially in Cherry Grove and The Pines, gay communities where the fun never stops. There's something about a car-free island that really gets people turnt, without worrying about the designated driver or calling an Uber. These tiny towns—with only 200 year-round residents—turn into the sites for wild bacchanalias in the summer, with bachelorette parties spilling out of restaurants and nightclubs filled with half-naked strangers writhing on the dance floor.

Kismet

SURF'S OUT

1 Bay Walk, Kismet, New York 11706 • 631.583.7400

This cute blue and white restaurant and bar has live music acts throughout the summer on the covered patio. It serves salads, sandwiches, and seafood standards like fish tacos and seared scallops. There's also a non-traditional sushi bar that makes sushi bowls and sushi burritos, along with a selection of specialty rolls. It's a local vibe and a fun place to hang out. If you're at Robert Moses beach, you can make the trek over (about 2 miles) to get out of the sun for a little bit.

Atlantique

THE SHACK

245 Central Walk, Atlantique, New York 11706 • facebook.com/theshackatlantique

This beachside fast-food shack serves fried food and rum drinks to a party-hearty crowd. With live music and a large outdoor space, this is the best place to party in Atlantique.

Ocean Beach

ISLAND MERMAID

780 Bay Walk, Ocean Beach, New York 11770 • 631.583.8088 • islandmermaid.com

At this bayside eatery, you can watch the sunset while dining on grilled octopus salad, crab cakes, or pan-seared sea scallops. Come for dinner and stay for the signature rum punch, made with coconut rum, dark rum, Hypnotiq, and a secret combination of tropical juices. There's live music on Sundays and Thursdays and a DJ every weekend. Tuesday night means Drag Queen Bingo.

FLYNN'S

1 Cayuga Street, Ocean Beach, New York 11770 • 631.583.5000 • flynnsfireislandny.com

Flynn's is a lively waterfront bar and restaurant in Ocean Beach, with live music and DJs turning the deck into a dance floor most summer weekends. Stop by for the raw bar, burgers, or seafood dishes before the party gets started. There's a special prix fixe menu just for bachelorette parties that includes an open bar, if that's any indication of the kind of wild night you could have here.

THE SANDBAR

479 Bay Avenue, Ocean Beach, New York 11770 • 631.583.0388

A colorful beach bar by day, The Sandbar is known for live music, DJs, and a packed dance floor with multicolor lights and a smoke machine that goes on once the sun goes down. Friendly bartenders and a party-hearty clientele give this bar a fun atmosphere, as long as you don't mind loud music, crowds, and sticky floors.

// Summer cocktails with a twist at Ruschmeyer's

Cherry Grove

CHERRY'S ON THE BAY

158 Bayview Walk, Bay Shore, New York 11706 • 631.597.7859 • cherrysonthebay.com

What may seem like a boring old seafood restaurant during the day gets pretty turnt once the sun goes down. "Dinner and a show" takes on another meaning here, with drag shows, DJs, and boudoir bingo weekly during the summer. Cherry's is known for wild nights and the best dance party on Fire Island.

ICE PALACE CHERRY GROVE

1 Dock Walk, Cherry Grove, New York 11782 • 631.597.6600 • icepalacefi.com

Fire Island's most Vegas-y gay nightclub, Ice Palace stays open till the early morning with DJs and X-rated entertainment.

The Pines

SIP N TWIRL

36 Fire Island Boulevard, Fire Island Pines, New York 11782 • 631.597.3599 • facebook.com/sip.n.twirl

Sip N Twirl is the most rocking gay club in The Pines, with a disco ball and DJs playing techno until the early morning.

THE BLUE WHALE HARBOR WALK

Bay Shore, New York 11706 • 631.597.6500

As the sun begins to set, the crowd at Blue Whale gathers to get the night started with beachy cuisine and tropical cocktails in plastic cups. Their "low tea" parties are legendary, boozy afternoons. Try it on piano bar night or when nothing's going on to experience a more mellow vibe.

THE PAVILION

36 Fire Island Boulevard, Sayville, New York 11782 • 631.597.6500

In an extremely cool architectural building that looks like a wooden sculpture, The Pavilion is a gay bar that turns from a sunset cocktail spot to a massive sweaty dance party full of half-naked strangers once the sun goes down.

Where Party Animals Should Stay

BLUE WATERS HOTEL

642 Bayberry Walk, Ocean Beach, New York 11770 • 631.583.8295 • bluewatershoteloceanbeachfire island.com.

This adults-only hidden gem has 21 cozy rooms with private bathrooms across from the ferry terminal. The best part about this hotel is the rooftop sundeck, where you can lounge in sun chairs and relax, or have a cocktail from the full-service bar and restaurant downstairs. From $300.

The Jersey Shore

While Long Island certainly deserves credit for some of the wildest parties in New York, the Jersey Shore practically invented the concept of the sloppy summer—so much so that it spawned a party-hearty reality show franchise that lasted for seventy-one episodes, a couple of movies, a handful of book deals, one Etsy shop, and a lifetime of spin-offs. For those looking to recreate the *Jersey Shore* experience, look no further than the boardwalks of Point Pleasant, Seaside Heights, and Atlantic City. And while those destinations are incredible party locales, there's not much else to recommend there. Asbury Park, however, has blossomed into a shore town with soul, giving people a place to party like it's 1999 while also offering stylish places to stay and an amazing restaurant scene.

JERSEY SHORE | *Legendary Music Clubs and Boardwalk Bars*

Long Branch

LE CLUB AVENUE

23 Ocean Avenue, Long Branch, New Jersey 07740 • 732.759.2900 • leclubavenue.com

This ultra-luxe restaurant and club in Long Branch's Pier Village is the snazziest place in town, with white booths, tall ceilings, and a huge space with chandeliers and greenery everywhere. The menu is French, with boeuf bourguignon, salade niçoise, and trout amandine. The nightclub gets going after dinner, with indoor and outdoor spaces in this multilevel venue with a rooftop pool. The private beach club below has towels, umbrellas, loungers, and cocktails.

Asbury Park

ASBURY PARK YACHT CLUB

1000 Ocean Avenue, Asbury Park, New Jersey 07712 • 732.455.3460 • apyachtclub.com

A hipster take on the nautical theme, Asbury Park Yacht Club is a restaurant, bar, and music venue. There's live music a few nights a week, with local and touring indie bands. The menu is short and sweet, with a variety of bar snacks: mini corn dogs with sriracha mayo, lobster mac and cheese, Thai chicken lettuce wraps, and fried green tomatoes.

THE STONE PONY

913 Ocean Avenue, Asbury Park, New Jersey 07712 • 732.502.0600 • stoneponyonline.com

Asbury Park's legendary music club has been graced by local legends like Bruce Springsteen and Steve Van Zandt before they were famous. Open since 1973, the bar and venue hasn't skipped a beat, hosting acts big and small in their intimate venue and outdoor summer stage.

Come to see throwback bands like Modest Mouse or Saves the Day, or brush up on the classics with bands like Start Making Sense, a Talking Heads cover band. Tickets generally range from $25 to $75 for indoor and outdoor concerts.

ASBURY LANES

209 4th Avenue, Asbury Park, New Jersey 07712 • 732.361.6659 • asburylanes.com

Brought to you by New York City's Bowery Presents, Asbury Lanes is a super-modern music venue, bar, and bowling alley reminiscent of Williamsburg's Brooklyn Bowl. There's usually a concert on Fridays and Saturdays, with tickets starting around $25–$30. There's an on-site restaurant serving hipsterfied diner food like meatloaf, fried chicken, and pastrami hash, as well as a fully stocked bar. The state-of-the-art bowling facilities are $30 per hour, but the lanes are sometimes closed during a show. Call ahead to make a reservation.

BEACH BAR

1300 Ocean Avenue, Asbury Park, New Jersey 07712 • 732.455.8500 • theanchorsbend.com

Asbury Park's Beach Bar is not as simple as the name might suggest. This bar inside the Asbury Convention Hall is directly on the boardwalk and the beach, blasting music and pouring cocktails all day long on weekends and holidays. It's massive, with a long deck that wraps around the building, extending on to the beach. On the other side of the building, the Anchor's Bend is a mirror image of Beach Bar, with booze, snacks, and tables on the sand.

HOUSE OF INDEPENDENTS

572 Cookman Avenue, Asbury Park, New Jersey 07712 • 732.977.5284 • houseofindependents.com

Off the boardwalk in downtown Asbury Park, House of Independents is a music venue, lecture hall, and movie theater with a huge range of events from concerts to fundraisers to a recurring '90s-themed dance party on weekends.

ASBURY PARK FESTHALLE & BIERGARTEN

527 Lake Avenue, Asbury Park, New Jersey 07712 • 732.997.8767 • asburybiergarten.com

The authentic Festhalle & Biergarten brings a little bit of Germany to Asbury Park with communal tables, live music, and over 90 different domestic and international beers. The space is massive, with indoor and outdoor seating in a gorgeous historic brick building. It's cozy in the winter, sunny in the summer, and a rowdy good time. There's an extensive menu serving the usual suspects like pretzels and wiener schnitzel, but also on offer are steamed mussels, oysters, steak, and BBQ ribs.

WONDERBAR

Ocean Avenue, Asbury Park, New Jersey 07712 • 732.455.3767 • wonderbarasburypark.com

The iconic and historic Wonder Bar, located right off of the boardwalk, is famous for its "yappy hour," the dog-friendly happy hour where pets take over the outdoor seating area. The vintage-chic decor (and frankly creepy logo) makes this one of the most photogenic bars in Asbury Park, and the food menu fits the space with burgers, hot dogs, wings, and pork rolls.

PORTA

911 Kingsley Street, Asbury Park, New Jersey 07712 • 732.776.7661 • pizzaporta.com

Porta is one of the places in town credited with putting Asbury Park "back on the map," and it's no wonder why. This pizza place and bar in a hipster warehouse setting is undeniably cool—and the crowds agree. The massive space is usually packed on weekends, with people eating wood-fired pizza and drinking cocktails at the picnic tables out in the spacious yard.

SALVATION

210 5th Avenue, Asbury Park, New Jersey 07712 • 732.774.7100 • theasburyhotel.com/salvation

This sophisticated rooftop bar at the ultra-hip Asbury Hotel might be the town's most chichi watering hole, with fancy cocktails and a great sunset view. Go here for an afternoon drink or an after-dinner night cap. It can get loud on weekends, and there's a dress code (no athletic wear or tank tops), but the music is good and the vibe is fun.

PARADISE NIGHTCLUB

101 Asbury Avenue, Asbury Park, New Jersey 07712 • 732.988.6663 • paradisenj.com

The wildest nightclub in Asbury Park, Paradise is like something you might expect to find in Atlantic City (except better, since it's in Asbury Park). It's first and foremost a gay club, but anyone is welcome here, with disco balls, drag queens, smoke machines, and DJs playing bangers until the early morning. There's usually a cover charge to get in on Fridays and Saturdays.

Where Party Animals Should Stay

THE EMPRESS HOTEL

101 Asbury Avenue, Asbury Park, New Jersey 07712 • 732.774.0100 • asburyempress.com

The Empress Hotel is practically on the boardwalk, with easy access to the beachside bars and music venues. It's not unstylish, with a pool and an oddly swanky lobby with a tiki bar that seems to be popular at any time of day, on any day of the week. The hotel is connected to Paradise Nightclub, and the pool scene here can be wild on the weekends. From $109.

6

Escapes for Nature Freaks and Health Nuts

The Best Parks, Preserves, and Activities on Long Island

With all the restaurants, bars, and beautiful people on Long Island, it can be easy to forget what makes this place so special: incredible natural beauty. For such a small region of the state, the terrain is incredibly varied, with beautiful white beaches, rocky cliffs, pine-filled forests, and lush wetlands. With a few exceptions, Long Island's state parks and preserves fly mostly under the radar, meaning that if you choose to visit, it's not unheard of to have the place to yourself, especially in the off season.

Here's everything you need to know about how and where to experience Long Island's great outdoors.

≡ Long Island and the Hamptons

In Montauk, rocky cliffs drop off into the Atlantic Ocean below, making for prime surf. The state parks here are small but diverse, with coastline, forests, and sand dunes. Throughout Montauk and the Hamptons, you can charter boats for booze cruises or fishing trips, or rent kayaks, surfboards, and paddle boards.

MONTAUK | *Dramatic Coastlines and Surfer Vibes*

Places

HITHER HILLS STATE PARK ⭐ AUTHOR'S PICK

164 Old Montauk Highway, Montauk, New York 11954 • 631.668.2554 • parks.ny.gov/parks/122

Between Montauk and Amagansett, the 1,755-acre Hither Hills State Park highlights the breathtaking natural beauty of Long Island's South Fork, stretching from the ocean to the Napeague harbor with forest, dunes, and beach. The highlight here is undoubtedly the walking dunes, a wilderness area of sandy hills filled with oak, shad, and pine trees. The landscape is unlike the rest of Long Island, and winding trails take you to beautiful vistas overlooking the dunes and water. There are also campsites for those who wish to spend the night, but the best way to experience the walking dunes is by packing a picnic and visiting at sunset.

MONTAUK LIGHTHOUSE AND MONTAUK POINT STATE PARK

2000 Montauk Highway, Montauk, New York 11954-5600 • montauklighthouse.com; parks.ny.gov/parks/61

At the eastern tip of Long Island's South Fork, Montauk State Park feels like the end of the world. Rugged and windy, it's a little bit of Maine in New York, with rocky cliffs leading down to the Atlantic Ocean below. On a clear day, you can see Block Island in the distance. The best reason to visit the park is the lighthouse, a national historic landmark and the oldest lighthouse in New York State, built in 1976. Entry to the lighthouse is $11 (the view from the top is stunning!), or you can just take a look at the outside for free.

>> Insider Tip: Take a walk around the point on the rocks below the lighthouse to get up close to the waves crashing below. There's a path cut into the jetty, but watch your step—the rocks can be slippery.

// Get lost in the Napeague Walking Dunes for a sense of how the Hamptons looked before the billionaires arrived

SHADMOOR STATE PARK 🌸 *AUTHOR'S PICK*

900 Montauk Highway, Montauk, New York 11954 • 631.668.3781 • parks.ny.gov/parks/16

The sandy cliffs at this state park are a striking backdrop for a stroll on the beach near Ditch Plains in Montauk. The 90-acre park has 2,400 feet of sandy oceanfront, along with hiking trails and picnic tables.

Activities

AIR + SPEED SURF SHOP

795 Montauk Highway, Montauk, New York 11954 • 631.668.0356 • airandspeedclothing.com

Montauk's hipster surf shop has rentals for all your surfing needs, including surfboards, wetsuits, boogie boards, and beach cruisers to get you to the beach. They also have their own line of shirts and hats. Ask about surf lessons.

AUSTIN'S SURF CAMP

austinssurfcamp.com • montauksurfcamp@gmail.com

Austin's Surf Camp offers private a group surf lessons for kids and adults. They'll provide boards and wetsuits, making this a great option for absolute beginners. If you're out here for the season with kids, ask about their summer camp.

BYOGA/FITNESS CLASSES

83 South Elmwood Ave Suite 1B, Montauk, New York 11954 • 631.483.5200 • byogahive.com

If Montauk locals seem eerily happy and relaxed to you, you're right—they are. But the secret to their happiness is open to visitors too. BYoga is indisputably happy yoga, where all walks of life are welcome to practice. If you're intimidated by New York City yoga studios, come here to experience one of their judgement-free vinyasa classes for all levels.

COREY'S WAVE SURFING

516.639.4879 • coreyswave.com

This surf company has surfing and stand-up paddleboard lessons. Call to book a group lesson for a special event, like a bachelorette party. Surfboards and wetsuits are provided.

DEEP HOLLOW RANCH HORSES

8 Old Montauk Highway, Montauk, New York 11954 • 631.668.2744 • deephollowranch.com

Deep Hollow Ranch is, improbably, the oldest working ranch in the United States. The historic stables offer beach and trail rides for beginner and advanced riders of all ages. Fans of the television show *The Affair* might recognize these stables.

HAMPTONS SURF CO.

631.495.1162 • hamptonssurf.co

This year-round surf school founded by professional big wave surfer Kurt Rist has a summer camp for kids, as well as one-on-one or group lessons for all ages. Surfboards and wetsuits are provided.

TICK CHECK

Long Island is tick paradise, and some of them carry diseases. Do thorough checks after you're in brush or tall grass, and if you've been bitten, see a doctor. If the bite looks like it could be problematic, your doctor will prescribe a heavy-duty dose of antibiotics. Bites from infected ticks can lead to Lyme disease, with varying outcomes.

// Montauk's Hither Hills State Park has miles of hiking trails that can be explored in any season

MONTAUK BIKE SHOP

725 Montauk Highway, Montauk, New York 11954 • 631.668.8975 • montaukbikeshop.com

Montauk Bike Shop rents mountain bikes, road bikes, and beach cruisers, as well as hiking and biking tours for all levels.

MONTAUK FISHING CHARTERS

352 West Lake Drive, Montauk, New York 11954 • 631.523.8862 • susiee.com

Montauk Fishing Charters has 20 full-time charter boats in various sizes, available for sport-fishing charters that include bait, tackle, and ice. They'll even clean and bag your catch for you, so you can bring it home and cook it. Call to inquire about booze cruises, private parties, or overnight trips.

MONTAUK SALT ROOM

552 West Lake Drive, Montauk, New York 11954 • 631.668.7258 • montauksaltcave.com

The Montauk Salt Room is a room built out of, well, salt. Halotherapy, or salt therapy, is thought to relieve asthma, inflammation, or allergies. Call to book an appointment in the salt room, an otherworldly salt cave with mood lighting and reclining chairs. It's a relaxing experience, sometimes accompanied by singing bowls or other sound meditation.

MONTIKI CATAMARAN

631.668.2826 • sailingmontauk.com

Montiki is a catamaran sailboat with three different tours. The two-hour Discover Montauk tour takes you out for a relaxing afternoon sail, while the three-hour Sail & Swim tour is a more active sail, with options to get off the boat and swim or kayak. There's also a daily sunset cruise and a Sunday morning yoga cruise. Call to ask about private charters.

PLAZA SPORTS

716 Montauk Highway, Montauk, New York 11954 • 631.668.9300 • plazasurfandsports.com

This downtown spot shop is the place to go for all your adventure needs. The huge store has everything from surfboards and wetsuits to bathing suits and beach games to cheesy souvenirs. There's also hiking and biking gear, as well as bike rentals. Check the sale section—you might find a great deal on something you didn't even come in here for.

PUFF & PUTT FAMILY FUN CENTER

659 Montauk Highway, Montauk, New York 11954 • 631.668.4473 • puffnputt.com

Family-friendly Puff & Putt is more than just a mini-golf course, offering sailboat and kayak rentals. Beginners are welcome to try out the canoes, kayaks, stand-up paddle boards, sunfish, and a hobie cat.

UIHLEIN'S MARINA & BOAT RENTAL

444 West Lake Drive, Montauk, New York 11954 • 631.668.3799

For those interested in being captain of their own ship, Uihlein's has a fleet of 18 boats (fishing boats, wakeboard boats, and cruising boats) for rent. A valid driver's license (no boat license necessary) and a deposit are required; for those who need a refresher course, instructors are available for $50 per hour. You can also rent jet skis, tubes, water skis, wakeboards, and paddle boards at the marina.

VIKING FLEET

5126, 462 West Lake Drive, Montauk, New York 11954 • 631.668.5700 • vikingfleet.com

With some of the biggest boats in Montauk, Viking Fleet offers fishing trips, ferry service, and whale watching tours. Book online for half-day and full-day fishing trips, or call to charter a private trip. In addition to a sunset cocktail cruise and a lighthouse tour, Viking Fleet offers whale-watching trips—overnight adventures that take passengers to the Great South Channel to spot whales, dolphins, turtles, and seabirds.

Where Nature Freaks and Health Nuts Should Eat

JONI'S ⭐ AUTHOR'S PICK

28 South Etna Ave #9, Montauk, New York 11954 • 631.668.3663 • jonismontauk.com

Popular with the post-yoga crowd, Joni's has made-to-order juices, smoothies, wraps, and sandwiches for sale at the counter in this cute and colorful cafe. Eat in at the communal table or outdoor picnic tables or take your goodies to go. Vegans and vegetarians will love dishes like the Thai rice paper wrap with ginger tofu, shredded carrots, mushrooms, pea shoots, spinach, and peanut sauce. There's also meat on the menu, like the popular grilled shrimp tacos with salsa, avocado, cilantro, and sour cream, served with a lime on corn tortillas.

Where Nature Freaks and Health Nuts Should Stay

GURNEY'S MONTAUK YACHT CLUB RESORT

32 Star Island Road, Montauk, New York 11954 • 631.668.3100 • gurneysresorts.com/montauk-yacht-club

This full-service waterfront resort has 107 rooms overlooking Lake Montauk. This is a great resort for active travelers, with a fitness center, indoor and outdoor pools, tennis courts, and a spa, as well as a marina with boat rentals and charters. The rooms are modern and preppy, with striped wallpaper, fluffy beds, and simple white furniture. There's a free shuttle to take guests to the beach or into town, but there's more than enough right here to keep you occupied for a day. There's a casual and an upscale restaurant, as well as a cool yacht club–themed bar called the lighthouse, inside the actual lighthouse that's part of the building. From $270.

AMAGANSETT, SAG HARBOR, AND THE HAMPTONS | Sailboats and Surfboards

Amagansett | Activities

AMAGANSETT BEACH & BICYCLE COMPANY

624 Montauk Highway, Amagansett, New York 11930 • 631.267.6325 • amagansettbeachco.com

There's a wide selection of bikes for rent at Amagansett Beach & Bicycle Company, including cruisers, road bikes, mountain bikes, hybrids, and even tandems. Locks and helmets are included, and buggies and baby seats are available too. They also offer kayak and mountain bike tours of Accabonac Harbor and Hither Hills State Park.

MANDALA YOGA

156 Main Street, Amagansett, New York 11930 • 631.267.6144 • mandalayoga.com

Mandala Yoga has daily classes, with weekend classes for all levels, as well as ayurvedic treatments and occasional holistic workshops.

SPRINGS GENERAL STORE BOAT RENTALS

29 Old Stone Highway, East Hampton, New York 11937 • 631.329.5065 • springsgeneralstore.com

Located on Accabonac harbor, the General Store in Springs offers kayak rentals and tours. Take a kayak out for a spin in the calm marshy waters of the harbor, or join a tour to be led by an expert. The general store has a small cafe that can pack you a picnic for your trip.

Sag Harbor | Activities

BREAKWATER YACHT CLUB

51 Bay Street, Sag Harbor, New York 11963 • 631.725.4604

This non-profit community sailing center has camps and races for kids, as well as private sailing lessons for all ages. There's no experience required for lessons; you'll be taught by an expert instructor on a JY15 or J70 sailboat.

GLOBAL BOARDING WATER SPORTS

50 West Water Street, Sag Harbor, New York 11963 • 631.537.8601 • globalboarding.com

Sag Harbor's Global Boarding has kayak rentals, fishing charters, stand up paddle board rentals, sunset boat charters, and surf lessons. For those interested in learning to wakeboard or waterski, they have instructors who can take you out and get you started.

// Sag Harbor is a great starting point for sunset sails

SAG HARBOR CYCLE COMPANY

34 Bay Street, Sag Harbor, New York 11963 • 631.725.1110 • sagharborcycle.com

Rent hybrid bikes or road bikes at this Sag Harbor shop that also organizes weekly themed rides.

WEEKEND WARRIOR TOURS & OUTFITTERS

8 Main Street, Sag Harbor, New York 11963 • 631.725.5950 • weekendwarriortours.com

Weekend Warriors rents kayaks and paddleboards or leads groups on active multisport adventures including yoga, kayaking, biking, or hiking.

YOGA SHANTI

32 Bridge Street, Sag Harbor, New York 11963 • 631.725.6424 • yogashanti.com

TriBeCa's trendiest yoga studio has a location in Sag Harbor, where beginners and experts can join a class. Yoga Shanti also offers workshops and retreats in the Hamptons and beyond.

East Hampton | Places

CEDAR POINT COUNTY PARK ⭐ AUTHOR'S PICK

5 Cedar Point Road, East Hampton, New York 11937 • 631.852.7620

Jutting out onto a narrow strip of land in Gardiner's Bay, Cedar Point Beach in Cedar Point County Park is one of the East End's most picturesque bay beaches. It's a trek to get to, but rewarding once you're there, with calm waters and views of Shelter Island. It's great for fishing, picnicking, or simply walking out to the lighthouse at the end of the peninsula.

East Hampton | Activities

BERMUDA BIKES

36 Gingerbread Lane, East Hampton, New York 11937 • 631.324.6688 • bermudabikes.com

Bermuda Bikes in East Hampton rents hybrid and road bikes. If you have kids in tow, you can rent kids' bikes, child seats, trailers, or tandem bikes.

KHANH SPORTS

60 Park Pl, East Hampton, New York 11937 • 631.324.0703 • khanhsportseh.com

Khanh sports is the place to go for the latest beach toys: kadima paddles, spikeball, frisbee, boogie boards, paddle boards, kayaks, and more. They also have bike rentals for mountain bikes, cruisers, and hybrids, as well as those elliptical-style bikes.

PADDLE DIVA

219 Three Mile Harbor Hog Creek Road, East Hampton, New York 11937 • 631.329.2999 • paddlediva.com

Paddle Diva has stand-up paddle board lessons, rentals, and classes, as well as SUP yoga. If you're looking for a fun group activity for a special event, they can customize multisport wellness retreats as well as adventure tours for experienced paddlers.

Bridgehampton | Places

SOUTH FORK NATURAL HISTORY MUSEUM AND NATURE CENTER

377 Bridgehampton-Sag Harbor Turnpike, Bridgehampton, NY 11932 • 631.537.9735 • sofo.org

Bridgehampton's Natural History Museum and Nature Center might be kid-focused, but that doesn't mean adults can't also enjoy this 40-acre nature preserve with a butterfly garden, wildflower garden, and purple martin nesting site. The adjacent Long Pond Greenbelt has a 6-mile trail through the wetlands, and there are also nature walks through the property. Inside, the small museum has dioramas and multimedia educational exhibits about local flora and fauna. Admission is $10.

Bridgehampton | Activities

MAIN BEACH SURF & SPORT

352 Montauk Highway, Wainscott, New York 11975 • 631.537.2716 • mainbeach.com

Main Beach is a local outfitter with everything you need for a day in the sun, including surf-board, stand up paddle board, and kayak rentals. Ask about surf lessons or adventure tours—SUP or kayak trips that end with an epic clambake on the beach.

Southampton | Activities

FLYING POINT SURFING SCHOOL

flyingpointsurfschool.com • 516.885.6607

Get a private surfing lesson or sign up for surf school with Flying Point, offering lessons from Southampton to Montauk.

HAMPTONS MINI GOLF

668 County Rd 39, Southampton, New York 11968 • 631.283.2158 • hamptonminigolf.com

Hamptons Mini Golf has eighteen holes of putt-putt with hazards that feature iconic East End landmarks like the East Hampton windmill and the Montauk lighthouse. Open until 10 p.m. on weekends; course rates are $15 per person.

// Surfboards lined up and ready for wave

HAMPTONS WATER SPORTS

1688 County Rd 39, Southampton, New York 11968 • 631.283.9463

Hamptons Water Sports goes beyond the usual surf lessons and kayak rentals to offer clinics of windsurfing, kitesurfing, and foil—a surfboard with a long rudder that uses a paddle. Windsurfing has a notoriously steep learning curve, so learn the ropes of surfing or stand-up paddleboarding before you try this.

ROTATIONS BICYCLE CENTER

32 Windmill Lane, Southampton, New York 11968 • 631.283.2890 • rotationsbicyclecenter.com

This Southampton bike shop has road bikes, cruisers, and hybrids for rent, along with accessories like trailers and child seats. Ask about renting one of their Fat Bikes, with a super light frame and fat tires designed for biking on the beach.

Westhampton | Places

CUPSOGUE BEACH COUNTY PARK

906 Dune Road, Westhampton Beach, New York 11978 • 631.852.8111

At the tip of Westhampton Beach Peninsula, Cupsogue Beach County Park is a popular summertime destination, with rolling dunes and beautiful white sand. If you walk to the very tip of the peninsula, you can see Smith Point State Park across the inlet. Lifeguards are on duty, and there are campgrounds for those who wish to spend the night.

Westhampton | Activities

SKYDIVE LONG ISLAND

135 Dawn Drive, Shirley, New York 11967 • 631.208.3900 • skydivelongisland.com

Adrenaline junkies can get their kicks at this skydiving center. Tandem jumps are $298, and on a clear day, you'll see amazing views of the Hamptons and Fire Island.

Where Nature Freaks and Health Nuts Should Eat

BREADZILLA ⭐ AUTHOR'S PICK

84 Wainscott NW Road, Wainscott, New York 11975 • 631.537.0955 • breadzilla.com

Stock up for your day of adventure with the East End's best sandwiches at Breadzilla. Sandwiches range from your standard ham and cheese to interesting combos like the fresh grilled albacore tuna steak with homemade puttanesca sauce on a roll, or the crispy duck wrap with avocado, spicy carrots, greens, and mango salsa. Breadzilla makes all their own breads and pastries, so pick up some cupcakes or cookies for dessert. If you're looking for a picnic, there's also a case full of fancy local and imported meats and cheeses, and they even sell cutting boards.

Where Nature Freaks and Health Nuts Should Stay

BARON'S COVE

31 West Water Street, Sag Harbor, New York 11963 • 844.227.6672 • baronscove.com

This upscale waterfront resort is super stylish, thanks to a recent update. Suites with water views have a nautical theme, and the on-site restaurant and bar are must-visits. For active guests, the resort has a saltwater pool and tennis courts, as well as kayak tours and stand-up paddleboard lessons. For those interested in surfing or visiting the beach, complimentary shuttle service, beach chairs, umbrellas, and towels are available for guests to use.

☰ *Shelter Island and the North Fork*

Shelter Island and the North Fork have marshy inlets and freshwater ponds that are the stuff of birders' dreams, where pine forests meet the Long Island Sound. Given Long Island's proximity to New York City, the rich flora and fauna found here can be surprising.

SHELTER ISLAND | *Birding and Kayaking on Calm Waters*

Places

SYLVESTER MANOR

80 North Ferry Road, Shelter Island, New York 11964 • 631.749.0626 • sylvestermanor.org

Sylvester Manor is a historic Shelter Island estate that's been turned into an educational farm and preserve. Stop by the farmstand to buy veggies and see the chickens and pigs, or take a stroll around the grounds to see the koi pond and gardens. There are walking trails through the 243-acre estate, as well as occasional concerts and public events.

MASHOMACK NATURE PRESERVE ⭐ *AUTHOR'S PICK*

79 South Ferry Road, Shelter Island, New York 11964 • 631.749.1001

This 2,100-acre nature preserve is home to ospreys, piping plovers, and rare plants. With coastline, marshes, fields, and forests, it's as diverse a landscape as you can find on Shelter Island, with over 20 miles of hiking trails (note that dogs and bicycles are not allowed). Come here to get off the beaten path and experience Shelter Island's coastal wildlife.

Activities

PICCOZZI FUEL & BIKE SHOP

177 North Ferry Road, Shelter Island Heights, New York 11965 • 631.749.0045 • jwpiccozzi.com

Piccozzi's is Shelter Island's spot for bike sales, repairs, and rentals. You can rent by the hour, the half-day, or the full day.

SHELTER ISLAND KAYAK TOURS

80 Burns Road, Shelter Island, New York 11964 • 631.749.1990 • kayaksi.com

A kayak is one of the best ways to explore Shelter Island's marshy coastline, and Shelter Island Kayak Tours offers rentals and guided tours. Grab a map and hop on a kayak to explore the Coecles Harbor Marine Water Trail.

THE NORTH FORK | *Rocky Beaches and Calm Inlets*

Orient | Places

LAVENDER BY THE BAY ⭐ *AUTHOR'S PICK*

7540 Main Road, East Marion, New York 11939 • 631.477.1019 • lavenderbythebay.com

East Marion's Instagram-worthy lavender fields are a must-visit on any trip to Orient. After you frolic with the birds and the bees in the gorgeous and aromatic fields, you can stop by the farm shop to purchase local products. Lavender by the Bay has essential oils, pillow mist, soaps, and dried bundles to take home.

ORIENT BEACH STATE PARK

40000 Main Road, Orient, New York 11957 • 631.323.2440 • parks.ny.gov/parks/106

With marshes and a rare maritime forest with prickly pear cactus, Orient Beach State Park is a birder's paradise, with osprey, herons, and egrets. The park is popular with families, with opportunities for swimming, kayaking, windsurfing, hiking, biking, and picnicking.

Orient | Activities

EAGLE'S NECK PADDLING COMPANY

40000 Old Main Road 83, Orient, New York 11957 • 631.407.3504 • eaglesneckpaddling.com

Rent a kayak from Eagle's Neck to explore the waters surrounding Orient Point, or join a guided tour. Eagle's Neck offers sunset and full moon tours, as well as hourly rentals at Orient Beach State Park.

Greenport | Activities

DAN'S BIKES

131 Front Street, Greenport, New York 11944 • 212.380.1119 • greenportbikerental.com

Renting mountain bikes and hybrid bikes by the day or week, Dan's brings the rentals to you, dropping off at hotels or rentals and even the train station or jitney stop anywhere between Mattituck and Orient on the North Fork. Send them a text to reserve your bike rental, which includes a basket, helmet, lock, and light.

Southold | Places

CUSTER INSTITUTE

Main Bayview Road, Southold, New York 11971 • 631.765.2626 • custerobservatory.org

Custer Observatory is open to the public every Saturday night for tours and stargazing with telescopes. A museum, gift shop, and library are located on-site, and the observatory hosts concerts, lectures, and events.

HORTON POINT LIGHTHOUSE AND NAUTICAL MUSEUM

3575 Lighthouse Road, Southold, New York 11971 • 631.765.5500 • southoldhistoricalsociety.org

The 58-foot tall Horton Point Lighthouse was built in 1857. The lower level is the Southold Historical Society's Nautical Museum, with antique lighthouse equipment, marine-themed art, and vintage sailing supplies. Admission to the lighthouse and museum is $5.

Southold | Activities

PECONIC WATER SPORTS

64150 Main Road, Southold, New York 11971 • 631.680.0111 • peconicwatersports.com

Charter a boat with a crew for fishing, wakeboarding, or water-skiing at Peconic Water Sports. There are jet ski tours that can take you out to Orient Point (60 minutes) or on a circumnavigation of Shelter Island (90 minutes). Rent a pontoon party boat or a 22-foot speed boat for a day of cruising around on your own, or ditch the motorsports with a stand-up paddleboard or kayak.

Where Nature Freaks and Health Nuts Should Eat

SALT WATERFRONT BAR AND GRILL ⭐ *AUTHOR'S PICK*

63 Menantic Road, Shelter Island, New York 11964 • 631.749.5535 • saltshelterisland.com

In the marina at the Island Boat Yard, Salt is an upscale dockside restaurant, with indoor and outdoor tables. Order something from the sushi bar to start, and then dive into seafood dishes like the "dock to table" fish of the day or the Cajun-spiced Naw'lins lobster roll. The setting is sophisticated seaside, with wooden accents and nautical flags, and the service is friendly.

// Though Shelter Island is small, the few restaurants are surprisingly good

Where Nature Freaks and Health Nuts Should Stay

DERING HARBOR INN

13 Winthrop Road, Shelter Island Heights, New York 11965 • 631.749.0900 • deringharborinn.net

Shelter Island's Dering Harbor Inn has studios, one-bedrooms, and two-bedroom suites, many with water views. The inn has a heated pool and tennis courts, as well as a sloping lawn with Adirondack chairs looking out over the sandy beach and the docks below. A yoga studio and gym are available on-site for active travelers, and the property has bikes available for rent. From $360.

FIRE ISLAND | *Incredible Coastal Wilderness*

Fire Island's coastline is home to a rare sand forest, with opportunities for bird watching, camping, and hiking.

Places

FIRE ISLAND LIGHTHOUSE

Captree Island, New York 11702 • 631.321.7028 • fireislandlighthouse.com

At 168 feet tall, the Fire Island Lighthouse is the tallest lighthouse on Long Island. Located between the car-free town of Kismet and Robert Moses State Park, the lighthouse is walkable from the Fire Island communities or the Robert Moses parking lot. The lighthouse has special events throughout the year, like holiday parties and guided nighttime tours. Admission costs $8.

SUNKEN FOREST PRESERVE ⭐ *AUTHOR'S PICK*

Fire Island, New York 11782 • 631.597.6183 • nps.gov/fiis/planyourvisit/sailorshaven.htm

Located in Sailor's Haven, the Sunken Forest is a must-see for any visitor to Fire Island. This wild, beachy landscape is unlike anything else you'll see in New York State, or even the world, with a 1.5-mile trail that takes you through the rare maritime holly forest. The forest is about 200–300 years old and started with small beach plants that got their nutrients from the air and water. Now, the forest is home to holly, sassafras, and juneberry trees. Sailor's Haven can be accessed by foot from other parts of Fire Island, or by ferry from Sayville. There's also a public marina, if you choose to bring your own boat. Facilities at Sailor's Haven and the Sunken Forest are open from May to October, when the ferries are in service. From October to May, the boardwalk is still open.

WATCH HILL

Fire Island, New York 11782 • 631.597.6455 • nps.gov/fiis/planyourvisit/watchhill.htm

Watch Hill is located on an isolated stretch of the Fire Island National Seashore. It's one of the only true wilderness areas on Long Island, and the only place where you can go backcountry camping in the Otis Pike Fire Island High Dune Wilderness. You can also find easier camping at the Watch Hill Campground (but keep in mind there are no cars on Fire Island—you'll

SPECTATOR SPORTS

BELMONT STAKES • June • belmontstakes.com

The second Sunday in June, spectators grad their hats and head to the horse races in hopes of betting on a winner.

MONTAUK SHARK TAG TOURNAMENT • June • marinebasin.com

At this annual fishing tournament, boats compete to see who can reel in the biggest shark.

THE HAMPTON CLASSIC HORSE SHOW • August • hamptonclassic.com

At this prestigious horse show, celebrities are as much of a draw as the world-class equestrian events.

PORT JEFFERSON DRAGON BOAT FESTIVAL • September •
portjeffdragonracefest.com

Teams of paddlers propel lightweight boats through the water to the rhythm of beating drums at this annual festival.

still have to carry everything from the ferry to your campsite a few steps away). In addition to camping, Watch Hill offers ranger tours, like guided kayak tours of the salt marsh. There is also a self-guided nature walk along the dunes. The ferry, visitor center, marina, and general store are only open seasonally, so make sure to plan your trip between May and October. The marina is open to the public. Call ahead and make a reservation to bring your own boat.

WILDERNESS VISITOR CENTER

Fire Island, New York 11782 • 631.281.3010

Next to Smith Point County Park, the Wilderness Visitor Center is the access point for the Otis Pike Fire Island High Dune Wilderness, 1,380 acres of beachfront wilderness area. The visitor center has maps, books, and information about backcountry camping and ranger-led programs. The wilderness area is accessible year-round from the Smith Point parking lot.

Activities

OCEAN BEACH HARDWARE

482 Bayberry Walk, Ocean Beach, New York 11770 • 631.583.5826 • oceanbeachhardware.com

Ocean Beach Hardware rents beach cruisers and trikes (with huge baskets) with daily, weekly, and monthly rates.

Where Nature Freaks and Health Nuts Should Eat

CASINO CAFE AND BAR DAVIS PARK NEAR WATCH HILL

1 Trustees Walk, Davis Park, New York 11772 • 631.597.6150 • casinocafefireisland.com

The beachfront Casino Cafe is just steps from the dunes in Davis Park, near the Watch Hill Visitor Center. Since 1945, the Casino has been serving seafood in a beautiful setting. The vibe here is casual, but you won't find any fried clam strips on the menu, with dishes like mahi mahi tacos, baked shrimp and feta, grilled octopus salad, and linguine with clams.

Where Nature Freaks and Health Nuts Should Stay

FIRE ISLAND HOTEL & RESORT

25 Cayuga Walk, Ocean Beach, New York 11770 • 631.583.8000 • fireislandhotel.com

With clean and comfortable rooms just steps from Ocean Beach, Fire Island Hotel & Resort is a solid, if not stylish, choice. Rooms range from tiny studios to bigger suites that sleep up to four people. There's a pool for when the ocean's too cold for swimming, as well as a beach rental shop with beach chairs and umbrellas, along with beach games like volleyball.

☰ *Greater Long Island*

There are many ways to experience Long Island's natural beauty, and the best way is by boat. Outfitters all over the island rent kayaks and canoes for exploring quiet rivers, inlets, and bays, while charter companies can take you on a scenic sail or speedboat ride (or rent you a vessel and let you be the captain). For those looking for a bit more adrenaline, you can try surfing, jet skiing, and even skydiving. Active types can soak up the yacht club vibes at resorts around the area, and yoga classes let you stretch it all out in the morning.

GREATER LONG ISLAND | *Parks and Beaches on the Long Island Sound*

Riverhead | Activities

HAMPTON DIVE CENTER

369 Flanders Road, Riverhead, New York 11901 • 631.727.7578 • hamptondive.com

The divemasters at Hampton Dive Center can lead experienced divers to some of the best lobster boat shipwrecks in the North East. The shop has everything you need for a dive and can get you set up with lessons for beginners or continuing education classes for experienced divers.

PECONIC PADDLER

3301, 89 Peconic Avenue, Riverhead, New York 11901 • 631.727.9895 • peconicpaddler.com

Riverhead's Peconic Paddler has kayak, canoe, and paddle board rentals for anybody wanting to get out onto the water in Peconic Bay. They can also arrange a drop-off or pickup for you, so you don't have to worry about making a loop or fighting the current on the way back.

Wading River and Surrounds | Places

WILDWOOD STATE PARK

790 Hulse Landing Road, Wading River, New York 11792 • 631.929.431 • parks.ny.gov/parks/68

Wildwood State Park has over 600 acres of shoreline bluffs on the Long Island Sound, with sandy beaches and shady picnic areas. There are also hiking trails through the forest, with vistas of the deep blue Long Island Sound. Campsites are available for those who wish to spend the night.

// Greenport's harbor is home to interesting antique watercraft

ROCKY POINT STATE PINE BARRENS PRESERVE

S Highway 25A, Rocky Point, New York 11778 • 631.444.0270

Rocky Point's 6,000 acres of pine forest has easy hiking, horseback riding, and biking trails through the preserve. It's open year-round but closed to recreational activities during deer hunting season in January. In winter, there are cross-country and snowshoe trails.

Stony Brook | Places

AVALON PARK AND PRESERVE

Harbor Road, Stony Brook, New York 11790 • 631.689.0619 • avalonparkandpreserve.org

Part sculpture park, part nature preserve, this 76-acre tranquil green space has walking trails, wildflower meadows, sculptures, and interesting events. Join an outdoor yoga class or visit during one of the skylabs, a stargazing event at the Avalon Barn. Don't miss the selfie-tastic "Letters to Heaven" sculpture.

Oyster Bay | Places

OYSTER BAY NATIONAL WILDLIFE REFUGE

Oyster Bay, New York 11771 • 631.286.0485

In Oyster Bay's National Wildlife Refuge, visitors can sail, kayak, fish, or explore the shoreline. The refuge includes salt marsh and freshwater wetlands, making this a varied ecosystem and a natural haven for waterfowl.

// Colorful lures hope to bring in local fish like fluke and striped bass

Oyster Bay | Activities

CHRISTEEN

1 West End Avenue, Oyster Bay, New York 11771 • 516.922.7245 • thewaterfrontcenter.org/christeen

America's oldest oyster sloop has been restored to her former glory by Oyster Bay's Water-Front Center, offering harbor tours and sunset cruises. Ask about private charters and events on this gorgeous 1883 boat.

Babylon | Activities

THE MOON CHASER

3500 East Ocean Pkwy, Babylon, New York 11702 • 631.265.1848 • themoonchaser.com

Captree State Park's Moon Chaser takes passengers on an excursion through the Great South Bay on this 65-foot boat. Afternoon tours take place every Wednesday and Thursday and cost $15 per person.

Where Nature Freaks and Health Nuts Should Eat

OCEAN

333 Bayville Avenue, Bayville, New York 11709 • 516.628.3330 • cometotheocean.com

Dine on raw oysters, PEI mussels, or ahi tacos to start before moving on to lobster, steak frites, or a burger. The location and setting feels a bit more like Palm Beach than Long Island, with palm trees, tropical cocktails, and a sandy beach with sunloungers.

Where Nature Freaks and Health Nuts Should Stay

DANFORD'S HOTEL & MARINA

25 East Broadway, Port Jefferson, New York 11777 • 631.928.5200 • danfords.com

This waterfront resort in Port Jefferson has 86 cute and comfortable rooms with a nautical theme. Wave Seafood Kitchen, the onsite restaurant, serves upscale seashore classics like crab cakes, fried calamari, and linguine with clams. The marina location means that hotel guests have easy access to the water, and the hotel is a short drive from North Shore beaches on the Long Island Sound. From $269.

≡ *The Jersey Shore*

NEW JERSEY | *Beyond the Gym*

The Jersey Shore lacks the outdoor wilderness opportunities of Long Island, but in the land of GTL (gym, tan, laundry—popularized by the TV show Jersey Shore) there are still a few ways to stay active.

Activities

DJ'S CYCLES

644 Ocean Avenue, Long Branch, New Jersey 07740 • 732.870.2277 • djscyclesnj.com

DJ's offers hourly and daily bike rentals in downtown Long Branch.

ROOFTOP YOGA AT THE ASBURY HOTEL

210 5th Avenue, Asbury Park, New Jersey 07712 • 732.774.7100 • theasburyhotel.com/wellness-fitness

You don't have to be a hotel guest to sign up for a rooftop yoga class at the fashionable Asbury Hotel. Offered Friday, Saturday, and Sunday, classes take place at their rooftop cinema. Mats and water are available.

KUR WELLNESS STUDIOS

412 Bond Street, Asbury Park, New Jersey 07712 • 732.361.8956 • kurstudios.com

Kur Wellness is somewhere between a yoga studio and a spa, offering fitness classes, massages, ayurvedic treatments, facials, and yoga workshops.

7

Escapes for Fashionistas

The Hamptons and Long Island might possibly be the most fashionable summer destination in the country, and this enclave of wealthy people with (mostly) good taste means that if you like to shop, you've come to the right place.

While the rest of Long Island and Fire Island are definitely not destinations for fashion (people are still dressed fabulously, but they brought those clothes from New York City), the Jersey Shore should not be overlooked.

☰ *Montauk and the Hamptons*

In a land of models, celebrities, and designers who call this area home, there's some excellent shopping to be had, and not all of it is out of your price range. In the towns of Southampton and East Hampton, the streets are filled with boutiques from major designers. These stores on Main Street pay for a year's worth of prime rental space, but in many cases only stay open for a few busy months during the summer. If the math doesn't quite make sense to you, you're right: in some cases, these huge brands are losing money but gaining brand recognition and the bragging rights to say they have a storefront in the Hamptons. But those stores aren't the reason why the shopping here is good—you can buy all that stuff online and in malls in every major city in America, anyways.

This is a land of philanthropy, which means two things: there are tons of fundraisers and events for the well-connected to attend—and they can't be photographed in the same thing twice, plus, donating to their local thrift store makes them feel good.

Because of the astronomical rents and the lack of a robust year-round economy, pop-ups are extremely popular. Galleries and hotel boutiques will often have guest curators come in to stock their shelves, and everyone from lifestyle influencers to celebrities host trunk shows throughout the summer. The airstream boutique is a popular concept here—keep your eyes peeled at your favorite Montauk bars for a trailer filled with goodies.

>> Insider Tip: Keep your eyes peeled for garage sales and estate sales. There are some serious second-hand treasures in this part of the world.

// Don't miss garage sale season in the Hamptons, usually in late May and early June

MONTAUK | *Designer Pop-Ups and Hipster Finds*

BLUESTONE LANE BEACH COLLECTIVE

786 Montauk Highway, Montauk, New York 11954 • 718.374.6858 • bluestonelane.com/coffee-shops/montauk

This cult favorite New York City coffee shop has brought its Australian style to Montauk with a summer retail shop. It's still a coffee shop with espresso and small bites, but the space also serves as a clothing boutique, showcasing coveted surf fashion from some of Australia's trendiest labels. Here, you can shop for bikinis, sunglasses, and surfboards, all with a coffee in hand.

CYNTHIA ROWLEY

696 Montauk Highway, Montauk, New York 11954 • 631.668.807 • cynthiarowley.com

Cynthia Rowley is a Montauk local, and this boutique sells surfer-chic pieces that are actually functional—rash guards, bathing suits, and cover ups all in cool prints and color blocks. The main thing to buy here are Rowley's super-stylish wetsuits. The multicolor neoprene suits have long sleeves and a bikini bottom and are far from the sexless pieces you'll find at a regular surf shop. They're so chic, you'll want to wear one even if you don't surf.

GURNEY'S FASHION COLLECTIVE

290 Old Montauk Highway, Montauk, New York 11954 • 631.668.2345 • gurneysresorts.com/montauk

Gurney's Montauk Resort is the ultimate fashion pop-up, with different designers or brands taking over their retail space—sometimes for just a weekend, and sometimes for the whole summer. Past pop-ups include collaborations with Haute Hippie, Katie Kime, and Armor Lux.

THE SURF BAZAAR AT SURF LODGE

183 Edgemere Street, Montauk, New York 11954 • 631.668.1035 • thesurfbazaar.com

Selling beachy clothing, cover ups, and bathing suits, this sporty boutique at the Surf Lodge has everything you might need for a stylish day in the sun and a casual night out. Styles tend toward the comfortable and functional, which is perfect for a low-key weekend in Montauk.

ROOM 09 AT HAVEN

533 West Lake Drive, Montauk, New York 11954 • 631.668.7000 • r09m.com

In a repurposed guest room at the Haven Hotel in Montauk, this casual-chic concept store sells everything from trendy minimalist jewelry to art and home decor. With vintage pieces and locally made items, it's easy to find something truly unique here. The store is often host to pop-ups and live musical performances.

Where Fashionistas Should Eat

THE HIDEAWAY
⭐ *AUTHOR'S PICK*

364 West Lake Drive, Montauk, New York 11954
• 631.668.6592 • thehidewawaymontauk.com

Literally hidden away in a semi-defunct marina in Montauk, this Mexican eatery is cute beyond words. With plastic floral-printed tablecloths and bar stools, blue walls, and colorful umbrellas, this is the most Insta-grammable lunch in Montauk, and one that's still slightly under-the-radar. The menu here is super simple, but also authentic, with a focus on tacos and burritos—don't forget to order the chips and guac. After paying $18 for three tacos, you might be disappointed that the food comes served on paper plates on plastic trays, but it all adds to the ambience here.

// Like many Montauk restaurants, The Hideaway is picture-perfect

Where Fashionistas Should Stay

THE CROW'S NEST

4 Old West Lake Drive, Montauk, New York 11954 • 631.668.2077 • crowsnestmtk.com

This secluded celebrity hot spot is a popular restaurant and bar with an attached hotel. Overlooking Lake Montauk, rooms here eschew the "all white everything" look that's so popular with other Montauk hotels to create rooms that are a cozy riot of color and patterns. From tie-dye to ikat to block printing and paisley, every fabric here is a different pattern and a different color, but somehow it's totally chic. Rooms all have balconies overlooking the lake and the restaurant—the perfect place to watch the sunset with a glass of rosé in hand. From $250.

// With lanterns and couchs, The Crow's Nest is one of the coziest places for a summertime drink

AMAGANSETT, SAG HARBOR, AND THE HAMPTONS | *Vintage, Decor, and Designer Duds*

Amagansett

INNERSLEEVE RECORDS

199 Main Street, Amagansett, New York 11930 • 631.604.6248 • innersleeverecords.com

Amagansett's record shop feels like the lone holdout from the days before celebrities in this beachy town. Walking in here feels like being transported to the '90s, but with records instead of CDs and minidisc players. The shop is surprisingly huge, and the selection is too—it feels like they've got one of everything. They also sell record players and stereo equipment.

LOVE ADORNED ⭐ *AUTHOR'S PICK*

156 Main Street, Amagansett, New York 11930 • 631.267.7720 • loveadorned.com

Amagansett has always been the "low-key" Hampton, but that reputation has changed a bit as it's become a celebrity enclave. Love Adorned in Amagansett Square fits Amagansett perfectly—it's cool, creative, low key, but mostly beyond your price range. Mostly selling one-of-a-kind handmade and vintage jewelry alongside eccentric-chic home goods, it's the place to go for something truly unique that you'll have forever.

PILGRIM SURF + SUPPLY

4 Amagansett Square, Amagansett, New York 11930 • 631.267.3598 • pilgrimsurfsupply.com

You don't have to be a surfer to shop at Pilgrim, although they definitely sell surfboards and wax. In addition to gear, the shop sells cool utilitarian clothing with a unisex look, as well as Brooklyn-y beach essentials: swimsuits, sunglasses, totes, sunscreen, and hats.

Sag Harbor

AYR BEACH HOUSE

25 Madison Street, Sag Harbor, New York 11963 • 631.899.3775 • ayr.com

This popular boutique brings a little bit of Abbot Kinney to Sag Harbor, with made-in-America denim and simple cotton t-shirts. The name is short for "All Year Round" and the company strives to create clothes that won't go out of style, no matter what season. The clothes here aren't cheap by any standards except Hamptons standards, but they are a good deal, considering it's the kind of high-quality simple stuff that will become a wardrobe staple.

BLACK SWAN SHOP

26 Main Street, Sag Harbor, New York 11963 • 631.377.3012

At this antique store in Sag Harbor, you'll find beachy kitsch alongside quality mid-century and Americana pieces. Decently priced, the store is a slightly cluttered treasure trove of fun souvenirs, or, if you're in luck, heirloom-quality furniture.

JOEY WÖLFFER

11 Madison Street, Sag Harbor, New York 11963 • 631.725.1436 • joeywolffer.com

Curated from the owner's world travels, this boutique by Joey Wölffer (of Wölffer Estate Wine) is a treasure trove of internationally inspired home goods and accessories, with a few vintage pieces thrown in, too. The store also sells a line of Wölffer-designed handbags that recreate a vintage 1970s style with fringe, suede, and beading. Keep your eyes peeled for the Styleliner, a mobile trunk show inside of a truck that can be found at special events.

LOVE SHACK FANCY

117 Main Street, Sag Harbor, New York 11963 • 631.808.3995 • loveshackfancy.com/pages/sag-harbor

Love Shack Fancy is the place to try for frivolous, romantic frocks. Almost everything here is floral-printed or has some kind of ruffle on it (in most cases, all of the above) but somehow it works. The vibe here is decidedly Vogue instead of Laura Ashley—the ultra-feminine styles might not be everyone's cup of tea. Still, it's nice to check out the fairytale quality of the dresses here. It's a must-stop shop if you have a wedding coming up and nothing to wear.

RUBY BEETS SHOP

25 Washington Street, Sag Harbor, New York 11963 • 631.899.3275 • rubybeets.com

This pristine white furniture shop mixes old and new in an expertly curated selection of home goods. With a mix of sleek modern pieces and French country cottage-style, the whole store seems to fit together as if it's been put together by an interior designer (because it has been). Go here for style inspo for when you build your dream home.

East Hampton

AERIN

7 Newtown Lane, East Hampton, New York 11937 • 631.527.5517 • aerin.com/aerin-easthampton

Aerin Lauder is the latest socialite lifestyle guru to follow in the footsteps of Gwyneth Paltrow, and this East Hampton store is a delight to browse. It's all about sumptuous homegoods, home decor, signature scented candles, and a few Hamptons wardrobe essentials, like sundresses, sun hats, and summery statement earrings. Come here when you've been invited to somebody's house for the weekend and you need to show up with a perfectly Hamptons hostess gift.

ARF THRIFT & TREASURE SHOP

17 Poxabogue Lane, Sagaponack, New York 11962 • 631.537.3682 • arfhamptons.org

All proceeds at this donation-based thrift store benefit the Animal Rescue Fund of the Hamptons, which is a "no kill" animal shelter providing services to Long Island's East End. With an ever-changing selection of donated furniture, clothing, jewelry, books, and more, it's worth poking around to see what's for sale. You can search for treasures here, or you can stop by the adoption center on 124 Daniels Hole Road, to take home a new family member.

BLUE & CREAM

60 The Cir, East Hampton, New York 11937 • 631.329.1392 • blueandcream.com

This high-end boutique for men and women sells beachy frocks from a variety of designers including Zimmerman, Self-Portrait, and 3.1 Phillip Lim. They also have their own line, which features simple silhouettes in luxurious fabrics, like silk dresses and cashmere sweaters.

BLUE MERCURY

67 Main Street, East Hampton, New York 11937 • 631.324.0330 • bluemercury.com

A one-stop shop for makeup and skincare, this high-end store sells everything you need in the beauty department, with products made from high-quality ingredients. Selling luxury brands like Nars, La Mer, and Diptyque alongside some more affordable (but still quality) products, this is the place to go to treat yourself. Everybody deserves a $80 sunscreen for their face, especially if you're going to spend your days at the beach.

KIRNA ZABETE

66 Newtown Lane, East Hampton, New York 11937 • 631.527.5794 • kirnazabete.com

A favorite of gallery girls, Kirna Zabete sells quirky and over-the-top statement pieces like pink lambswool jackets and glittery tights. Everything here is full of pizzazz, like gaudy-chic costume jewelry, handbags in improbable shapes, and sequined pants from brands like Gucci, Altuzarra, and Proenza Schouler. Be ready to spend a small fortune on something unforgettable.

LVIS

95 Main Street, East Hampton, New York 11937 • 631.324.1220 • lvis.org

With all the money in the area, the Hamptons is a treasure trove of vintage finds—as long as you know where to look. The Ladies Village Improvement Society, or LVIS for short, is a donation-based thrift store with (mostly) reasonable prices on clothes and homewares. They'll accept and sell almost anything, so you'll have to do a bit of searching, but it's not hard to strike gold here.

MALIA MILLS ⭐ *AUTHOR'S PICK*

55 Main Street, East Hampton, New York 11968 • 631.604.1568 • maliamills.com

Malia Mills has become the gold standard for expertly made, comfortable, and simple bathing suits that are somehow flattering on every body type. The silhouettes feel timeless, and the cozy-chic dresses and jumpsuits for sale make for the perfect day-to-night weekend outfit. Just keep in mind, you'll need to throw down some serious cash to nail this effortless look.

THE MONOGRAM SHOP

19 Newtown Lane, East Hampton, New York 11937 • 631.329.3379 • themonogramshops.com

One of East Hampton's oldest stores, The Monogram Shop is the ultimate gift shop for things you didn't even know you wanted monogrammed: ice buckets, coasters, cheese boards, and tissue box covers can be found among usual suspects like glasses, stationery, and towels. Many Hamptons homes have custom reusable plastic pool cups from here. If you're not in the mood for something monogrammed, it's worth a stop for fun gifts and home decor. There's also a cute selection of baby stuff.

REFORMATION BEACH HOUSE

85 Main Street, East Hampton, New York 11937 • 855.756.0560 • thereformation.com

The uniform of downtown cool girls, Reformation has opened up a summer shop in East Hampton. Reformation is about fashion with a conscience: trend-setting silhouettes designed and made in America, from recycled and sustainable fabrics. From simple cotton dresses and jumpsuits to wedding-worthy silk gowns, Reformation should probably be your first stop if you're suddenly invited somewhere and have nothing to wear. It's not cheap, but it's definitely the most affordable clothing store on Main Street in East Hampton.

RRL

57 Main Street, East Hampton, New York 11937 • 631.907.9201 • ralphlauren.com

While Ralph Lauren definitely falls under the category of "stuff you can find online," there's something very special about this well-curated shop. Ralph Lauren owns a house in the Hamptons, so it's only natural that this store feels like you're walking into somebody's home. The clothes here will make you nostalgic for another era and will look best driving your classic woody jeep to a beach picnic with some tartan blankets and a wicker basket full of real glasses.

WHAT GOES AROUND COMES AROUND

48 Main Street, East Hampton, New York 11937 • 631.324.0874 • whatgoesaroundnyc.com

The most high-end vintage boutique in the area, this is the place to visit if you're looking to drop a bundle of money on a one-of-a-kind item for a special occasion. The selection is sparse but highly curated, so it's worth a pop-in whenever you're in town to see what the latest find is—especially if you suddenly have an extra $600 to spend on a T-shirt.

Bridgehampton

CARBON38

2424 Montauk Highway #1541, Bridgehampton, New York 11932 • 631.919.5444 • carbon38.com/hamptons

Athleisure is big in the Hamptons, especially with the unnaturally fit, unnaturally tanned, and unnaturally blonde yoga moms. Carbon 38 is where Hamptonites go for the perfect legging that can take them from Pilates to the coffee shop to the beach club to pick up the kids. Try this store for sportswear that looks like streetwear. Hint: chic exercise clothes are not just for athletes—anybody who has ever been on a plane for more than three hours knows the power of spandex.

WYETH

3654 Montauk Highway, Sagaponack, New York 11962 • 631.604.2103 • wyeth.nyc

You can tell by the font on the sign outside that this place is going to be good, and inside, it does not disappoint. With a focus on mid-century furnishings and objets d'art, this is a fun place to browse, but the price tags are absolutely whopping—it's the kind of place where decorators shop for clients for whom money is no object. Seriously, the cheapest thing in this place is a $1,000 set of vintage coasters. Museum-worthy collectibles include perfectly crafted pieces by Charles and Ray Eames, George Nakashima, Hans J. Wegner, and Wyeth's own design team.

Southampton

SUGARFINA

89 Main Street, Southampton, New York 11968 • 631.850.3038 • sugarfina.com

A favorite with the fashion set, this Instagram-famous candy shop sells luxury candy, aesthetically packaged. Far from your average pay-by-the-pound candy shop experience, everything here comes perfectly packaged in clear plastic containers that turn this candy store into a sort of temporary art installation. This is a candy store for grown-ups, offering fun treats like rosé-infused gummy bears that are almost too pretty to eat. Almost.

CABANA

53 Jobs Lane, Southampton, New York 11968 • 631.353.3234 • cabananewyork.com

With festive summer clothing, shoes, and accessories, Cabana is the place to go for irresistible summer frocks. Combing new designer clothing with vintage luxury items, this industrial space is easily the most fashionable place in town.

L'OBJET A LA PLAGE

9 Main Street, Southampton, New York 11968 • 631.259.2644 • l-objet.com

L'Objet stocks everything you need to create an Instagram-worthy table scape. With modern china, stemware, cutlery, and linens, this is where the chicest hosts in the Hamptons come to turn their dining tables into works of art. There are also home accents like throws and pillows, along with a selection of quirky-cool luxury gifts like absurdly cool letter openers and paper weights.

Where Fashionistas Should Eat

WÖLFFER SAG HARBOR

29 Main Street, Sag Harbor, New York 11963 • 631.725.0101 • sagharbor.wolfferkitchen.com

At this vineyard-to-table restaurant in Sag Harbor, local ingredients come first in perfectly-executed American and Mediterranean dishes. Indulge in seafood starters like raw oysters or ceviche before dining on entrees like striped bass with artichoke and basil relish or sea scallops with corn and fava bean succotash. There's also a classic steak frites on the menu, and though you should probably pair your meal with a bottle of Wölffer Estate wine, there's an extensive wine list with new-world and old-world wines, curated by people who definitely know what good wine is.

Where Fashionistas Should Stay

THE MAIDSTONE HOTEL ⭐ *AUTHOR'S PICK*

207 Main Street, East Hampton, New York 11937 • 631.324.5006 • themaidstone.com

The Hamptons are full of upscale, homey inns, but this one is by far the most stylish on the East End. While The Maidstone (not to be confused with the private beach club of the same name) might look like your average bed-and-breakfast on the outside, inside it is full of loud prints, stylish furniture, and great art. Rooms range from cozy nooks in the main house to spacious cottages with private entrances, gardens, and fireplaces. The style definitely falls into the category of "edgy-preppy," but it's completely unstuffy. The Maidstone Hotel has somehow managed to be both classic and cool, making this one of the hottest hotels in the Hamptons. From $395.

☰ *Shelter Island and the North Fork*

On Shelter Island and the North Fork, it's the small-fry one-off boutiques that make this a shopping destination, with artists and designers curating a hip selection of fashion finds—sometimes even from their own travels or closets. Vintage lovers will find unbelievable pieces (some at unbelievably high prices) in boutiques, antique shops, and thrift stores scattered throughout the North Fork.

SHELTER ISLAND | *Laid-Back Style*

MARIE EIFFEL

8 Grand Avenue, Shelter Island Heights, New York 11965 • 631.749.0707 • marieiffel.com

You might recognize the name Marie Eiffel from the coffee shop and market in town, and this shop by the same owner sticks with the French theme. With breezy linen clothes and funky jewelry, this clothing store sells everything you need to complete your effortless island wardrobe.

MARIKA'S ECLECTIC BOUTIQUE

6 South Ferry Road, Shelter Island, New York 11964 • 401.862.6607

This quirky furniture store is hard to miss, with pieces spilling out the door of this little yellow cottage and into the vast parking lot and front lawn during the summer. Items range from shabby to chic, with some seriously valuable treasures sourced from estate sales alongside items (allegedly) scavenged from the town dump. Everything about Marika's is truly wonderful, and it's hard to come here and not fall in love with something.

THE NORTH FORK | *Furniture, Decor, and Eclectic Style*

Greenport

ALEX VINASH AT AMERICAN BEECH

300 Main Street, Greenport, New York 11944 • 631.477.6571 • americanbeech.com/shop

The lobby of American Beech Hotel is home to a boutique that is an absolute riot of color. Everything in this Miami-style shop selling dresses, jewelry, shoes, and accessories is made by Spanish designer Alex Vinash, whose whimsical creations, often involving colorful floral embroidery, make it hard to pass by this place without peeking in. The shop is surprisingly affordable for what you're getting (although far from cheap), and everything here is full of personality.

BEALL & BELL

430 Main Street, Greenport, New York 11944 • 631.477.8239 • beallandbell.com

Greenport's favorite antique store is a hot spot for interior designers looking for a bargain, with new pieces on sale every Thursday. They specialize in well-made, timeless pieces, usually with a mid-century vibe. Shop here for quality pieces to outfit any New England home.

LIDO

132 Main Street, Greenport, New York 11944 •
631.477.2350 • lidoworld.com

This bohemian store has gifts and clothes for the world traveler, with products inspired by travels in Bali, Thailand, India, and beyond. It focuses on high-quality, natural materials and fair-trade products. There are also vintage rugs and clothing sourced from around the world. Try here for that perfect beachy kaftan.

ORENDA

29 Front Street, Greenport, New York 11944 •
631.477.6793 • orendagreenport.com

// Greenport's streets are lined with antique shops

Orenda sells jewelry and gifts with a bohemian vibe. Owned by local jewelry designers, this artisan boutique also sells crystals and objets d'art.

THE TIMES VINTAGE ⭐ AUTHOR'S PICK

429 Main Street, Greenport, New York 11944 • 631.477.6455 • timesvintage.com

This is a classic vintage store, where you'll find everything you need to fill your craving for '70s prints. All sizes of sheepskin coats, flannels, jeans, and of course, psychedelic paisley dresses round out the collection here, with some rare finds for those willing to take their time and look around. Clothes are clean, well-organized, and in mostly good condition, so it's a worthwhile stop, even for the thrift store-averse.

THE WEATHERED BARN

41 Front Street, Greenport, New York 11944 • 631.477.6811 • theweatheredbarngreenport.com

Greenport's Weathered Barn is the ultimate in farmhouse-chic. This store has everything you need for a cool, countryside home, from natural soaps and fragrances to silverware and linens to spices and tea. This is the place for a homey hostess gift for your most down-to-earth friend.

Southold

WHITE FLOWER FARMHOUSE

53995 Main Road, Southold, New York 11971 • 631.765.2353

This cozy Southold shop sells new, vintage, and repurposed home goods and furniture, mostly painted white. The monochromatic interior is picture-perfect, with bleached wood and rustic touches like vintage jars and aluminum planters. Go here for all your shabby-chic home decor needs.

Where Fashionistas Should Eat

BASSO CICCHETTI—WINE BAR

300 Main Street, Greenport, New York 11944 • 631.333.2175 • bassogreenport.com

In the courtyard of American Beech, this intimate wine bar serves small plates and simple Italian dishes in a cozy space. Perfect for an off-season date night, it's hard to be unhappy here, eating imported cheese and charcuterie and drinking local wine by candlelight. The restaurant also stocks a selection of imported gourmet foods, perfect for whipping up your own Mediterranean feast at home.

THE BEST BOOK STORES ON LONG ISLAND

BOOK HAMPTON • East Hampton • bookhampton.com

HARPER'S BOOKS • East Hampton • harpersbooks.com

HARBOR BOOKS • Sag Harbor • harborbookssgh.com

CANIO'S BOOKS • Sag Harbor • caniosbooks.com

SOUTHAMPTON BOOKS • Southampton • southampton-books.com

BLACK CAT BOOKS • Shelter Island • blackcatbooks.com

BURTON'S BOOK STORE • Greenport • burtonsbooks.com

BOOK REVUE • Huntington • bookrevue.com

LOCUST VALLEY BOOKSTORE • Oyster Bay • locustvalleybookstore.com

DOLPHIN BOOKSHOP • Port Washington • thedolphinbookshop.com

TURN OF THE CORKSCREW • Hempstead • turnofthecorkscrew.com

Where Fashionistas Should Stay

SOUNDVIEW INN

58775 Route 48, Greenport, New York 11944 • 631.477.1910 • soundviewgreenport.com

THE fashionable destination for those visiting the North Fork, the Soundview Inn got a complete makeover by Brooklyn-based Studio Tack in 2017, making this seaside motel into a chic vacationland. Rooms are rustic-chic, with wood paneled walls and cozy linens. The hotel has a sit-down restaurant, a poolside lobster shack, and a cozy piano bar that feels like something from another era.

≡ *The Jersey Shore*

Contrary to popular belief, it's not all neon tank tops on the Jersey Shore—stylish boutiques in the town of Asbury Park sell a well-curated selection of chic clothes, homegoods, and accessories.

JERSEY SHORE | *Instagram-Worthy Decor and Chic Designer Finds*

Asbury Park

BACKWARD GLANCES

658 Cookman Ave #20, Asbury Park, New Jersey 07712 • 732.774.0007 • backwardglances.com

This basement vintage shop is more costume than style, but that doesn't mean it's not worth checking out. Here you can find super psychedelic prints, wacky styles, and cheesy (but fun!) novelty items like fruit-shaped coin purses and superhero lunch boxes.

HOLD FAST RECORDS

611 Cookman Avenue, Asbury Park, New Jersey 07712 • 732.988.0066 • holdfastasburypark.net

With Asbury Park's storied musical history, it's only fitting that there's a great record shop here. Selling used and new vinyl, Hold Fast Records has been around for 10 years, ushering in Asbury Park's second (or maybe third) renaissance as a hip destination for those in the know.

INTERWOVEN

511 Cookman Avenue, Asbury Park, New Jersey 07712 • 732.775.1713 • interwovenap.com

Interwoven manages to create the perfect balance between designers of the moment and those you've never heard of before. With a huge range of prices, most of them affordable,

1 Luxe homewares at Red Moon

2 Costumes and vintage finds at Backward Glances

3 Asbury Park's Interwoven has styles for all price ranges

this boutique sells clothing, swimsuits, accessories, beauty products, and shoes for both men and women.

PATRIAE

713 Bangs Avenue, Asbury Park, New Jersey 07712 • 732.774.4341 • patrieastudio.com

Almost everything at this home goods store seems to be made with natural products: jute and cotton textiles, carved wooden bowls, and other functional and artistic homewares made from shells, bone, rope, and wood. There's a wide selection of indigo-dyed tablecloths and quite a bit of dishware. Shop here to make yours the chicest kitchen on the block.

REBEL SUPPLY COMPANY

550 Cookman Avenue, Asbury Park, New Jersey 07712 • 732.455.5080

This vintage shop specializes in band tees, Doc Martens, and collectibles with a rock-n-roll vibe. The store is super clean and uncluttered, making this a great vintage experience for those who are wary of digging through bins to hunt for treasure.

RED MOON ⭐ AUTHOR'S PICK

300 Emory Street, Asbury Park, New Jersey 07712 • 732.361.8919 • redmoonshop.com

Straight out of Brooklyn, this unbelievably chic store sells earthen homeware, all-natural high-end beauty products, and a small selection of handmade clothing and shoes. Every single article here is thoughtfully placed in this minimalist-chic space with hanging plants. The biggest problem you'll have here is walking in, needing everything, and leaving with nothing because you couldn't possibly decide what to get. Go here to shop for a wedding present for your coolest friends.

Where Fashionistas Should Eat

TALULA'S PIZZA
⭐ AUTHOR'S PICK

550 Cookman Ave #108, Asbury Park, New Jersey 07712 • 732.455.3003 • talulaspizza.com

The best pizza in New Jersey, this brick-oven joint serves pizza with bougie ingredients like squash blossoms and fennel. Don't worry— you can still get a margherita or pepperoni here, and it will be top notch, made with ingredients sourced from local farms and purveyors. For starters, try a simple salad or a ricotta toast, and don't forget the bread and

// Talula's is the best fancy pizza on the Jersey Shore

butter. While there's certainly stuff besides pizza on the menu, and it's definitely delicious, you would be remiss in not ordering at least one pizza. Sticking with the theme of conscious consumption, the drinks menu is full of natural wines and nanobrews. The decor is stylish, simple, and utilitarian, with exposed brick, a communal table, and metal stools. Try to come here on your first day in town, because it's so good that you might want to cancel all your other plans just so you can come back for breakfast/lunch/every meal until you leave. It's one of those restaurants that's worth planning a trip around. If you come to Asbury Park and don't eat at Talula's, you're doing it wrong.

Where Fashionistas Should Stay

THE ASBURY 🌟 *AUTHOR'S PICK*

210 5th Avenue, Asbury Park, New Jersey 07712 • 732.774.7100 • theasburyhotel.com

Before The Asbury, Asbury Park was slowly transforming into a hip weekend getaway for cool New Yorkers. After The Asbury, this town has become a full-blown scene for some of the most fashionable people in the city—and they can all be found at the Asbury. The lobby is well-lit with huge greenhouse-style windows over comfy lounges, while the lobby bar gets the party started with craft cocktails. Rooms are minimalist chic, and the kind of thing somebody might create if they were creating chic college dorms for the post-college crowd: white painted floors, accent chairs, and futon couches in case you have a friend crash for the night. There are, in fact dorm rooms here, with a few rooms that bunk up to eight people. With movies on the roof, a happening pool party scene, and a rooftop bar, you might forget that there's a whole town out there for you to explore. From $250.

Escapes for Love Birds

While not famous as a romantic destination, Long Island is the perfect place for a couple to retreat—or even for a minimoon. While New Jersey and Fire Island are the places to go for fun, Long Island is the place to go for love.

Long Island is full of romantic summer activities—strolling through a sculpture park or nature preserve, wine tasting on the North Fork, or renting kayaks and enjoying the calm waters of the bay.

There's something magic in the air out here during the summer, but don't discount the off-season, either. Once the crowds go home and the kids go back to school, there's a sense of serenity that takes over. Instead of chugging rosé at a beach party, it's sipping red wine in front of a fireplace or going to the beach and snuggling under blankets.

Love on Long Island can be simple or over-the-top. While a seven-course dinner and a five-star hotel might be one couple's idea of romance, others might enjoy curling up next to a bonfire on the beach after a day of surfing or sailing together.

With its proximity to New York City, Long Island shouldn't be discounted as a place to spend your mini-moon or anniversary—there's more than enough to keep you occupied for a long weekend, but it's also the perfect place to do absolutely nothing at all.

Whatever your relationship status is and whatever season it is, Long Island has something for everyone.

≡ Montauk and the Hamptons

Long Island's South Fork is full of romantic opportunities—long walks on the beach, world-class food and wine, and chic and cozy hotels. And for those who are unattached, beware—a fair share of New Yorkers have met their significant others out here somewhere: at an all-night party in the Hamptons, a farmstand on the Northfork, or at a bar in Montauk. During the off-season, the cozy inns of the East End become warm and welcoming spots to spend a weekend (at a greatly discounted price).

MONTAUK | Low-Key and Cozy Vibes

Where Lovebirds Should Eat

THE CROW'S NEST ⭐ AUTHOR'S PICK

4 Old West Lake Drive, Montauk, New York 11954 • 631.668.2077 • crowsnestmtk.com

Set on a beautiful sloping hill on Lake Montauk, The Crow's Nest is one of those painfully chic see-and-be-seen restaurants. Serving lunch and dinner, the menu here is New American with a Mediterranean slant. As with the best restaurants on the East End, there's a strong focus on local and seasonal ingredients, like Montauk scallops, local zucchini, and wine from Wölffer Estate down the road. Eat inside at rustic reclaimed wood tables, or opt for a seat outside under the string lights—either way, it's a pretty as a picture here, especially by candlelight.

// Rooms at The Crow's Nest look out onto the bar and restaurant's outdoor tables

Where Lovebirds Should Stay

GURNEY'S MONTAUK RESORT & SEAWATER SPA

290 Old Montauk Highway, Montauk, New York 11954 • 631.668.2345 • gurneysresorts.com/montauk

One of the only Montauk hotels that's open year-round, Gurney's is also the most luxurious. While Montauk abounds with chic converted motels, Gurney's is one of the only proper resorts, with a restaurant, bar, and spa right on the beach. With deluxe rooms, suites, and cottages all with an ocean view, this is the kind of place where you can check in on a Friday and never leave the hotel grounds. The indoor saltwater pool is open year-round, and the top-notch spa facilities are the perfect place to indulge in a massage.

AMAGANSETT, SAG HARBOR, AND THE HAMPTONS | *Luxury Hotels and Candlelit Dinners*

Where Lovebirds Should Eat

THE PALM

94 Main Street, East Hampton, New York 11937 • 631.324.0411 • thepalm.com/restaurants/east-hampton

The ultimate date night destination, the Palm exemplifies old-school luxury. In the Historic Huntting Inn, the setting couldn't be more classic—dark wood paneling, white tablecloths, and everything you need for an intimate dinner. The menu matches the vibe, with steaks, seafood, and Italian specialties. There's an updated spin on the classics here, with quality ingredients and plenty of fresh salads to satisfy the Hamptons set.

ALMOND

1 Ocean Road, Bridgehampton, New York 11932 • 631.537.5665 • almondrestaurant.com

On Friday and Saturday nights, you'll see people spilling out of this inviting bistro. It's been a popular Hamptons mainstay since it opened in 2001, working with local ingredients to create straightforward, unpretentious meals in a buzzy and welcoming setting. Dine on Long Island duck, striped bass, or Korean-style BBQ short ribs for dinner, and don't miss out on dessert—the chocolate pot de creme is what dreams are made of.

PIERRE'S RESTAURANT

2468 Main Street, Bridgehampton, New York 11932 • 631.537.5110 • pierresbridgehampton.com

Pierre's is a Hamptons classic, providing ladies who lunch with a place to gossip 7 days a week, 365 days a year. The vibe is St. Tropez meets Hamptons, with white tablecloths, bistro chairs, and a few tables set up on the sidewalk for those who want to see and be seen. For brunch and lunch, indulge in lobster Benedict, Croque Monsieur, and steak frites. Come

BEACHY WEEKEND GETAWAYS FOR BIG SPENDERS: WHERE AND HOW TO TREAT YOURSELF

Getting Here

BY PLANE AND HELICOPTER For the extra fancy, it's possible to book a seat on a helicopter or seaplane departing from Manhattan with **Blade**. Helicopters depart from East 34th Street and West 30th Street, and seaplanes depart from East 23rd Street. The trip takes about 45 minutes. Helicopters land at either the Meadow Lane Helipad in Southampton or the East Hampton Airport. Seaplanes only land at the East Hampton Airport. Eastbound flights are offered on Thursday, Friday, and Saturday, and westbound flights are offered on Saturday, Sunday, and Monday.

Prices average a whopping $800 for a seat on one of these flights, but they can fluctuate way higher, especially on holiday weekends. Download the app or check the website for schedules and prices: Flyblade.com.

Shoreline Aviation is another option for the wealthy among us, with seaplane flights to Montauk. Flights depart on Friday, return Sunday, and cost around $850 each way. Shoreline Aviation sometimes offers flights to Fire Island Pines for around $700. The schedule is irregular, and the prices are subject to change, so go online to book. Check the website for prices and schedules: shorelineaviation.com.

Where to Eat

LE BILBOQUET

1 Long Wharf, Sag Harbor, New York 11963 • 631.808.3767

A Hamptons outpost of the Upper East Side dining institution that the *New York Post* once called "the snobbiest restaurant in New York," this restaurant brings a little bit of New York City attitude to the Hamptons. With an epic location on the wharf, some seriously stylish design, and a dress code, this is not the place to go for a casual meal. Expect to pay top dollar for decadent delicacies like foie gras and champagne—with a view that includes million-dollar yachts and million-dollar facelifts. Whether the old-timers like it or not, this style of over-the-top dining has descended on Sag Harbor. If you have the money, it's worth the experience—if only for the satisfaction of making it past the door to see how the other half lives for a night.

DOPO LA SPIAGGIA

6 Bay Street, Sag Harbor, New York 11963 • 631.725.7009 • dopolaspiaggia.com/sagharbor

With locations in Sag Harbor and East Hampton, Dopo is the quintessential bougie Hamptons Italian joint, complete with occasional celebrity sightings, carefully plated tiny portions, and a jaw-dropping wine list. But if you don't mind the prices, this is a fun place to eat. The atmosphere is lively, and you can't go wrong with dishes like burrata and spicy tuna tartare with avocado. Come here to dress up, sip champagne, and dine on squid ink pasta in a beautiful setting surrounded by beautiful people.

NICK & TONI'S

136 Main Street, East Hampton, New York 11937 • 631.324.3550 • nickandtonis.com

THE spot to see and be seen in East Hampton, this institution also happens to be one of the best fine-dining destinations in the area. The food, atmosphere, and wine certainly live up to the establishment's reputation (and the price) as one of Long Island's best restaurants.

TOPPING ROSE HOUSE

1 Bridgehampton-Sag Harbor Turnpike, Bridgehampton, New York 11932 • 631.537.0870 • toppingrosehouse.com/restaurant

This restaurant by Jean-Georges is located in the chic Topping Rose House, a super-luxe hotel in one of Bridgehampton's most striking mansions. The formal dining room is chic and surprisingly modern, with lime green banquettes and minimalist tables. The cuisine here is a bit more inventive than what you might find elsewhere, with appetizers like burrata with strawberry compote, arugula, basil, and black pepper of the crispy salmon sushi with chipotle mayo. Entrees include duck with slow-roasted tomato with sour cherry mole, or the cheeseburger, dolled up with yuzu pickles, onions, and Russian dressing.

75 MAIN

75 Main Street, Southampton, New York 11968 • 631.283.7575 • 75main.com

High prices, celebrity clientele, and clubby atmosphere make this a place to see and be seen in Southampton. Along with Hamptons staples like watermelon salad and local littleneck clam pasta, 75 Main is well-known for its black truffle burger, with Romano cheese, Italian black truffle, and roasted garlic aioli.

SANT AMBROEUS

30 Main Street, Southampton, New York 11968 • 631.283.1233

Elegant and chic, Sant Ambroeus serves some of the most consistently good food in Southampton. The green-and-white striped awning outside leads into a bright and airy cafe, where you'll find impeccable Italian fare at astonishingly high prices. Start with a caprese salad or salmon crudo with shaved fennel and pink peppercorn before moving on to linguine with clams or tagliatelle with veal ragu. The ambiance and the quality of the food are unmatched in Southampton's fine-dining scene. It's only open on weekends during the winter.

PETER LUGER GREAT NECK

255 Northern Boulevard, Great Neck, New York 11021 • 516.487.8800 • peterluger.com

A suburban outpost of Brooklyn's most famous steakhouse, Peter Luger delivers high-quality cuts of beef in a sophisticated setting. The prices here are astronomical, but so is the quality— you truly get what you pay for. The menu here is simple, with an iceberg or Caesar salad to start, and a choice of beef, pork chops, chicken, salmon, or lobster, all served with a la carte sides.

Where to Stay

TOPPING ROSE HOUSE

1 Bridgehampton-Sag Harbor Turnpike, Bridgehampton, New York 11932 • 631.537.0870 • toppingrosehouse.com

One of the most luxurious 5-star hotels on Long Island, Topping Rose House is a historic mansion on the outside and a sophisticated modern resort on the inside. With only sixteen guest rooms and a striking pool area that looks like it comes straight out of a modern design magazine, the hotel exudes an air of exclusivity with spacious and comfortable guest rooms, a spa, and a see-and-be-seen on-site restaurant by Jean-Georges. From $595.

Where to Play

SAG HARBOR SAILING

51 Pine Neck Avenue, Sag Harbor, New York 11963 • 631.725.5100 • sailsagharbor.com

Charter a 34-foot or 27-foot sailboat for a sunset cruise or an overnight trip with Sag Harbor Sailing. Experienced sailors can take the boat out on their own, or you can hire a captain.

SAIL MONTAUK

32 Star Island Road, Montauk, New York 11954 • 631.522.5183 • sailmontauk.com

With private sailing charters, overnight trips, sailing lessons, and bareboat rentals, Sail Montauk will get you out on the water in style.

nighttime, the lights are dimmed, and romance fills the air of this lovely French restaurant. Dinner is over the top, with decadent dishes like steak tartare, duck a l'orange, and lobster fricassee, with an extensive (and expensive) French wine list to match. Pierre's is authentic and old-school, with a completely different vibe from the new age coastal American restaurants that are ubiquitous out East.

Where Lovebirds Should Stay

1770 HOUSE

143 Main Street, East Hampton, New York 11937 • 631.324.1770 • www.1770house.com

Exemplifying cozy countryside luxury, 1770 House is a boutique hotel with a history. Originally built as a private estate in 1663, the house was converted to an inn in 1770. There are six rooms plus a carriage house, all individually decorated with antiques, sumptuous linens, and patterned wallpaper. You'll find a fireplace and cozy reading nooks in the public spaces and a tavern serving comfort food. The inn is welcoming and unpretentious, with friendly staff and excellent service. Visit in the off-season to truly appreciate this charming, romantic inn. From $249.

// The dock in Greenport

≡ Shelter Island and the North Fork

There's nothing more romantic than eating and drinking delicious food in a beautiful place, which makes Shelter Island and the North Fork one of the best options for a romantic getaway. It's almost impossible to find a mediocre meal here, and if you happen upon one, you'll be so smitten with the waterfront location that you won't even notice or care. Spend a day wine tasting and farm-hopping, or get active on a tandem kayak to explore the Peconic Bay.

SHELTER ISLAND AND THE NORTH FORK |
Old-School Charm and Off-Beat Menus

Where Lovebirds Should Eat

RAM'S HEAD INN RESTAURANT

108 South Ram Island Drive, Shelter Island Heights, New York 11965 • 631.749.0811 • theramsheadinn.com

With a beautiful location on Ram Island, The Ram's Head Inn is worth a visit, even if you're not staying there. The dining room is grandma-chic, with patterned wallpaper and antique chairs. Request a table out on the patio during dinner for a view of the sloping lawn and water. The menu is old-school, with classics like Caesar salad, Shrimp Fra Diavolo, and rack of lamb. Sunday brunch is a treat, with decadent options like duck confit hash, lobster mac and cheese, and banana bread French toast.

NOAH'S

136 Front Street, Greenport, New York 11944 • 631.477.6720 • chefnoahs.com

One of Greenport's most well-known dining destinations, Noah's serves innovative food and wine inspired by the chef's time spent in Sonoma. Seafood is the star of the show here, with a raw bar that includes local oysters, little neck clams, jumbo shrimp, and yellowfin tuna. Opt for grilled monkfish or octopus skewers, or try out the crab cake (a local favorite) or the Lobster Roll (voted the best lobster roll on the East End in 2017).

Where Lovebirds Should Stay

THE CHEQUIT

23 Grand Avenue, Shelter Island Heights, New York 11965 • 631.749.0018 • www.thechequit.com

It's not the buzziest hotel on Shelter Island (that award goes to Sunset Beach), but the newly-updated Chequit is certainly stylish. A low-key, relaxed, and preppy-chic atmosphere permeates the hotel, with a mix of classic antiques and bright, modern design elements. The rooms here are nearly perfect, with fluffy white beds, chic rugs, and millennial pink walls. Rooms range from cozy standard kings to a sprawling loft suite with a private terrace. From $175.

☰ *Greater Long Island*

On Greater Long Island, historic mansions and literal palaces beckon—Oheka Castle is probably one of the most romantic places to spend the night any time of year. From dimly lit classic steakhouses to trendy new fine dining, restaurants on Long Island have romance in spades. (Not to mention, almost all of them serve raw oysters, which are supposedly an aphrodisiac). Skip the beach and spend the day walking the grounds of historic estates or walking through lush gardens.

// Farm-fresh flowers are a lovely
(if short-lived) souvenir

GREATER LONG ISLAND | *Palace Hotels and Vintage Steakhouses*

Where Lovebirds Should Eat

OLD FIELDS GREENLAWN

81 Broadway, Greenlawn, New York 11740 • 631.754.9868 • of1956.com

This old-school steakhouse got a hip revamp, turning a Long Island fixture into a retro-chic dining destination that wouldn't be out of place in Brooklyn. The menu has gotten an update, while still serving comfort food, like crab cakes with chipotle corn puree and buttermilk chicken with honey maple glaze for appetizers. Entrees include fish and chips, short rib risotto, and almond-crusted mahi-mahi. For steaks, there are four options to choose from, all served with a side of mashed potatoes. There's also a location in Port Jefferson.

Where Lovebirds Should Stay

OHEKA CASTLE ☆ *AUTHOR'S PICK*

135 West Gate Drive, Huntington, New York 11743 • 631.659.1400 • oheka.com

Oheka Castle is the most improbable and impressive hotel on Long Island. This opulent historic hotel is actually a castle, built in the 1920s by financier Otto Hermann Kahn. The grounds are absolutely magnificent, with over 400 acres of landscaping. The suites are completely over-the-top, with oil paintings in gilt frames, crystal chandeliers, and overstuffed furniture. There's nothing subtle about Oheka, but it's hard not to have a smile on your face when you see this place. It's the perfect place for a romantic weekend getaway (or even a minimoon or marriage proposal!). From $395.

Escapes on a Budget

How to Visit Long Island and the Jersey Shore Without Going into Debt

Over 20 million people live in the New York, New Jersey, and Pennsylvania tri-state area. With summer temperatures reaching upwards of 100 degrees in the cities, the beach beckons—and the people come. During summer weekends (especially holidays) on Long Island and the Jersey Shore, you'll find that even dumpy motels are charging $400/night and over-priced and mediocre restaurants have a line around the block. Many times, businesses in these small beachside communities make their entire year's profit during July and August—some don't even bother to open between Labor Day and Memorial Day.

Long Island's unbelievable parks and beaches are all yours, and there's no better spot for a picnic. Set up camp and stay for the day, swimming, reading, and sunbathing, and you won't even notice that you haven't spent any money. When the sun goes down, head into town for some cheap eats and expensive drinks—while there are restaurants that won't break the bank, there's nowhere to get a cheap drink on Long Island, even at the dive bars.

But having a cheap weekend doesn't mean sleeping in your car and eating cold burritos (although that sounds fun too). In fact, it can be quite the opposite: many "fancy" activities are actually free.

Dress up for a night on the town and poke your head into the galleries. While museums charge admission, galleries don't, and if the gallerists don't recognize you from the *New York Post*, they realize you're probably not going to buy anything, so they'll either be snooty and ignore you or give you a friendly tour. If you happen upon a gallery during an opening night— you're in luck, because that means free wine. Hang out just long enough to people watch and get a buzz (but not so long that it's creepy).

Throughout Long Island and the Jersey Shore, adorable Main Streets lined with cafes and shops are waiting to be strolled. If you're on a budget, seek out bookstores and second-hand shops, where the price tags won't cause a heart attack.

A weekend at the beach doesn't have to be expensive, as long as you know where to go and how to spend it.

≡ *Montauk and the Hamptons*

While everybody knows the Hamptons is far from a budget destination, even small beachside communities can have hotels and restaurants with astronomical prices. But, if you know what to eat (sandwiches) and what to sacrifice (chicness), it's possible to visit without breaking the bank. And don't forget that state parks and beaches are free, so if you're out here to enjoy nature and not to be seen at the hottest restaurants, you'll do just fine.

MONTAUK | *Local Seafood Favorites*

Where Those on a Budget Should Eat

THE DOCK BAR & GRILL

482 West Lake Drive, Montauk, New York 11954 • 631.668.9778 • thedockmontauk.com

One of the only restaurants in Montauk with a significant number of menu items for under $10, The Dock is the best deal in town. Expect standard bar fare like chicken wings and jalapeno poppers, plus some fancy surprises like clams casino and fried soft shell crab. It's a local crowd here, so be nice and leave your New York City attitude at the door.

// Kids at play in the surf

Where Those on a Budget Should Stay

DAUNT'S ALBATROSS MOTEL

44 South Elmwood Avenue, Montauk, New York 11954 • 631.668.2729 • dauntsalbatross.com

One of the cheapest but definitely not the most depressing lodging options in Montauk, Daunt's Albatross is a family-run motel just one block from the beach. Rooms are clean, although dated (and not in a vintage-chic way), but if the weather's good, this cheap and cheerful motel is the perfect place to lay your head. There's even a pool for when the ocean's too cold to swim in. From $99.

AMAGANSETT, SAG HARBOR, AND THE HAMPTONS | *Low-Key and Local*

Where Those on a Budget Should Eat

SAMS ☆ *AUTHOR'S PICK*

36 Newtown Lane, East Hampton, New York 11937 • 631.324.5900 • samseasthampton.com

Even in the coldest, bleakest months of winter, Sam's is a cozy nest of warmth, laughter, and Italian comfort food. The food here is authentic Italian American, served in large portions: eggplant parm, spaghetti a la vongole, and thin crust pizza. With massive and affordable (for the Hamptons) glasses of red wine, it's hard not to become a regular here. Don't forget to order the garlic bread—it's out of this world.

ESTIA'S LITTLE KITCHEN

1615 Bridgehampton-Sag Harbor Turnpike, Sag Harbor, New York 11963 • 631.725.1045 • estias.com

One of Sag Harbor's best-kept secrets, Estia's Little Kitchen is a local favorite. It's not some gleaming Hamptons hotspot, but it's a cozy little cabin serving unpretentious food without any hype. Estia's keeps it simple, with local ingredients and modest prices. Breakfast, lunch, and dinner have a Latin flair, with dishes like chicken mole and paella. Go with a group so you can order the chili chicken nachos without spoiling your appetite.

Where Those on a Budget Should Stay

COZY COTTAGES

395 Montauk Highway, Wainscott, New York 11975 • 631.537.1160 • thecozycottages.com

In the land of $500 per night bed and breakfasts, it's hard to find something affordable. While Cozy Cottages are still expensive, they're the cheapest option you'll find in the Hamptons. The property has a hot tub and provides beach passes, umbrellas, and towels. The cottages are clean, but dated and unstylish, with linoleum floors and polyester duvets. But it's the location that counts, and Cozy Cottages is just a five-minute drive from the beach. From $165.

// BYO board games for extra fun at the beach

☰ *Shelter Island and the North Fork*

Shelter Island and the North Fork are just as expensive as the Hamptons when it comes to day-to-day vacation necessities like food and drinks. Just getting things to Shelter Island is an extra step in the process, making it so that almost nothing is cheap. But in Greenport and the North Fork, there's a year-round community of regular people who don't spend $9 on a latte.

SHELTER ISLAND AND THE NORTH FORK |
Old-School Prices

Where Those on a Budget Should Eat

THE DORY

185 North Ferry Road, Shelter Island Heights, New York 11965 • 631.749.4300

The Dory is a must-visit on Shelter Island. It's a dive bar with soul (and surprisingly good food). Request a table on the covered back patio overlooking the water and order from the menu of seafood basics and pub fare, like fish and chips or burgers.

Where Those on a Budget Should Stay

THE BLUE INN

7850 Main Road, East Marion, New York 11939 • 631.477.2800

Between Greenport and Orient on the North Fork, this adorable little motel has clean and cozy rooms. Choose from queen or double standard rooms, or upgrade to a cottage, apartment, or suite, complete with a kitchenette where you can stock up at a farm stand and cook some of your own meals. From $135.

FIRE ISLAND | *Counter-Service Cult Favorites*

Fire Island is tricky—it's so casual that it feels like it's got to be cheap, but somehow, the prices are astronomical, even though you're drinking out of a plastic cup and not wearing any shoes. It's just the price of paradise, however short-lived the season is. The key is to drink at dives and never sit down for a meal.

Where Those on a Budget Should Eat

TOWN PIZZA

317 Bay Walk, Ocean Beach, New York 11770 • 631.583.7774

Town Pizza is the only pizza place on Fire Island, serving lunch, dinner, and late-night slices every day in the summer. They do a brisk business, with a line out the door for slices. There's nothing fancy here, but you won't be disappointed with classic Neapolitan and Sicilian pies with standard toppings like mushrooms, peppers, and sausage. It's the best deal in town for those on a budget. If you're out late, don't miss out on the phenomenon of the "cold slice." Contrary to what you might think, it's not a piece of pizza pulled from the fridge, but a plain cheese slice, heated to perfection and then topped with a handful of cold shredded mozzarella. It's the ideal antidote for a belly full of booze. Call ahead to order pies for pickup.

Where Those on a Budget Should Stay

CLEGG'S

478 Bayberry Walk, Ocean Beach, New York 11770 • 631.583.9292 • cleggshotel.com

Clegg's is a simple bed and breakfast in Ocean Beach, but just a few steps from the ferry slip, the location couldn't be more convenient. The rooms are surprisingly cute for Fire Island, but basic, with no television or phones and shared bathrooms down the hall. If your budget allows, you can upgrade to a suite with a private bathroom and kitchenette. From $119.

7 BEST FREE THINGS TO DO ON LONG ISLAND

1. **THE DAN FLAVIN ART INSTITUTE** • Bridgehampton • diaart.org
   ⭐ *AUTHOR'S PICK*
2. **BAILEY ARBORETUM** • Lattingtown • baileyarboretum.org
3. **NASSAU COUNTY MUSEUM OF ART'S SCULPTURE PARK**
   • Roslyn • nassaumuseum.org
4. **BAYARD CUTTING ARBORETUM** • Oakdale • bayardcuttingarboretum.com
   (no fee for pedestrians)
5. **AMERICAN GUITAR MUSEUM** • New Hyde Park • americanguitarmuseum.com
6. **FIREBOAT FIRE FIGHTER MUSEUM** • Greenport • americasfireboat.org
7. **GRUMMAN MEMORIAL PARK** • Calverton • grummanpark.org

☰ *Greater Long Island*

Staying away from the Hamptons and Fire Island is your best bet for saving money. There's plenty to do on Greater Long Island that doesn't break the bank, like visiting a public beach, strolling through parks and gardens, or satisfying your seafood craving at a greasy roadside stand.

GREATER LONG ISLAND | *Seafood Shacks and Roadside Stands*

Where Those on a Budget Should Eat

BIGELOW'S SEAFOOD

79 North Long Beach Road, Rockville Centre, New York 11570 • 516.678.3878 • bigelows-rvc.com

This classic New England-style clam shack serves a selection of fried seafood like clams, scallops, cod, popcorn shrimp, flounder, and even smelt. Portions come with a choice of fries or coleslaw, and everything is served on a paper plate.

Where Those on a Budget Should Stay

HOTEL INDIGO

1830 West Main Street, Rt. 25, Riverhead, New York 11901 • 631.369.2200 • indigoeastend.com

Riverhead is situated at a fork in the road, where Long Island splits into the North and South Forks. It's an ideal location for somebody who wants to see the wineries of the North Fork and the beaches of the South Fork, without spending an arm and a leg to stay in a boutique Hamptons Hotel. Hotel Indigo is cute and modern, with Saturday night rates in high season for under $200, which is less than half of what you'll pay somewhere in the Hamptons. The rooms at this fairly new hotel are simple and comfortable, and there's even a pool.

☰ *The Jersey Shore*

JERSEY SHORE | *Drool-Worth Delis*

Where Those on a Budget Should Eat

FRANK'S DELI

1406 Main Street, Asbury Park, New Jersey 07712 • 732.775.6682 • franksdelinj.com

Serving classic Jersey pork rolls and overstuffed club sandwiches, Frank's Deli in Asbury Park offers a lot of bang for your buck. Open for breakfast and lunch every day, this is the place to stop in for a greasy bacon egg and cheese to counteract last night's overindulgences. Or you can get some sandwiches, soups, and salads to bring to the beach for a picnic. The luncheonette famously appeared on an episode of Anthony Bourdain's *Parts Unknown*.

Where Those on a Budget Should Stay

HOTEL TIDES

408 7th Avenue, Asbury Park, New Jersey 07712 • 732.897.7744 • thehoteltides.com

A far cry from the snazzy new hotels popping up in Asbury Park, this humble Victorian B&B is one of the best deals in town. With comfortable (but not exactly stylish) rooms that offer everything you need and no more, this hotel usually sells out far in advance of the weekend. Unlike other houses-turned-hotels in the area, Hotel Tides has a pool, a bar, and a restaurant. From $140.

TOP 4 FREE THINGS TO DO ON THE JERSEY SHORE

1. **SEA GIRT LIGHTHOUSE, SEA GIRT** • seagirtlighthouse.com
   This historic lighthouse is open for tours on Sundays, where visitors can see the living quarters, office, and tower.
2. **TWIN LIGHTS HISTORIC SITE, HIGHLANDS** • twinlightslighthouse.com
   Atlantic Highlands' twin lighthouse stands watch over Sandy Hook. On a clear day, New York City is visible in the distance.
3. **MARINE MAMMAL STRANDING CENTER, BRIGANTINE** • mmsc.org
   The sea life museum at the non-profit animal rescue center has educational displays.
4. **DISCOVERY SEASHELL MUSEUM, OCEAN CITY** • 609.398.2316
   This museum and shop sells and displays seashells from all over the world.

10

Escapes for Thrill-Seekers

How to Visit the Scariest and Weirdest Places on Long Island and the Jersey Shore

Every place has its own urban legends and fairytales. But for some reason, Long Island seems to have a disproportionate amount of ghost stories and hauntings. From shipwrecks and the Revolutionary War to the mansions of the Gilded Age and terrifying psychiatric centers of the 20th century, Long Island is full of spooky settings—including a site that inspired the hit Netflix series *Stranger Things*.

Fall is an especially fun time to visit Long Island, when corn mazes and pumpkin patches pop up in the farmlands. High-budget haunted houses come to life for a few months for those who enjoy shocking frights, but there's also a subtle spooky feeling in the air.

From elaborate mansions to psychiatric centers and laboratories, Long Island is full of spooky abandoned buildings. Many of them aren't accessible, but you might be able to get close enough to peek inside.

>> Insider Tip: For those interested in more, websites like weirdus.com, liparanormalinvestigators .com, and atlasobscura.com all feature the weirdest spots on Long Island.

MONTAUK AND THE HAMPTONS | *Abandoned Buildings and Storied Shipwrecks*

CAMP HERO ⭐ *AUTHOR'S PICK*

1898 Montauk Highway, Montauk, New York 11954 • parks.ny.gov/parks/97

Camp Hero is an abandoned former army base on Montauk that was the inspiration for the laboratory in the Netflix show *Stranger Things*. The defunct military base has a 120-foot radio tower, and the facility was supposedly a place where scientists conducted human experiments, with far-flung tales about alien abductions, psychic powers, and inter-dimensional travel. It's now a 45-acre public park.

AT SEA: SHIPWRECKS, BURIED TREASURE, AND SECRET ISLANDS

THE *SS OREGON*

The *SS Oregon* was a transatlantic ocean liner that wrecked off the coast of Long Island when it crashed into a smaller ship, the *Charles R. Morse*, in 1883. The passengers of the ocean liner were all rescued with no casualties, but the smaller ship disappeared under the waves and there were no survivors. The *Oregon* can be explored only by expert scuba divers.

THE *JOHN MILTON* SHIPWRECK

34 James Lane, East Hampton, NY 11937

In 1855, the *John Milton* ran aground during a winter storm on the rocks of Ditch Plains in Montauk. The ship was in its way home after a three-year voyage to Virginia, Peru, and San Francisco. There were no survivors, and frozen bodies of the crew that washed onshore in the days following the wreck were buried in the South End Cemetery in East Hampton.

GARDINER'S ISLAND

In the Long Island sound, off the coast of Shelter Island, is another, smaller island called Gardiner's Island. This island is, improbably, privately owned by the family for which it's named. The island is small, but valuable (in 1989, its value was estimated at $125 million), although it's never been on the market—the Gardiner family and their descendants have lived here since 1639. It's largely undeveloped, with over 1,000 acres of old-growth forest. The island is also home to the oldest surviving wooden structure in New York State, a carpenter's shed built in 1639. It's an island full of true fairy tales, with buried treasure, pirates, and priceless inheritances. While you can't visit, if you're on a boat or a jet-ski, you can get a close look at the island.

SHELTER ISLAND AND THE NORTH FORK |
Historic Homes and Mysterious Islands

WICKHAM FARMHOUSE

27320 Route 25, Cutchogue New York 11935 • 631.734.7122 • cutchoguenewsuffolkhistory.org

This tiny 1704 farmhouse is part of the Cutchogue-New Suffolk Historic Council. The historic home is open for tours, where visitors report feeling cold spots and seeing lights turn on and off.

PLUM ISLAND

Ask anybody on Long Island who has gotten a tick bite and they'll probably know about the theory involving Plum Island. Located off the coast of Long Island, Plum Island is the site of the mysterious Plum Island Animal Disease Center, part of the US Department of Agriculture. The high-security research center is owned by the US government and controlled by the Department of Homeland Security (that part is fact). But legend has it that Plum Island was where Lyme disease originated. Allegedly, Lyme was originally created by scientists trying to create the ultimate biological weapon—one that would slowly and insidiously, undetected, wreak havoc on enemies' mental and physical health. Although testing was isolated to Plum Island, conspiracy theorists believe that a few deer swam out to the island, became infected, and swam back to the mainland to spread the disease all over New England. The mystery of Plum Island has captivated the imaginations of many, providing the settings for novels, TV shows, and horror films.

>> Insider Tip: Pick up a copy of *Plum Island* by Nelson DeMille.

While you can't actually visit Plum Island, the best way to catch a glimpse of the creepy buildings is by riding the Cross-Sound Ferry from Orient Point on the North Fork of Long Island to New London, Connecticut. If you have your own boat, you can take a day trip out—just don't get too close.

GREATER LONG ISLAND | *Houses with History*

WARDENCLYFFE LABORATORY AND TOWER, SHOREHAM

56 New York-25A, Shoreham, New York 11786 • teslasciencecenter.org/wardenclyffe/

Wardenclyffe is the site of Nikola Tesla's turn-of-the-century Long Island Laboratory. Backed by J. P. Morgan, Tesla built an 187-foot-tall radio tower in order to experiment with wireless telegraphy. Only a few years later, the project ran out of money and the property was seized and turned over to a manufacturer until 1987. When it looked as if the site would finally be demolished in 2013, a nonprofit group raised enough money to buy the grounds and erect a statue of Tesla. The site is still hazardous and undergoing industrial cleanup, but you can see the statue and the remains of the tower from the road.

KINGS PARK PSYCHIATRIC CENTER, KINGS PARK

W 4th Street, Kings Park, New York 11754

This abandoned psychiatric center even looks creepy—a brick building, with broken windows and overgrown plants. Opened in the late 1800s, KPPC had almost 10,000 patients at its peak in the 1950s before it was closed for good in the 1990s. It's illegal to enter the building or the grounds, but people have reportedly heard screams coming from the building.

MOUNT MISERY AND SWEET HOLLOW ROAD

Sweet Hollow Road, Melville, New York 11747 • 631.854.4423

Near Huntington, New York, Mount Misery (the highest peak on Long Island at 400 feet above sea level) and Sweet Hollow Road are the settings for spooky stories that go back centuries. There are a few legends surrounding how Mount Misery got its name. In the time of the early farming communities of the 18th century, this was unfarmable, rocky land that often broke the wheels on wagons, making traveling through it miserable. There were stories of evil spirits, strange lights, and animal sacrifices during those early days. Sweet Hollow Road, which runs near Mount Misery, is also full of strange stories, like a woman in white who appears in the middle of the street, running cars off the road. In some stories, she's the ghost of a woman who was killed while changing a tire; in others she's the ghost of a woman from a nearby insane asylum who set her room on fire and burned down the building with all the patients still inside. You can explore the creepy woods of Mount Misery and drive on Sweet Hollow Road by visiting West Hills County Park.

HALLOWEEN ON LONG ISLAND

From pick-your-own apple farms to terrifying haunted houses, Long Island has lots of spooky activities in the fall. Get lost in a corn maze and drink some apple cider.

HARBES FAMILY FARM PUMPKIN PATCH • harbesfamilyfarm.com

Pick your own pumpkins at this family-friendly farm.

RISE OF THE JACKOLANTERNS FESTIVAL ⭐ *AUTHOR'S PICK* • therise.org

This brilliant and impressive display of jack-o-lanterns takes place at Old Westbury Gardens.

HANK'S PUMPKINTOWN • hankspumpkintown.com

Visit for pumpkins, apple cider doughnuts, and corn mazes—everything you need for a wholesome fall weekend.

HORSEABILITY'S HAUNTED HAY BARN • horseability.org/hauntedhaybarn

This seasonal haunted house in a barn benefits equine facilitated programs.

DARKNESS RISING • darknessrising.org

Darkness Rising is a seasonal haunted house that benefits local nonprofits.

BAYVILLE SCREAM PARK • bayvillescreampark.com

Every fall, Bayville Adventure Park turns into a terrifying haunted theme park.

GATEWAY'S HAUNTED PLAYHOUSE • gatewayshauntedplayhouse.com

This haunted theater attraction benefits the Performing Arts Center of Suffolk County.

DEEPWELL'S HAUNTED MANSION • deepwellshauntedmansion.com

Every October, this possibly haunted history farm house opens its doors for a scary haunted house.

DARKSIDE HAUNTED HOUSE • darksideproductions.com

With indoor and outdoor attractions, this is one of the biggest and scariest haunted houses on Long Island.

RESTLESS SOULS HAUNTED HOUSE • restlesssoulsli.com

You get four separated haunted attractions for the price of one at this haunted house benefitting local nonprofits.

CHAMBER OF HORRORS • chamberofhorrorsny.com

Long Island's largest haunted attraction ups the ante with "full contact" and "kill the lights" nights.

MARY'S GRAVE AND SHEP JONES ROAD

Harbor Road, Stony Brook, New York 11790

According to legend, there is an unmarked grave in the Avalon Preserve. Mary was a young woman who was murdered (there are various stories on how and why) and then buried on property that is now part of the Avalon Preserve. According to stories, Shep Jones Road, near the murder site, will play tricks with your mind, starting out as a paved road and then turning into a windy, bumpy dirt path.

LAKE RONKONKOMA

Ronkonkoma, New York

Local lore says that a Native American princess, banned from marrying her lover, rowed out into the middle of the lake and drowned herself in rebellion. Her ghost now roams the lake, taking the life of one young man every year. The lake has indeed seen many drowned bodies, and it is supposedly connected to the bay and the ocean via underground tunnels, making it so the victims are never found.

THE CHANDLER ESTATE

Mount Sinai, New York 11766

Also known as "Satan's Trails," the Chandler estate was once a snazzy resort that was reportedly visited by Marilyn Monroe. The resort was eventually turned into an apartment complex that burned down, and there have been reports of Satanic activity on the property.

KING ZOG'S KNOLLWOOD ESTATE

Jericho, Oyster Bay Road, East Norwich, New York 11732

The ruins of this Syosset estate once belonged to King Zog of Albania, a dictator who fled from his country and purchased the estate from a Wall Street financier with a bag full of gold and rubies (as the story goes) in 1951. The king never actually lived here, but the estate was a safe place for his family. The estate was sold a few years later, and the new owner eventually demolished it in 1959. It's now part of the Muttontown Preserve, but the ruins are reportedly the site of satanic rituals—a human skeleton was found near the ruins in 2001.

SAGTIKOS MANOR

677 Montauk Highway, Bay Shore, New York 11706 • sagtikosmanor.org

The Sagtikos Manor Historical Society provides tours of this forty-two-room estate where George Washington once spent the night in 1790. The house was the site of a Revolutionary War skirmish, and the ghosts of these soldiers are thought to haunt the house.

// Foggy Georgica Pond

AMITYVILLE HORROR HOUSE ⭐ *AUTHOR'S PICK*

The white Dutch Colonial house at 112 Ocean Avenue in Amityville is the house that spawned an entire horror franchise. It was in this house, in 1974, that Ronald DeFeo Jr. killed his wife and five children. In 1975, Kathy and George Lutz moved into the house—and this is where the story gets weird. The Lutz family reported being terrorized by paranormal spirits, witnessing phantom sounds and odors, doors and windows slamming with no provocation, an infestation of flies in the dead of winter, and green slime oozing from the walls. After a month in the house, the family left without any of their belongings. What happened on their last night in the house is still a mystery; it's so frightening that they refused to talk about it. The true story became a book that became a book series that became the basis for over 15 horror films. Nowadays, you can drive past the house, but there's not much to see.

Where Thrill Seekers Should Eat

COUNTRY HOUSE RESTAURANT

1175 NorthCountry Road, Stony Brook, New York 11790 • countryhouserestaurant.com

This homey restaurant inside a converted house has a resident ghost. According to the story, a young woman was alone in the house when British troops took over the home during the revolutionary war. She let them in, but when they left, the townspeople decided she was a spy and murdered her, burying her on the property. She has been known to haunt the kitchen, where you can sometimes hear her crying.

KATIE'S

45 West Main Street, Smithtown, New York 11787 • katiesofsmithtown.com

The building that holds this Smithtown, New York bar was built on the site of a hospital that burned down in 1909. Katie's has been open since 2000 (although the building dates back to the 1920s), and people have experienced slamming doors, phantom footsteps, and shadowy figures dressed in old-timey clothing. This haunted bar is still in business, with live music every Tuesday night.

Where Thrill Seekers Should Stay

MONTAUK MANOR

236 Edgemere Street, Montauk, New York 11954 • 631.668.4400 • montaukmanor.com

In the 1920s, there was a real estate developer with a plan to turn Montauk into the Miami of the north. The first step in that plan was to build Montauk Manor, an enormous Biltmore-esque hotel on 12 acres that is unmissable in Montauk—perched on a hill, you can see it from all over town. After the stock market crash of 1929, the hotel fell into disrepair, but it has since been restored. Visitors claim hearing eerie drumbeats and seeing a figure of a man in the shadows on the hotel's fourth floor. From $144.

Perfect Weekend Itineraries by Destination

How to Spend a Weekend in Montauk

Surfers and Scenesters

Montauk is, quite possibly, the coolest beach town in the country. Located on the very end of Long Island, this small community of fishermen and surfers braves extreme winters in order to live in a place that's a little slice of paradise for 4 months out of the year. When the weather warms up, Montauk is the place to see and be seen for New Yorkers.

This low-key community attracts a wealthy crowd of celebrities and pseudo-celebrities to legendary nightlife spots like the Surf Lodge. Like many resort communities, there's sometimes animosity between the "summer people" and the year-round folks, so it's important to be respectful when you're visiting: don't leave any trash on the beach, don't drive like a maniac, and don't turn your partying into somebody else's problem.

// Oars on display at Ruschmeyer's

From dive bars to bougie seaside hotels, almost everything in Montauk is stylish, even if it's trying hard not to be. There's something sublime about this place that almost feels like a little slice of California in New York: laid-back vibes, overcast skies, epic waves, and a natural beauty that's unlike the rest of the East Coast, with scrubby pine trees and windswept beaches backed by sandy cliffs. It's really hard not to like it here. Come for a weekend and you'll start planning your next trip back before you even leave.

FRIDAY

Leave New York City on a 4 p.m. train, which will get you to Montauk in time for dinner. Go big tonight with dinner at **The Crow's Nest**, one of the choicest and best dining experiences in town. The hotel and restaurant have an outdoor dining area strewn with lanterns and a menu that focuses on local ingredients like fluke and scallops. Keep your eyes peeled for celebs and make a reservation a few weeks in advance. After dinner, if there's not a concert going on, visit the **Surf Lodge** for a nightcap. The buzzy bar and hotel are packed on weekends, but if you can get in and find a place to hang out, the vibe is really fun.

SATURDAY

In the morning, work off last night's indulgences with a yoga class at **B Studios**. Get a post-yoga smoothie next door at **Joni's** before heading to the beach a few blocks from town. Beach access is public, but you can't park there without a permit. Lay out, watch surfers, or go for a long walk. If it's too cold or too rough to swim, walk over to **Montauk Beach House** to have cocktails by the pool.

Have a lobster roll for lunch at **Hooked**, a fast-casual seafood joint that elevates simple beachy dining with locally sourced ingredients and a de-emphasis on fried things. There's even a kale salad on the menu.

If you're feeling ambitious, visit the lighthouse at **Montauk Point State Park**, on the very eastern tip of Long Island. The red lighthouse on a rocky beach with a blue-sky background is the perfect photo op. And if you climb up to the top, you can see all the way to Block Island on a clear day.

Back in town, spend the afternoon sampling Montauk's finest at **Montauk Brewing Company**. Their simply designed cans have taken over the party scene—there's a 100 percent chance of spotting a Montauk ale at any backyard barbecue east of New York City. Sample a flight or choose your favorite and sit outside.

When the sun starts to get low in the sky, make your way to **Montauket**, a low-key semi-divey bar on the water with the best view of the sunset. Grab a beer or a cocktail before heading out the back door onto the patio to snag a seat for the show—and see if you can resist the urge to take a photograph (you can't, it's beautiful).

After the sun has set, it's time for a night of rowdy fun. First, for dinner at **Ruschmeyer's**, a summer-camp chic hotel, bar, and restaurant that's full of nostalgia and yummy drinks. Order a pizza or one of the fresh seafood entrees before getting the party started with a pitcher of watermelon margaritas. After dinner, it's time for lawn games, s'mores, and drinks on the lawn. End the night the way the locals do, with a mudslide or a $1 beer down by the docks at **Liar's**, one of the only bars in town that's open late.

SUNDAY

Sunday is for being lazy. After a plate of pancakes and a hangover-curing greasy breakfast at **John's Pancake House**, visit **Ditch Plains** beach in the morning to watch the surfers (or if you're feeling ambitious—schedule a lesson!) and walk to **Shadmoor State Park** to see the drip castle-esque sand bluffs. While away the afternoon at **Montauk Beach House**, which is a hip hotel/bar with a happening pool scene and usually some fashionable pop-up boutiques and partnerships. If it's not beach weather, book a spa appointment at **Gurney's Montauk Resort & Saltwater Spa** and show up early to swim in the indoor saltwater pool that's open year-round.

Watch one last sunset during an early dinner at **Duryea's Lobster Deck**, a seafood restaurant specializing in lobster with a raw bar. Snag a table out on the dock for the best views. After dinner, it's time to catch a ride back to the city.

≡ *How to Spend a Weekend in Amagansett, Sag Harbor, and East Hampton*

The Perfect Hamptons Weekend

"The Hamptons" has reached an almost mythical status in pop culture. Nearly everyone has heard of this playground of the super wealthy, and even if they've never set foot here, they've probably seen it on gossip websites, reality TV, and design magazines.

The Hamptons officially refers to East Hampton, Bridgehampton, Southampton, and Westhampton, but there are a lot of micro-communities located between these towns that fall under the umbrella too: Wainscott, Watermill, Sagaponack, Noyack, North Haven, Springs, Napeague, and Georgica to name a few. Unlike these "in between" communities, Amagansett and Sag Harbor are towns in their own right, and although they'll both vehemently deny they are part of the Hamptons, they are, whether they like that distinction or not.

East Hampton, Amagansett, and Sag Harbor are the farthest east Hamptons. While

// Dogs are allowed on Hamptons beaches before 10 a.m. and after 6 p.m. in the summer

East Hampton is probably the most well-known, Sag Harbor has a bustling main street area with a robust year-round community. Amagansett is a quiet, artsy celebrity enclave with just one sleepy street through town. Here's how to make the most of your time on a weekend visit to the Hamptons' eastern towns.

FRIDAY

Base yourself in **East Hampton** for the weekend for easy access to both Sag Harbor and Amagansett. Arriving on Friday evening, try to get a walk-in table outside at **EMP Summer House**, the summer pop up restaurant from famed Eleven Madison Park, one of the best restaurants in the world. They're strict about reservations, but the outdoor seating is first-come first-served with a much more "affordable" menu of burgers, hot dogs, and lobster rolls.

If that doesn't work out, make the quick jaunt to **Amagansett** (you're already halfway there) for dinner at **Wölffer Kitchen**, a vineyard-to-table restaurant by the creators of Wölffer Estate

Wines. It's chic but casual, with local ingredients in a comfortable setting. There aren't many options in the way of nightlife in East Hampton, but if you'd like an after-dinner drink, visit **Moby's** on East Hampton Point for a cocktail. This waterside restaurant and bar occasionally has live music.

SATURDAY

During the summer, you'll want to spend as much time as you can at the **beach**. After grabbing a coffee and a quick breakfast at **Goldberg's Famous Bagels** in East Hampton, it's time to hit the beach. Both Amagansett and East Hampton have public beaches for residents, so choose whichever one is the most convenient for you. If you have a rental, they might have a resident parking pass you can use. If not, hop on a bike or hotel shuttle to take you to the ocean.

Make sure to bring everything you'll need if you're at a beach without facilities: towels, umbrella, water, drinks, sunscreen, and something to eat. You can stop at a deli in town like **Villa Italian Specialties** to pick up some sandwiches, or you can eat something at one of the beachside snack bars—there's one at **Atlantic Beach**, and you might find a food truck parked at some of the other beaches in town. Swim, sunbathe, read a book, bodysurf, or go for a long walk along the beach, looking at the mansions, trying to guess which famous person lives there.

When you've had your fill of sun, make an afternoon visit to **The LongHouse Reserve**. This 16-acre sculpture garden is a bizarre dreamland of sculptures by artists as different as Willem de Kooning and Yoko Ono. It's one the Hamptons' best-kept secrets—it's rarely crowded, and the lush grounds are full of secret sculptures. With the map in hand, it's almost like a high-end scavenger hunt.

Before the sun goes down, make your way to **Sag Harbor** for a sunset drink. You can hang out at the bar at the stylish **Baron's Cove** or choose from a handful of drinking and dining establishments to have a drink and an appetizer—but don't spoil your dinner! After the sun goes down, take a stroll around Sag Harbor's main drag, window-shopping and popping into bookstores and galleries that stay open late on Saturday nights in the summer. If you're lucky, you might stumble upon an opening.

When you're ready for dinner, **Sag Pizza** is probably the best pizza in the Hamptons—wood-fired pizza with the perfect amount of char and a pile of high-quality local ingredients. Order a clam pie and a margarita, and get your veggies in with an arugula salad.

After dinner, it's time to check out one of Sag Harbor's classic watering holes: **The American Hotel**. This iconic bar has played host to writers and artists throughout the years, and you never know who you'll see belly up to the bar, swapping stories with old-timers about the way things used to be out here.

If you have the energy for a night out, head to **Amagansett** for the original nightlife spot in the area, the **Stephen Talkhouse**. This huge indoor/outdoor bar and music venue is always crowded, even if there's not a concert. Listen to music, do a little dancing, or catch some fresh air in the backyard before calling it a night.

SUNDAY

You've had your day at the ocean, so now it's time to check out the bay side of Long Island. Pick up a coffee or a juice and a light breakfast at **Jack's** in Amagansett before driving east toward **Montauk**. Your destination is the **Napeague Walking Dunes**, part of Hither Hills State Park, between Amagansett and Montauk. From Highway 27, take a left on Napeaugue Harbor Road and park on the shoulder at the end. There are trails right off the road that take you through the walking dunes, sandy hills filled with oak and pine trees. It's somewhat of an otherworldly landscape, and very different from the ocean beach that's less than a mile away. Spend about an hour getting lost in the Dunes, and then make your way back to the car. On the way back to Amagansett, pull over for lunch at the **Clam Bar**, an institution in this part of Long Island, serving fried clams and clam chowder. It's a seasonal restaurant, with outdoor seating—grab a table with an umbrella.

For those who want something a little more active, **Springs General Store** has kayaks for rent, where you can drop a boat in the water behind the store and explore the nooks and crannies of **Accabonac Harbor**. If you're feeling lazy, the beach is calling. Get a change of scenery from yesterday by choosing a different beach and going for one last swim in the ocean.

// Farm fresh flowers for sale at Balsam Farms

Before heading home, fuel up with a hearty meal of tacos, nachos, or a burrito at **La Fondita**, a counter-service restaurant in a chic repurposed garage with great decor. Don't skip dessert—the Mexican wedding cookies will make a great snack for the drive home.

How to Spend a Weekend in Bridgehampton and Southampton

A Luxurious Weekend

Southampton might be the fanciest Hampton of them all. Located closer to the city than East Hampton and Montauk (but still east of the Shinnecock Canal—the great divider), this town is full of historic estates and mansions. While the town of **Bridgehampton** is on Highway 27, Southampton's downtown is not, giving it a feeling of a Main Street in small town America—only Guccified. Southampton is 15 minutes from Bridgehampton and 30 minutes from Westhampton.

FRIDAY

You've had a big week, and Friday is a time to treat yourself. After making the trip out to Bridgehampton from the city, splurge on a fancy dinner. The Hamptons has fancy dinners in spades, but **Pierre's** is a classic choice, an old-school restaurant that's been around for decades, serving quintessential French dishes 365 days per year. Start with oysters before moving on to steak frites or lobster fricassee, and pair your dinner with something special from the wine list.

SATURDAY

In the morning, prepare for your day at the beach by picking up sandwiches from **Breadzilla**, a popular Bridgehampton deli with a menu full of interesting sandwich combos. Substitutions are frowned upon, but even picky eaters can find something to munch on here, with simple items like grilled cheese alongside the spicy tuna sandwich. Everything here comes on homemade bread, and there are homemade pastries, too.

At **Sagg Main Beach**, you can pay to park even if you're not a resident, and there are showers and bathrooms you can use to change and rinse off. The beach is gorgeous and rarely crowded, with a wide dun-back strip of sand that slopes into the ocean. Spend as much time as you want here, relaxing, playing games, swimming, or going for a walk along the beach. In the afternoon, when you feel you've had enough, freshen up and make your way to **Madoo Conservancy**, an artist's home and garden that's now open to the public on Saturday afternoons to walk around and explore. The gardens are a mix of styles, with Japanese pagodas alongside modern sculptures.

After your stroll through the gardens, it's time for a bit of wine tasting. Your first stop is **Channing Daughters**, a low-key and unpretentious winery with a huge selection of rosé. Taste them all and pick your favorite to take home as a souvenir. Next, get a table at **Wölffer Estate** and settle in for a leisurely afternoon. You can order the cheese plate and a flight of wines as you sit out on the back patio, admiring the sunset over the vines.

After the sun sets, it's time to visit the town of Southampton. Take a stroll along main street to do some window shopping (or actual shopping—many of the stores are open late on Saturday nights) at designer showrooms and art galleries.

For dinner, get a table at **Jue Lan Club**, an over-the-top fancy-Chinese restaurant serving dim sum and Hamptonified versions of your favorite takeout dishes, like lobster fried rice. The later the better here, as the restaurant turns into a bit of a scene after dinner, and you can hang around drinking cocktails in this super-chic nightclub.

SUNDAY

In Bridgehampton, **Candy Kitchen** is the place to go for Sunday brunch. Dine on eggs, bacon, and pancakes at this retro-chic greasy spoon diner that's been serving milkshakes for over 90 years.

After you've gotten your fill, it's time to visit one of Bridgehampton's coolest free museums—the **Dan Flavin institute**. This permanent art installation in a firehouse uses neon to create a trippy sensory experience.

Continue your day of art at the **Parrish Art Museum**, a world-class museum in a modern barn-esque space that has a huge range of multimedia exhibits. Even if you don't find the art interesting, the building itself is exceptional.

Spend the afternoon at Southampton's **Flying Point Beach**. This windswept strip of sand is one of the most popular beaches in the area, but it's still easy to find a quiet spot to while away the last daylight hours of the weekend.

For Sunday dinner, stop into **Little Red**, an American bistro with burgers, flatbreads, and crab cakes to fill you up for the trip home.

☰ How to Spend a Weekend on Shelter Island

Enjoy the Simple Life

People like to say that Shelter Island is what the Hamptons were like 50 years ago. In some cases, that may be true. There are still some humble cottages here, many that cost under $1 million, with overgrown hedges, basketball hoops over the garage, and not a pool in sight. But that's not to say Shelter Island isn't stylish. Driving around, you'll see Victorian homes painted a kaleidoscopic rainbow of colors and modern creations that look like pre-fab houses that were put together without the instructions.

The pace of life on Shelter Island is significantly slower (some may even call it "boring"),

// Montauk's iconic red-and-white lighthouse is an excellent place to take photographs

// Tiny farmstands can be found all over Shelter Island

and with no ocean around, it's useful to have a boat (or at least a kayak) at your disposal to enjoy the water. Many of the hotels and resorts will have all sorts of recreational water toys for guests to rent, and rental houses usually come with a kayak or stand up paddleboard, especially if they're on the water.

But even if you're not an avid boater, life is good here. With a charming and tiny downtown area, super-chic hotels worthy of a romantic getaway, and one of the most stylish places to party in all of Long Island, Shelter Island is worth a visit. Add in a nationally recognized restaurant, surprisingly good coffee, and a natural setting that feels worlds away from New York City, and you've got the makings of a perfect place to spend a weekend.

FRIDAY

After taking the ferry over from **Greenport**, settle in for a casual night in town. Depending on what time of day you arrive, there are a few dining options. **The Dory** is usually open late, serving seafood standards in a charming old-school setting directly on the water. It's the kind of place to go for fried seafood and a strong Bloody Mary, but the food is surprisingly good and the local vibes make for fun people-watching. You might even make a few new friends. After dinner, stay on for a few drinks, or if you're looking for something a bit fancier, check out the bar at **The Chequit**, the "grande dame" of Shelter Island hotels and one of the chicest places to stay on the island.

SATURDAY

Start your weekend the way Shelter Island regulars do: With coffee and a french pastry at **Marie Eiffel's**. The line is long, and it can be extremely hectic from 9–11 a.m. on summer Saturdays, but it's the best place in town for a latte or a cappuccino and the pastries are melt-in-your-mouth delicious. There's a lovely deck out back where you can enjoy your coffee with a view of the water, and if you like something a little heartier for breakfast, they have sandwiches and wraps too.

After breakfast, rent a bike from **Piccozzi Fuel & Bike Shop** and pedal over to **Sylvester Manor**, a historic estate that has been turned into a nonprofit educational farm. Self-guided tours are available on Saturdays in the summer, where you can walk around the grounds and learn about the history of the house and farm. Keep an eye on the calendar for special events like farm-to-table dinners, concerts, and workshops.

Learning stuff can certainly work up an appetite, so the next stop is the **Shelter Island Farmers' Market**. Held each Saturday at the **Havens House Museum**, the market is a chance to taste some local foods, pick up some foodie souvenirs, and possibly plan a beach picnic.

Head a few doors down to **Elli's Country Store** to pick up anything you might have missed (don't forget the beer and rosé) at the farmers market and hop back on your bike for a ride to **Shell Beach**.

Since Shelter Island is located in a bay, the beaches here are not the sweeping sandy dunes with crashing waves that you'll find on the southern coast of Long Island. Instead, these beaches are rocky, yet calm. Shell Beach is located on a narrow spit of land in a sheltered bay, making this water a bit warmer and a bit calmer than its Hamptons counterparts. Relatively uncrowded, Shell Beach is the kind of place you'd want to spend an afternoon, reading, eating, and splashing around. If you happen to make a friend who has a boat, it's even better.

When you've had your fill of sand and sun, head back home to freshen up for the night. One of the best options for dinner on Shelter Island is **Salt**, serving elevated seafood classics and sushi in a marina setting. The decor is chic and nautical-themed, the wait staff are hip and friendly, and the food is delectable (although a bit on the pricey side). Start with a sushi appetizer and opt for the fresh "dock to table" entree.

After dinner, drink a nightcap next door at the quirky boat-turned-bar **The Shipwreck**, where you can get unpretentious drinks and listen to live music.

SUNDAY

Sunday morning deserves more than just a pastry for breakfast, so fill up on huevos rancheros at **Stars Cafe** to fuel up for a hike in **Mashomack Preserve**. The preserve has a few different choices for loop hikes, depending on your energy levels. Take it easy with a 1.5-mile loop, or challenge yourself with the 10-mile loop.

Once you've gotten your workout in, settle in for the afternoon at **Sunset Beach**, where you can lounge on the sand, go swimming, and indulge in fruity drinks and chilled wine at the excellent rooftop restaurant. When the sun gets low in the sky, Sunset Beach is where, unsurprisingly, you'll find the best place on the island to watch the sunset.

It's hard to leave this place, so stay until the evening and catch the final train home from Greenport.

☰ *How to Spend a Weekend on the North Fork*

A Foodie Feast

Long Island's North Fork fancies itself the "anti-Hamptons"—a place without pretension, where laid-back locals work hard to preserve the natural beauty of their surroundings while living a farm-to-table lifestyle.

It's all a bit of wishful thinking, however. Sure, there's no Prada store here (yet) but you'll find that New York City's artistic elite have infiltrated this part of Long Island, opening restaurants and hotels that wouldn't be out of place on the South Fork. That's not to say it's not peaceful and idyllic here—it is, with wineries, rocky beaches, and fresh seafood at every restaurant. Greenport is the hub of the North Fork, with boutique hotels and plenty of thoughtful restaurants with creative menus. From Greenport, you can easily explore the rest of the area in a relaxed weekend itinerary.

// With two streets, Greenport is one of the more happening towns on the East End

FRIDAY

Taking the bus or train from New York, you'll arrive in **Greenport** on Friday just in time for dinner. Although there's a lot to explore on the North Fork, Greenport makes an excellent base for wineries, farms, and the nearby town of Orient.

Get dinner at **1943**, an upscale pizza joint that's just as good (if not better) than Roberta's and Motorino's of New York City. It's located in a courtyard that's the hippest little corner of Greenport, with a hotel, boutique, and wine bar that are all worth exploring before or after dinner. Order a clam pie and a salad made with farm fresh ingredients, and then head next door to **American Beech** for a nightcap or two.

SATURDAY

There's a lot of ground to cover today. Rent bicycles or drive yourself to the nearby town of **Orient** for coffee and cookies at the Orient country store. Pick up some cookies to go, because once you've had one, you'll never stop wanting them. Cruise around town a bit, checking out the Victorian homes and **Orient Beach State Park** before heading back to Greenport for lunch. Serving the best oysters on Long Island (and possibly the state), **Little Creek Oyster Company** is located in a tiny bait shack in a parking lot by the docks. It's hard to find, but on summer afternoons it's easy to spot by the crowds of patrons dining at picnic tables outside. The menu here is really simple: raw oysters, raw clams, and the best clam chowder you've ever had: brothy and flavorful, with thinly sliced firm potatoes and not an ounce of gloppiness. Order a dozen oysters (or two or three dozen) and wash it all down with a local Greenport Harbor Ale. If raw seafood isn't your thing (condolences), you can get some killer tacos in town at **Lucharito**, a hipster Mexican restaurant with excellent food. Greenport is an increasingly stylish destination, with snazzy boutiques popping up all over town. Go window shopping for antiques at **Beall & Bell**, browse the gallery at **VSOP Art + Design**, and go hunting for vintage treasures at **The Times**.

Make your way east for the five-course tasting menu at **The North Fork Table & Inn** (reservations are essential). Dinner here is an unforgettable journey for your taste buds, with creative concoctions made with local, farm-fresh ingredients. In the height of summer, you'll find local fluke, corn, and tomatoes arranged into complex and utterly delicious dishes.

After dinner, check out the **Soundview Hotel**. Even if you're not staying there, the cocktail bar at least is worth a visit, with a bar that feels like a hipster country club. It's the perfect place for a nightcap, especially on a warm night, when the moon is reflected off the Long Island Sound and you can hear the waves lapping at the shore.

SUNDAY

Sunday is a day of leisure, and that means wine. The first grape vines were planted by the Hargrave family in 1973, and since then, the North Fork has emerged as the premier wine destination on the East Coast. The reds out here aren't too robust, but they've perfected the art of the rosé (hey, this is the land of summer, after all). The oldest vineyard (once owned by the Hargraves) is **Castello di Borghese**, which should be your first stop on the tour, for a primer course on North Fork wine culture. From there, make your way back to Greenport along Main Road from **Cutchogue** to **Southold**, stopping at whatever winery strikes your fancy. Many of them have tasting rooms with light bites, or a food truck parked outside.

Back in Greenport, have a final dinner at **Barba Bianca**, a seasonal dockside restaurant serving authentic Italian seafood. The setting is unbeatable and the flavors are impeccable—it's the perfect meal to prepare you for the ride home.

☰ *How to Spend a Weekend on Fire Island*

Quintessential Summer Vibes

Fire Island is a somewhat improbable place, and unless you've been here, it's hard to wrap your head around the idea of what might be America's most perfect summer destination. Fire Island is a barrier island on Long Island's south shore, between Long Beach and the Hamptons. The island is only 31 miles long and less than a quarter-mile wide at its widest point—it's almost all sand, with an elevation of just 3 feet above sea level. It's a delicate and beautiful place, with only 200 year-round residents, surreal sand forests, party-all-night LGBTQ clubs, fried seafood shacks, a private preppy enclave of beach mansions, and the tallest lighthouse on the island (that's reportedly haunted).

It's a bit tricky to get to Fire Island, and there are barely any hotels, making this somewhat of a hard nut to crack if you're visiting for the first time. The best way to experience Fire Island is with a local—renting a room from somebody with a house there, or visiting with friends who grew up going there.

The most wonderful thing about Fire Island is that there are no cars—everyone uses bikes, wagons, or their own two feet to walk around these tiny towns, connected by sidewalks and wooden boardwalks. Even though it's such a small place, its inaccessibility makes it impossible to see everything in just one weekend. But you can try.

// Fire Island's pristine beaches are unrivaled on the East Coast

FRIDAY

Taking the ferry to **Fire Island** can be a bit confusing—different ferry companies in different towns on the mainland take you to different parts of the island, so you have to know where you're going before you get there—there's not just one ferry dock that takes you across the bay.

Ocean Beach is the biggest town with the most tourism infrastructure, so it makes the most sense to base yourself there for the weekend. To get to Ocean Beach, take the ferry from Bayshore. You can leave your car in the parking lot (for a fee) or take the train. There a strict baggage restrictions and no bikes allowed, so plan accordingly and bring your groceries in canvas totes—no grocery bags are allowed on the boat either.

Once you've settled in for the night, take a walk to get the lay of the land. Ocean Beach is the hub of Fire Island, but it's fun to explore the quieter communities to the west. Take a long walk through Atlantique and Fair Harbor for dinner at **Le Dock**, one of the only fine-dining experiences to be had on the island. This seafood-focused restaurant on the bay has dishes like steamed mussels and steak, along with wine and cocktails. On your walk back home, stop by **the Shack** in Atlantique to see what's going on for the night. If the vibe is right, settle in for a nightcap before walking the rest of the way back to your accommodation in Ocean Beach.

SATURDAY

Fire Island has one of the most beautiful beaches in the country, and that's why you've come here. Get coffee and a pastry at **Rachel's Bakery** before setting up camp on the white sand beach at **Ocean Bay Park**. Laze away the morning, but pack up your valuables and throw on a coverup for a long walk to lunch in Cherry Grove.

You can walk along the beach or along the sidewalks and wooden boardwalks, winding your way past Point o'Woods, the private preppy enclave of summer homes. At **Sunken Forest**, there's a wooden boardwalk that takes you on a short loop through the surreal landscape of trees—a rare holly forest set between two dunes.

Beyond the Sunken Forest is **Cherry Grove**, about an hour's walk from Ocean Beach and an ideal place to stop for lunch. Cherry Grove is one of America's oldest gay communities, with a thriving arts scene. Check out flyers to see about any events in this tiny town, and if anything piques your interest, make a note to come back after dinner—you can always call a water taxi.

Sit down for lunch at the **Sand Castle**, one of the only beachfront restaurants on Fire Island with menu options besides fried fish. The offerings here are sophisticated, with fresh seafood and salads, along with craft cocktails (hey, you're on vacation and there are no cars to drive, so why not?). Stay as long as you'd like, and if you worked up a sweat on the walk over, go for a dip in the ocean.

The next stop on your long walk is the **Pines**, about 30 minutes past Cherry Grove. Also a trendy LGBTQ destination, the Pines has absolutely stunning homes. The theme here seems to be beachy modern, with architectural masterpieces somehow blending in perfectly with the natural surroundings and taking up a very small footprint. It is a design dreamland here. Have a drink at one of the bars at the marina while you wait for the water taxi back to Ocean Beach.

With two of the island's more sophisticated meals under your belt, it's time to take things down a notch with some good old-fashioned fried seafood, served on a paper plate. Grab a table at **Island Mermaid**, a local favorite bar and restaurant with oysters, fried fish, and some American pub grub.

After dinner, it's time to party, which means bar hopping between places that are literally steps apart. If you're not feeling the vibe at one bar, try the one next door. There are only a handful to choose from, but you'll find something that suits your mood.

If you get a case of the munchies, you can end your night the way everybody else does— with a slice at **Town Pizza** before bed.

SUNDAY

With all of yesterday's exercise behind you, it's time to chill on Sunday. Sleep in, hang out at the beach, and have a late lunch at **Island Mermaid** before catching the ferry back to the mainland. You'll see a little bit of everything on the menu here, with burgers, seafood, and salads alongside fancier items like seafood linguine, lobster, and tuna tataki. The restaurant's right by the ferry, so you can stay here until you see the boat pull in, savoring every last second of the weekend.

How to Spend a Weekend on Greater Long Island

A Historic Tour

If you've only visited eastern Long Island and the beaches, you'd be forgiven for thinking that the rest of Long Island is suburbia. There's not much to see from the window of the LIRR or on the side of the Long Island expressway. But once you get off the main roads and start exploring, you'll find Gatsby-esque mansions, lush gardens and parks, WASPy-glam north shore towns, and even some hidden oddities.

Greater Long Island is best for those with an imagination: somebody who can tour the historic Gold Coast estates and get a sense of what they were like at its height in the 1920s. There's a sense of mystery here, and those who will have the most fun exploring will be curious and intrepid.

There's a fair share of suburbia here too—not every town on Long Island can be worth a weekend, but if you have a car at your disposal, you'll be able to weave around the island, seeing the best of both coasts and everything in between.

FRIDAY

Base yourself in **Huntington** for the weekend, about halfway down the island on the North Shore. It's one of the bigger towns on Long Island, but it's not without charm—there are plenty of cute restaurants, and Huntington makes it easy to access the historic homes and nature preserves of the Gold Coast.

Arrive in time for dinner and head to **Swallow**, a buzzy downtown restaurant serving cocktails and small plates. Order dishes like burrata, calamari, grilled octopus, and charred beets while you sip on a cocktail or a local beer.

SATURDAY

After a coffee and a quick breakfast in the morning, hop in a car for a day of discovery. The first stop is Oyster Bay's **Planting Fields Arboretum**, over 400 acres of formal gardens, greenhouses, meadows, and forests. Spend as much time as you want walking around and exploring the site. In the height of summer, the gardens are in full bloom, but it's worth a visit in other seasons too.

When you've had your fill, it's time for a history lesson at Theodore Roosevelt's summer home—**Sagamore Hill National Historic Site**. The "summer White House," as it was once called, is full of natural history artifacts, as well as important antiques. Managed by the National Park Service, there are tours offered daily. After seeing leopard skins and buffalo on the walls, take one of the nature trails. Roosevelt was an avid birder, and the marshy beaches of the preserve make for a biodiverse landscape.

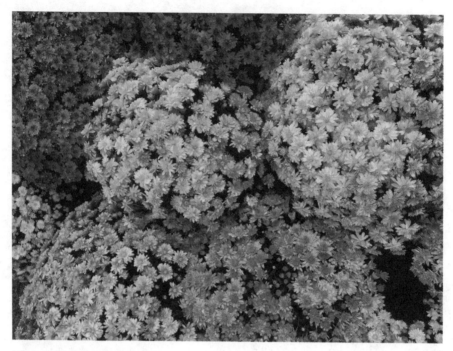

// Flowers in bloom in early summer

There's one last house on the schedule for today, and that's the unbelievable **Oheka Castle**. You might recognize this place from Taylor Swift's "Bad Blood" music video, but the palatial estate once owned by financier Otto Hermann Kahn is now a hotel. The castle was built in the French chateau style, and it is absolutely massive—at the time it was built, it was the second largest private home in the country (second only to the Biltmore Estate). Now, visitors can take a tour of the castle, spend the night in one of the opulent rooms, or stop by for a meal (that's why you're here). It's a popular event space, so call ahead to make a reservation and book a tour.

Once you've taken a stroll of the grounds and the castle, settle in for an over-the-top formal lunch in the hotel's grand restaurant—oysters, steak, and maybe even a bottle of champagne.

In the late afternoon, you can spend some time on the shore, walking along the **Long Island Sound**. There are small public parks all over, or if you're looking for something a bit more active, you can visit **Sunken Meadow Park**.

For dinner, go for something casual—the small town of Northport has a gem called **Tim's Shipwreck Diner**, which is the perfect antidote to Oheka Castle—small, homey, and serving greasy-spoon diner food. Have fish and chips or a burger and a beer, seated on a stool at the counter.

SUNDAY

Sunday is a beach day, so pack your bags and head south. If you're feeling brunchy, you can have a leisurely meal on the water at the upscale **Prime** restaurant overlooking Huntington Harbor.

From Huntington, the closest beach is also one of the best beaches on Long Island—**Robert Moses State Park**. This huge white sand beach at the southern end of Fire Island will definitely keep you entertained for a day. There are snack bars and bar bars on site, and if you're in the mood for a walk, you can visit the **Fire Island Lighthouse Preserve**.

At the end of your day in the sun, you can drive back through Jones Beach and Long Beach, stopping at **Pop's Seafood Shack** for one final bite of fried fish before the weekend's over.

≡ How to Spend a Weekend in Asbury Park

Hipster Charm

Asbury Park is New Jersey's capital of cool, and a town that keeps getting cooler every time you go back. This 1920s playground for the well-heeled was *the* place to spend the summer, with beautiful Victorian homes and a boardwalk with a casino and carousel. (The casino and carousel were eventually abandoned, and their gorgeous carcasses are still on the boardwalk today.)

In the '70s, this town had a second renaissance as the stomping grounds of Bruce Springsteen, playing legendary shows at the Stone Pony. In the '90s, however, Asbury Park lay fallow, with boarded-up buildings on Main Street and not much of a summer crowd.

// Asbury Park is almost too stylish for its own good

Now, the town is in its third incarnation as an artsy hipster destination. Downtown is thriving, with boutiques, restaurants, and music venues that are drawing in an ever-hipper crowd from New York City. Now's the time to visit this place, before it gets too cool for the rest of us.

FRIDAY

Leaving the city after work, you'll arrive in Asbury Park just in time for dinner. If you're visiting in late June or early July, you might be lucky enough to experience some daylight.

After settling in at your hotel or rental, make your way straight to the beach to have a cocktail with an ocean view on the boardwalk. There are a few options, but choose whatever can give you a view of the beach—check out the bars in the **Convention Hall** to see if there's anything available.

When it's dark out, venture a block over to **Porta**, one of the restaurants that put Asbury Park back on the hipster map. It's a huge warehouse-like space, with indoor and outdoor seating for perfect brick-oven pizzas and beer. The outdoor bar area turns into a bit of a scene on weekend nights, so stick around after you're done eating and have a cocktail at one of the picnic tables.

SATURDAY

In the morning, start your day with a coffee at **High Voltage**. With locations both in town and on the boardwalk, you can choose the one that works best for you. There are also pastries and a few dishes like avocado toast.

People who aren't interested in the beach probably shouldn't visit Asbury Park during the summer. Sure, there's a cute town to explore, but most of the action between Memorial Day and Labor Day takes place at the **beach and boardwalk**. The best part about spending the day at the beach at Asbury is that you don't have to be very prepared. You can buy or rent beach chairs and umbrellas, and there's a huge selection of beachfront restaurants and bars where you can get food, water, and most importantly, ice cold beer. Getting onto the beach at Asbury costs $7 per person (even if you're just walking on), so you'll want to spend at least a couple of hours there to make it really worth it. If you're not really a sand person, the boardwalk is free, so you can sit and people watch or post up at one of the waterside bars or restaurants.

When you're done with the beach, head into town to do a little shopping. From record stores to vintage boutiques, Asbury Park has some real gems.

Get your night started with some over-the-top craft cocktails at the modern Mediterranean-inspired **Reyla**. One of the chicest spots in Asbury Park, you can sip on floral-inspired boozy creations and snack on light bites like deconstructed falafel or house-made hummus, but don't spoil your dinner—you have big plans ahead.

Put your name in for a table at **Talula's**, which is definitely the best pizza in town and possibly the best pizza in the entire state of New Jersey. It's the kind of place where every single dish is intentionally crafted (no substitutions) and every ingredient is thoughtfully sourced. In fact, there's a list of their purveyors on the wall in the restaurant. You can opt for something simple like margherita or get something a little more creative like the Beekeeper's Lament, with tomato sauce, hot calabrian sopressata, mozzarella, and local honey. Either way, you'll get pizza that's crispy and chewy. There are a few choice appetizers and other dishes, but you'd be remiss to skip the pizza here. Pair a pie with a nice red selected from their natural wine list.

If you're looking for dessert after dinner, you can't do any better than the creme brûlée at **Pascal and Sabines**, or you can embrace the summer with a scoop at **Cookman Creamery**.

Asbury Park is renowned for music—especially the Springsteen-famous **Stone Pony**. The bar is still in operation and through the summer they host concerts at their summer stage, directly behind the boardwalk. See who's playing and book tickets in advance.

If nothing piques your interest, the new **Asbury Lanes**, next to the Asbury Hotel, is a Brooklyn Bowl-esque nightlife venue with concerts, drinks, and of course, bowling.

If you're in the mood for something a bit more sophisticated, you can visit the rooftop bar at **The Asbury Hotel**, a cool cocktail bar with great music and a fun crowd.

SUNDAY

The best way to cure your Asbury Park hangover is the way everybody else does it: with breakfast at **Toast**, where there's an extensive menu that will please everyone in your group. After breakfast, hang out by the Asbury Hotel pool, sipping on frozen drinks, lounging in a cabana, and watching the scene unfold.

When you're ready to venture out again, there's just one last stop: **The Asbury Festhalle** and **Biergarten**, an authentic German beer garden with over 60 imported and domestic beers to choose from. Hang out at the communal tables and eat some pretzels until it's time to go home.

// The boardwalk is the center of the action in Asbury Park

☰ How to See It All in One Weekend

From Castles to the Coast, the Best of Long Island

There's a lot to see and do on Long Island, but that doesn't mean you can't do it all in one weekend. You'll need your own car for this adventure, and you have to be good with a bit of hotel hopping and a lot of driving—but there will be delicious things to eat and beautiful things to see along the way.

FRIDAY

Start your adventure in **Montauk**, at the end of Long Island. Stay in one of Montauk's beachside hotels like **Hero Beach Club**, and make sure you arrive before sunset for drinks at **Montauket**, a waterfront dive bar with simple drinks and an amazing sunset view. Eat at **The Crow's Nest** for dinner, a chic and romantic restaurant on the water, serving fresh farm to table fare at reclaimed wood tables under the string lights. It's simple and stylish here, and has some of the best food in town. After dinner, visit **Ruschmeyer's** for boozy summer camp vibes with lawn games and a campfire. If you're in the mood to dance, hit up the late-night **Memory Motel**, a vintage motel with a packed dance floor. And if you're looking for something a little bit more low-key, visit **Liar's** for a mudslide and a bit of local flavor, tucked away in a marina.

// Fresh Long Island peaches for sale

SATURDAY

In the morning, take a stroll on **Ditch Plains Beach**, watching surfers, going for a swim, and walking down to **Shadmoor State Park** to see the sandy bluffs. Pack up and get in the car for the drive east, where you'll drive through Amagansett to **The Longhouse Reserve**, a sculpture garden and outdoor museum full of whimsical artworks hidden among lush greenery.

Stop for lunch at **EMP Summer House**, a summer pop-up of New York City's Eleven Madison Park. Although it's expensive and hard to get a reservation, there's a first-come, first-served patio area with a much more affordable menu—hot dogs, burgers, and lobster rolls.

After lunch, make your way to **Sag Harbor**, stopping along the way at **Channing Daughters Winery** to pick up the best souvenir you can get in the Hamptons: a bottle of rosé.

Take the ferry to **Shelter Island** for the afternoon and park yourself at **Sunset Beach**, an ultra-stylish hotel and restaurant. Sunbathe and lounge on the sand before snagging a seat at the upstairs bar of the hotel to drink sangria and watch the sunset.

Back in the car, get on the North Ferry this time for the ride to **Greenpoint**—check into the chic waterfront **Soundview Hotel** before heading into town for dinner at **1943**, a wood fired pizza restaurant with the area's best clam pie. After dinner, the speakeasy downstairs beckons with sophisticated bourbon cocktails. Have a final nightcap at the vintage-chic Soundview Bar before hitting the hay.

SUNDAY

In the morning, wake up early for the drive west. Stop in **Riverhead** at **Briermere Farms** to pick up a pie. Get one pie to eat tomorrow and another pie to freeze and pop into the oven on a dark and dreary winter day.

Make a lunchtime reservation at **Oheka Castle**, the former residence of Otto Hermann Kahn, which is now a hotel (with a restaurant and bar that's open to the public). Take a tour of the grounds to get a sense of Long Island's Gilded Age history before settling in for a decadent lunch.

In the afternoon, make the drive south to **Robert Moses State Park**, the southernmost tip of Fire Island and one of the most beautiful beaches in New York. You won't have time to stay very long, but you can go for a swim and take a look at the lighthouse before getting back in the car to drive home. Drive back to the city along highway 27, stopping at in **Amityville** to get a glimpse of the **Amityville Horror House**—a seemingly innocent home where a father once murdered his whole family. The house became famous after the family that bought the house moved out less than a month later, having been terrorized by demonic paranormal activity.

Lighten things up with a paper plate full of fried clams at **Bigelow's**, a roadside seafood shack in **Rockville Centre**, and toast your weekend, in which you managed to (almost) see it all.

// The chic outdoor dining space at The Crow's Nest in Montauk

Acknowledgments

I would not have been able to discover Long Island without the help of family and friends who have shared their homes and tables with me throughout the years: the Heuses (Melissa, Jim, Rebecca, Kiki, Molly, Pete, and William); the Olts (Meredith, Frank, Jackie, Alex, Anna, and Elizabeth); the Bacons and Williamses (Susan, David, Isabel, and Tony); the Williamses (Jackie, Big Gene, Gene, Nicole, Harry, Francesca, Philip, and Claire); and of course my fabulous in-laws: the Dukes (Idoline, Biddle, Ellie, and Angie); the Parkeses (Jane, Simon, and Homer); the Whitneys (Laura, Sophie, and August); Tom Scheerer and Mike Baldridge; and of course Gaga, whose wonderful home has become my most favorite place on earth.

To my friends and colleagues at Fodor's Travel: thank you for teaching me everything I know about writing a guidebook. I could not have written this book without the foundation of knowledge that I was lucky enough to receive from working at Fodor's, which is also where I met my fantastic editor, Róisín.

I'd also like to thank the Long Island Railroad, since I wrote most of this book during my many Friday afternoon and Sunday evening commutes.

Some of my favorite beachy memories are with my family—my sisters Monica, Carly, and Abby, and my mom and stepdad, Susan and Brad. I'll never forget our summers on the Jersey Shore, and I can't wait for our next trip to the beach together.

East Hampton has an extra special place in my heart because it's where I met my husband, where we first said "I love you," and where we got engaged. Haley, thank you for taking care of me while I worked nights and weekends on this book. I'll always love you.

// In the fall, come to the Hamptons for changing leaves and cozy vibes

Index